The Miegunyah Press

The General Series
of the Miegunyah Volumes
was made possible by the
Miegunyah Fund
established by bequests
under the wills of
Sir Russell and Lady Grimwade

'Miegunyah' was the home of
Mab and Russell Grimwade
from 1911 to 1955

David Unaipon, frontispiece with the handwritten manuscript in the Mitchell Library.

DAVID UNAIPON

Legendary Tales of the Australian Aborigines

DAVID UNAIPON

Legendary Tales of the Australian Aborigines

Edited by
Stephen Muecke *and* Adam Shoemaker

Melbourne University Publishing acknowledges the traditional owners of the unceded land on which we work, learn and live: the Wurundjeri Woiwurrung peoples of the Kulin Nation. We pay respect to elders past, present and future, and acknowledge the importance of Indigenous knowledge.

THE MIEGUNYAH PRESS
An imprint of Melbourne University Publishing Limited
Level 1, 715 Swanston Street, Carlton, Victoria 3053, Australia
mup-contact@unimelb.edu.au
www.mup.com.au

First published 2001
Paperback edition 2006
Reprinted twice 2024
Reprinted 2025

Text design by Sandra Nobes
Cover design by Phil Campbell
Printed in Australia by McPherson's Printing Group

A catalogue record for this book is available from the National Library of Australia

9780522852462 (paperback)

Contents

Illustrations

Introduction: Repatriating the Story

As a full-blooded member of my race I think I may claim to be the first—but I hope, not the last—to produce an enduring record of our customs, beliefs, and imaginings.

David Unaipon, from the Preface

It seems Australians missed the opportunity, three-quarters of a century ago, to publish a major work of Indigenous literature. This is the story of that missed opportunity, and why we have come to publish the work today.

David Unaipon is acknowledged as the first Indigenous Australian writer by virtue of the pamphlets he wrote, published and distributed from 1927. It has also been known for some years that he wrote a book-length manuscript in English. These stories, collected in manuscript and typescript as 'Legendary Tales of the Australian Aborigines', were written in 1924–25 and reside in the State Library of New South Wales. They are presented here for the first time in their original form, published under Unaipon's own name.

But the long-overdue nature of this text is only one dimension of its uniqueness. In all respects—whether one is considering content, ethnography, aesthetics or language—Unaipon's work is unlike that of any other Australian writer, regardless of race or cultural background. It is eclectic, reflecting as it does the author's journeys all over Southern Australia. It is syncretic, deploying elements of sources as varied as Christian sermons and European fairytales within the crucial framework of Indigenous Australian oral traditions. It is also strategic: a pattern of writing reflecting a pattern of escape from European institutional control, where the very act of collecting and writing stories—certain *types* of stories—became Unaipon's passport away from the constraints of the mission system in the 1920s.

Therefore, this 'authorised' version of Unaipon's tales reflects many things. It engages with the dilemma of a brilliant, creative person who was often frustrated as he sought to find an outlet for his brilliance during his lifetime. It engages with the paradox of an historical figure who, as 'the man on the fifty-dollar note', is better recognised today than he has ever been before while both his life story and the stories he wrote during his lifetime have not been made available. It also investigates mysteries and hitherto unanswered questions: how was it that David Unaipon had signed numerous contracts with Angus & Robertson in the mid-1920s to publish his stories, yet his book never appeared? How could it have been that the medical officer, coroner and amateur anthropologist, William Ramsay Smith, obtained the copyright to Unaipon's entire manuscript and edited it for an English edition under his own name, released under the title *Myths & Legends of the Australian Aboriginals* in 1930? Where does this trail of appropriation lead to today?

Our aim with this volume is to restore Unaipon's work, in two senses: to return it to a version that is as close as possible to the manuscript David Unaipon first produced, and to restore it as intellectual property to the original owners, the Ngarrindjeri community of South Australia, and to Unaipon's descendants. Both challenges are as political as they are creative. Both edge back into the past to demonstrate that it is always relevant to the present and future aspirations of the Ngarrindjeri. And, if this is to be a true repatriation, it must involve literally bringing the stories back to the people and country of their creation, to make the circle whole.

For us, as editors, David Unaipon is at the centre of this circle, but like the mats that have made the Ngarrindjeri women famous for their craft, his story is woven in with those of others. Unaipon was born on 28 September 1872 at the South Australian congregational mission then known as Point McLeay, the fourth of nine children. As a boy he was identified as a bright lad, and being the son of the first Indigenous convert and lay preacher, James Unaipon [Ngunaitponi] and his wife Nymbulda, he was seen as a suitable candidate for education. From the age of seven he attended the mission school; at thirteen he departed for

Ngarrindjerri women with baskets.
(M. Angas Collection, South Australian Museum)

The school at Raukkan. (M. Angas Collection, South Australian Museum)

Postcard of Point McLeay (Raukkan) Mission c. 1920.
(M. Angas Collection, South Australian Museum)

Banner from Point McLeay (Raukkan) Church.
(M. Angas Collection, South Australian Museum)

Adelaide to work for C. B. Young and his family, prominent members of the Aborigines' Friends' Association (AFA). This group had a long-standing association with the community at Point McLeay on Lake Alexandrina; the AFA had been formed in 1858 with the aim of ameliorating the living conditions of the Aborigines dwelling in the Lower Murray River region. By 1860 a small school and church had been established at Point McLeay, some community houses had been constructed and the influential missionary George Taplin had begun his work among the local people.

It is fair to say that all of the Ngarrindjeri, including David Unaipon, struggled over the years with the demands of two cultures that often pulled in different directions. For his part, Unaipon was heavily influenced by the five years he had spent in Adelaide between 1885 and 1890. It was during this period that his insatiable interest in science was strongly encouraged: the broad-based classical education which he received in Young's home encompassed philosophy, music, religion and scientific discovery, all of which were to become major themes of Unaipon's later life. However, it is vital to note that David Unaipon always focused upon these areas *within* the context of his indigeneity. As with his writing, Unaipon's sermons and his scientific inventions may have worn the external vestments of European culture, but their inspiration and the matrix for their application was undoubtedly an Indigenous one.

For example, it is known that David Unaipon spent a considerable amount of time in the South Australian Museum, studying his own and other cultures, building up the anthropology-like, comparativist style that permeates his writings about his people's way of life. As Dr Eric Wilmott put it, in the inaugural David Unaipon lecture in Adelaide in 1989:

> Like Albert Namatjira, he [Unaipon] explored the methods of the new Australians and focussed upon two of their areas of expression. The first of these was the use of English literacy and the second was science. Unaipon was in this sense the first Aboriginal scientist who concentrated his investigations upon Europeans. (1989: 6)

An index of Unaipon's scientific renown was that by the mid-1920s, when he had begun to write his 'legendary tales' in earnest, he had developed a number of important patent applications. (In all, from

1910 to 1944 he made ten separate applications for inventions as varied as an anti-gravitational device, a multi-radial wheel and a sheep-shearing handpiece.) The year 1924 was a pivotal one for Unaipon; a formal watercolour portrait of him by Benjamin Edward Minns in that year describes him, in large letters printed on the middle of the canvas, as a 'Scientist Lecturer'. It is noteworthy that Unaipon's achievements as an author—the basis for much of his contemporary renown and the underpinning for this current book—were not publicly recognised at that stage. Clearly, an introduction such as this cannot do full justice to David Unaipon's many-sided life, career and achievements.

What is striking is how that same many-sidedness is so evident in Unaipon's written *oeuvre*. To cite one instance, most of the stories in the manuscript version of *Myths & Legends* come from Unaipon's own Ngarrindjeri people, but some are from other Indigenous clans as far afield as Victoria, Central Australia and—in one case—from 'Mount Brown, Southern Queensland'. Similarly, the striking range of subject matter in Unaipon's manuscript—from quasi-anthropological analyses of tribal customs simply entitled 'Sport' and 'Hunting' to deeply philosophical treatises such as 'Immortality' and 'The Voice of the Great Spirit'—emphasises the ambitiousness, breadth and complexity of what he has written. Meanwhile, the often elaborate and ornate style of Unaipon's work defied all expectations of Indigenous literacy in the 1920s, just as it has confounded numerous critics to the present day.

Put another way, it is worth remembering that at the time when David Unaipon was first writing, the notion of an Indigenous person being an author was literally unheard of. (According to the standard accounts, we would have to wait until 1964 and 1965, when Kath Walker and Colin Johnson first published their books.) But before we get to the story of the manuscript, let us return to David Unaipon's life to explore just what an Indigenous person could be, how he and his people had to struggle to be 'valued' during the years when he grew up in South Australia.

How we recognise the nature of a person is not always clear, given the different cultures building up this sense of personhood with layers of rights, obligations and freedoms. For issues of copyright, an individual person is habitually the legal entity who can 'hold' such rights. In South Australia in the first part of the twentieth century, an Indigenous person's rights were extremely limited. They were citizens, unlike in other States, but there were restrictions on movement, on ownership of private property and so on. Authorship, therefore, was a right that Indigenous people were generally considered incapable of holding.

Let us consider, by way of contrast, an Indigenous system for the control and distribution of intellectual capital, the system from which Unaipon was emerging. We say emerging because his quick mind was able to grasp the way the European world worked, and he decided to succeed in it from an early age, learning languages, playing Bach on the organ, studying theology, mechanics and physics, practising oratory. Yet he was at the same time located within his Yaraldi culture (Warrawaldi on his father's side), with its own attitudes towards knowledge as a kind of property.

People have often contrasted Indigenous custodianship with Western authorship, and pointed out that the latter has a fairly recent history:

> Authorship is a predominantly Western category which orients criticism of literature toward the subjectivity of the individual creator. But in Aboriginal Australia, it is the case that *custodianship* displaces ownership of stories and songs toward a collective ownership—the idea being that individuals are temporarily in charge of various cultural things by virtue of being in a certain position in the society. They are then not so much the creators of traditions, but they are repeaters. They reenact or retrace the steps of ancestors, which includes singing their songs and telling their stories. Each adult person is likely to hold custodianship responsibilities as part of the general tribal repertoire of cultural tradition. These parts are then put together on the more important occasions for the performance of the traditions. (Muecke 1992: 44–6)

It is debatable to what extent the emphasis on the legal and aesthetic character of 'author' obscures more collective access to cultural material in contemporary societies. John Frow, for instance, in his argument against the progressive commodification of public domain material, finds in Indigenous societies a useful contrastive model for the 'regulation of cultural rights':

Point McLeay (Raukkan) from 'Lovers Lane'.
(M. Angas Collection, South Australian Museum)

Point McLeay (Raukkan) Mission Jubilee.
(M. Angas Collection, South Australian Museum)

The 'Glee Club' at Raukkan.
(Ramsay Smith Collection, South Australian Museum)

David Unaipon.
(M. Angas Collection, South Australian Museum)

> This is a model which is in many respects more fully developed than any other way of thinking about the social ownership of information; in particular, Australian Aboriginal societies have a highly elaborated formulation of the distinction between different classes of rights holders, including separate rights of production, rights of use, rights of knowledge, rights of divulgence of that knowledge and rights of ownership. (Frow 1998: 40)

All these rights need not necessarily reside in the same person, and often do not. The person who paints a painting could be different from the one who tells the story about it, or who sells it. In that sense, with Unaipon, we could have a case of man whose culture had prepared him to think in terms of limited and local rights; for instance, someone down the track (which the story is travelling) knows, and has the rights to, its continuation. And as he gets old, he will also have to pass on his story to someone else. Things are thus produced *to be handed over*, circulated rather than accumulated.

So, working in conjunction with others was not at all unusual for Unaipon. He did it with his own people and William Ramsay Smith. He worked when necessary with an interpreter, people traded stories with him and he eventually sold his manuscripts. He might also have been thinking, as he sent his material to Sydney, that something else should come back along that trade route. In the Indigenous system, it no doubt would have. That his manuscript should be made into a book takes it even further out of the Indigenous system for the circulation of things of social value, but perhaps something *is* finally coming back along that trade route as we put together David Unaipon's intellectual and cultural property to take back to the community. Like Unaipon's image on the fifty-dollar note, books are of symbolic importance, but for his people there can be far more important mechanisms than papers and books to determine *value* in a cultural trading economy.

Let us give one example. In the old days when a Ngarrindjeri child was born its navel cord was dried and treated, bundled in feathers and sent in exchange to another group of people with a new-born child. The two children, thus linked, then had a special life-long relationship: 'Gifts of food and weapons accompanied the exchanges, but the main role of the partners was to act as intermediaries in trade relations between their respective groups' (Bell 1998: 493). Linked by their navel cords, as it were, they regulate the exchange of goods, which may include knowledge.

Here is Unaipon's own account of this practice, from the story 'Nhung e Umpie'. He attributes its origin to Narroondarie, a God-like ancestor figure he compares to 'Budha, Mohamet and Christ':

> Now Narroondarie, as if inspired, instituted the custom of Nhung e umpie.
>
> Now, Nhung e umpie is a portion of the navel cord at birth from mother and child. Now, the gut or intestine is treated in a way that preserves it, for it is kept for a considerable time. It is then placed within a roll of Emu feathers and then wound round with fibre from the bark of the tree or mallee. This makes it safe and transferable from one hunting ground to another and when it is sent on its long mission as a bond of friendship. (135, this volume)

The part this ceremony plays in the moral development of the mother is significant. The statement is, for us, an example of Unaipon's intellectual achievement: 'insider' knowledge articulated with Western science and moral philosophy:

> Now, this gut or part of the intestine of mother and child has a great significance to us. We look upon it as coming from within a part of a woman where dwells all good wishes of pity and sympathy. There are two parts embodied in this one gut. First, that of the well-trained moral of perfect womanhood which is recognised with a great deal of reverence. (135, this volume)

He analyses the spiritual dimensions of the custom, and the comparison to Christian symbols has the effect of dignifying both cultures:

> Secondly, there is that portion of the childish innocence and purity which offers itself for a great development of life: to prove in itself as a challenge its capability to develop itself and to prove the inheritance of a mother's quality. Thirdly, the navel cord is symbolic of a string that binds the peculiarities of mother to child. As a mother and child are linked to each other before birth, so the Nhung e umpie must be linked as mother and child. The navel cord is a physical reality, so Nhung e umpie should be so: true love, true fellowship, true pity. Let this symbol so bind you. Now we look upon the navel cord with reverence, just as there is Christian reverence towards the house of

> God, its fount and Altar and Sacrament. It is an all-powerful custom that can bind any two tribes to a bond of good fellowship and brotherhood. Distance makes no difference; wherever it is conveyed and is submitted to a tribe, it is accepted with honour. It is a law in itself. (135–6, this volume)

To this day Ngarrindjeri people speak of this 'life line' and the way it relates to their *miwi*, the power of feelings. *Miwi* is a word to be uttered with respect, and is at the heart of religious practice. The anthropologist Diane Bell states that: 'The feelings associated with one's *miwi* are relied upon in identifying sacred places and truth' (Bell 1998: 490). The study carried out by Ronald and Catherine Berndt in the 1930s corroborates the importance of this concept (1993). And also, in Diane Bell's book, Tom Trevorrow said: 'It's all to do with where you're born and your life comes through your *umbiblical* cord to your body'. Bell continues: 'They always say "umbiblical" for umbilical and it is a rendering I've come to appreciate. With its evocation of "biblical" it seems an appropriate gloss for this sacred relationship' (Bell 1998: 225).

These ideas cause us to reflect on the arbitrary focus on the printed word, in Western cultures, for the establishment of cultural value and truth. As Unaipon says, the Ngarrindjeri system is more strongly embodied and interpersonal. Nhung e umpie constitutes trading relationships between people and governs in one respect the way they handle knowledge. Let us not forget that the disembodiment of knowledge in books has not removed all ritual. There are rituals associated with the Western category of author; the book launching as a social event anoints individuals as authors and functions to increase their social prestige and power. In our work of republishing and repatriating David Unaipon's work, we plan to use just such a ceremony to *hand over* the book to the community, in celebration of his memory.

A further, crucial element of repatriation relates to discovering exactly what happened in the past between David Unaipon, William Ramsay Smith and publishers Angus & Robertson. Only in this way can the full story be 'brought home' and the actions of the key players be brought to account. Up until now, speculation has surrounded the strategy used by Ramsay Smith to divest Unaipon of his manuscript. Much of this uncertainty centres around one key question: how was it possible for Ramsay Smith to take Unaipon's work from him, especially when he had a prior contract from Angus & Robertson to publish the manuscript

David Unaipon (right) with friend Mark Wilson.
(M. Angas Collection, South Australian Museum)

in his own name? The answer lies in the publisher's original correspondence files held in the Mitchell Library. The sequence of events is as complex as it is dramatic.

The first steps towards Ramsay Smith's appropriation were taken as early as 1924, fully six years before *Myths & Legends of the Australian Aboriginals* was published by Harrap in London. The trail begins with a personal, handwritten letter by Ramsay Smith to George Robertson on 22 January 1925, where the medical officer reveals that, in the second half of 1924, he met with the British publisher in Adelaide during the latter's Australian visit:

> About Myths: Mr. Harrap when here some months ago asked me to write a volume on Australian Aboriginal Myths to complete his series. He had been told that it was not possible to get such a volume done. After very serious cogitation I said I would undertake the work, and he set about at once to try to make arrangements with Mrs. Langloh Parker and others about using what has already been published.[1]

It is clear that Ramsay Smith had been 'commissioned' by Harrap in late 1924 to produce a book for its international series of 'Myths & Legends' (other titles concerned the myths of Mexico and Peru and also a Maori volume). It is with this foreknowledge that Ramsay Smith wrote to Robertson early the following year, essentially seeking his advice on existing sources of material. In his words:

> Mr. Harrap knows that the chief difficulties in producing a book will lie in being able to use materials already published. How matters may turn out I do not know; but I should be very glad to have your views on the subject, so far as you could venture to give them.

George Robertson's response on 6 February 1925 is highly significant. Not only does it prove that Angus & Robertson was already intending to publish a book of legends written by David Unaipon but that it was planned to attribute the work to Unaipon himself. Robertson writes:

[1] State Library of New South Wales, 'Angus & Robertson Papers', MSS 314, Ramsay Smith, vol. 76 (1925–28). All extracts of correspondence with William Ramsay Smith are taken from this manuscript.

> Dear Sir,
> My first feeling was that of being an intruder in your cabbage patch, but on second thought I came to the conclusion that our little book, with Unaipon's portrait, will help your more ambitious volume by preparing the way. I did not mention your letter to our dusky author, and Mr. Shenstone, the member of our staff who is looking after his book, tells me that he has gone (or is going) to South Australia to find someone to make a few illustrations. Probably you will see him.

Aside from the typically patronising connotations of the term 'our dusky author'—and the fact that Robertson voluntarily chose not to tell Unaipon about Ramsay Smith's correspondence—this short note is a crucial link in the unfolding chain of events. Unaipon's portrait—which to this day remains a frontispiece for the until-now unpublished Mitchell Library manuscript—was clearly intended to adorn a book of tales collected and written *by* David Unaipon; the phrases 'his book' and 'our author' further reinforce the conclusion that Angus & Roberston was entirely prepared to acknowledge the Indigenous authorship of the work. Furthermore, the reference to illustrations being located by Unaipon implies a contractual relationship, whereby Unaipon had been empowered to seek supporting material for his book. Finally, there is no doubt that—at least at this point—George Robertson was not entertaining the idea of combining the Unaipon and Ramsay Smith projects: the suggestion that 'our little book . . . will help your more ambitious volume' is unequivocal on this issue.

Later entries in the file bear out these hypotheses. There is incontrovertible evidence that, between 8 January 1925 and 3 July 1925, Angus & Robertson obtained the rights to twenty-eight separate stories 'sold and assigned' by Unaipon to them for £2/2/- per 1000 words. This rate of payment was entirely in keeping with the era; in fact, the total payment to Unaipon (£167/5/-) was a substantial sum at the time. Moreover, it was common practice for authors to sell and assign copyright to publishers such as Angus & Robertson during the first thirty years of the twentieth century, although many—Henry Lawson included—later came to regret their decision. The point is that during the first half of 1925, Unaipon was being treated in all respects as an author in his own right; there was no imputation that he was merely an 'informant', an 'unacknowledged source' or an 'invisible author'. In the light of all of this, what subsequently transpired was particularly unfortunate.

Ironically, when Ramsay Smith first wrote his tentative letter to Robertson in January 1925 he indicated that he had considered and rejected the idea of using David Unaipon as a source for his Harrap volume. In Ramsay Smith's words:

> On my part I got into communication with several others who have published contributions from time to time, and I also wrote to people who are well acquainted with the aboriginals in the Territory, Central Australia and hereabouts. I thought of David Unaipon, whom I have known well for upwards of twenty years, and I spoke with the former Superintendent of the Point McLeay Mission Station at which David lives; and he advised me to get in touch with Jacob Harris who is a full blood, a store house of folk-lore, a very trustworthy man and extremely well-educated.

One can only imagine Ramsay Smith's surprise when he received the response from Robertson, advising him that the man he had considered—and discounted—for his project was heavily involved in one of his own. (In the month of January 1925, in quite a remarkable spate of creative activity, Unaipon had submitted fourteen stories to Angus & Robertson, which represented nearly half the length of his eventual 80,000-word manuscript.) Ever the opportunist, Ramsay Smith was soon to find a way to bridge that gap to his advantage.

What happened next had all the elements of the great dramas of literary history where reputations, envy, pride (and prejudice) are in play. Having successfully produced a substantial series of stories for Angus & Robertson during the first six months of the year, Unaipon no doubt felt that he had established an effective and equitable working relationship with the Sydney-based publisher. For example, on 14 July 1925—just eleven days after he had submitted the manuscript for the four tales 'Gool Lun Naga (Green Frog)', 'A Wonderful Bun Bar Rang (Lizard)', 'Whowie' and 'Yara Ma Tha Who'—Unaipon wired the secretary of Angus & Robertson, F. S. Shenstone, from Narrung, South Australia:

> COLLECTING MYTH LEGEND RETURNING NEXT WEEK
> —UNIAPON [sic][1]

[1] State Library of New South Wales, 'Angus & Robertson Papers', MSS 314, David Unaipon, vol. 85 (1925–27). All extracts of correspondence with David Unaipon are taken from this manuscript.

This bespeaks an ongoing relationship; one in which Unaipon had a continuing commission to gather material on behalf of the publisher. In the same vein, Unaipon sent a follow-up telegram to Shenstone from Adelaide two days later:

> SEND ME SIX POUNDS COLLECTED LEGENDS ETC RETURNING NEXT WEEKS
>
> —TONY UNAIPON GPO

Shenstone immediately wired back, again signalling the continuing nature of the relationship:

> CANNOT SEND MONEY UNLESS YOU WIRE US NAME OF AN ADELAIDE BOOKSELLER WHO IS WILLING TO RECEIVE IT FOR YOU
>
> —ANGUS ROBERTSON

Unaipon's reply was just as swift:

> E.S. WIGG AND SON GRENFELL ST ADELAIDE
>
> —UNAIPON

In addition, Unaipon wrote a follow-up letter to his Angus & Robertson contact four days later:

> Adelaide
> South Australia
> 30/7/25
>
> Mr Shenton [sic]
> c/o Angus Robertson
>
> Sir
> I shall be delayed here (Adelaide) a little longer. I have requested the Government to allow my free pass upon their Railway through this state and to give me £75-00 for expenses in the other states; this is to give me an opportunity to collect you as many Legends & Myths as possible. I shall post you.
>
> Yours sincerely
> David Unaipon

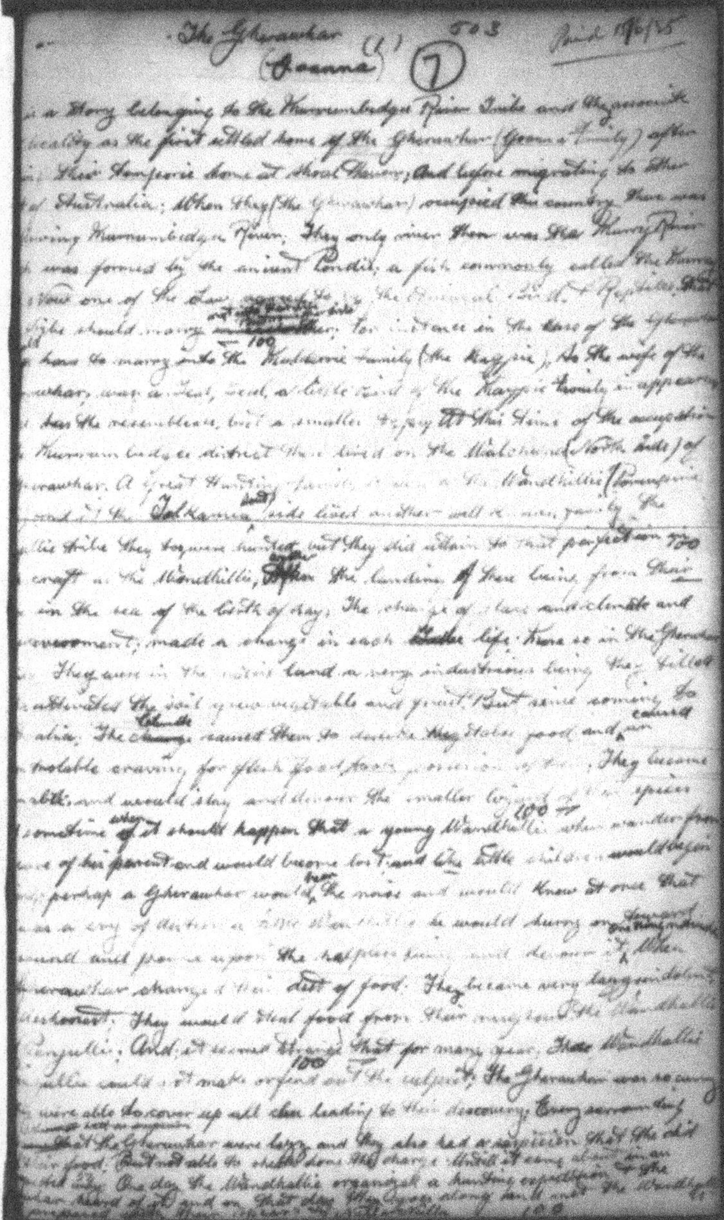

Pages from David Unaipon's manuscript, Mitchell Library.

What appears to have happened next was a change of heart in the Angus & Robertson boardroom; a realisation from the company that some limitations had to be placed upon what seemed to have become an open-ended arrangement. It is also evident from the correspondence that the editorial staff had come to the conclusion that the amount of material already sent by Unaipon was more than adequate for a book-length publication. Thus, Shenstone replied:

4th August, 1925.

Mr. David Unaipon,
c/o Messrs. E.S. Wigg & Son,
ADELAIDE, S.A.

Dear Mr. Unaipon,
We received your letter dated 30th ult., and Messrs. E.S. Wigg & Son have sent us your receipt for the £6 which we wired last week.

You will understand, of course, that the Aboriginal Legends which you are writing are to be submitted for our approval, and that we do not undertake to purchase the copyright of any except those approved by us. We mention this as we do not wish you to think that we are prepared to except [sic] an unlimited number of legends, and we do not wish you to incur any expense on our account. We shall be pleased to receive as many more of the legends as you care to submit, but have thought it as well to make the position clear to you.

Yours faithfully,

ANGUS & ROBERTSON LTD.
Secretary.

One can only conjecture if Unaipon ever received this letter. Two things are certain: he never replied to it nor acted in any way which indicated an awareness that restrictions had been applied to his story-gathering. Perhaps the key here lies in the differing cultural landscapes of, on the one hand, a European-Australian publisher and, on the other, an Indigenous man who believed he had entered into a binding trading relationship. From Angus & Robertson's point of view, the company could not simply sign a blank cheque over to Unaipon, authorising his untrammelled creative activity. But, from Unaipon's perspective, not only had an effective precedent been set for the 'trade route' he was travelling down, but he had already collected and written additional legends for the publisher—in other words, had fulfilled his part of the bargain—and expected Angus & Robertson to reciprocate. Therefore, the author sent three further telegrams in quick succession to Shenstone, on 7, 12 and 18 September, requesting him to: 'WIRE MONEY CARE WIGG AND SON', to acknowledge receipt of the latest instalment of legends—'DID MANUSCRIPT ARRIVE SAFE AND IN ORDER STILL COLLECTING'—and again, 'HAVE MANUSCRIPTS ARRIVED SAFELY IN ORDER'.

One can sense the mounting assertiveness in Shenstone's reply of 18 September 1925:

> RECEIVED PACKET MANUSCRIPT BUT MUST CONSIDER BEFORE ACCEPTING SEE LETTER FOURTH AUGUST ADDRESSED CARE OF WIGG.
> SHENSTONE

Far from mollifying Unaipon, this latest response served to unsettle him. The fact that his items of trade had been received by Angus & Robertson but that no commitment or recompense was forthcoming appears to have been confusing and disturbing. There is a clear undertone of earnest disquiet in his two subsequent telegrams, sent on 24 and 26 September:

> CAN YOU SEND ME TEN POUNDS BY WIRE.

> ARE MANUSCRIPTS SATISFACTORY WAITING TO SEND MORE.

Finally, Unaipon seems to have withdrawn into more formal language in his final telegram to Angus & Robertson, perhaps an index of his diminishing confidence in the relationship and in the value of his own writing:

> SHOULD MANUSCRIPT BE OF VALUE KINDLY INFORM ME AND SEND ME ITS WORTH THROUGH WIGG AND SON.

In a coincidence worthy of the climax of a Thomas Hardy novel, Unaipon's last telegram crossed with a letter of response from Shenstone —a letter that Unaipon *never received*. In his reply, dated 3 October 1925, the Angus & Robertson Company Secretary answered all of the author's questions:

> Mr. David Unaipon,
> General Post Office,
> ADELAIDE, S.A.
>
> Dear Sir,
> We have decided to purchase the copyright of the three Aboriginal Legends recently sent by you, and we now enclose the usual form of assignment covering same. Please sign and return the form to us and we shall then send you by wire the amount due to you after deducting the advance already made.
>
> The material so far supplied by you should, we think, be sufficient to make a volume of about the size we had in mind, and until we ascertain whether there is sufficient demand we do not intend to acquire the copyright of any more legends.
>
> Yours faithfully,
>
> ANGUS & ROBERTSON LTD.
> Secretary.

This is a crucial document for three reasons. First, it illustrates the fact that, at this stage, Angus & Robertson was still intending to publish the book of legends provided by Unaipon; the sense of closure implied by the second paragraph evidences its view that the project was nearing completion. Second, it is clear that the manuscripts were assessed, were deemed 'of worth', and that the publisher had every intention of remunerating the writer for his work. Third—and most important—for some inexplicable reason, Unaipon never picked up the letter from the Adelaide General Post Office. Perhaps, having despatched six telegrams to Sydney over the previous month, he was anticipating one in return. Possibly he was expecting any correspondence to be sent care of Wigg and Sons; or perhaps—most unluckily—he had just left Adelaide for the country the day before. The record shows that the mail was posted from Sydney on 3 October, was received in Adelaide on 6 October and was then returned 'Unclaimed' to Angus & Robertson on 20 October 1925.

FSS'MR

Mr. David Unaipon,

ADELAIDE, S.A.

Dear Sir,

We have decided to purchase the copyright of the three Aboriginal Legends recently sent by you, and we now enclose the usual form of assignment covering same. Please sign and return the form to us and we shall then send you by wire the amount due to you after deducting the advance already made.

The material so far supplied by you should, we think, be sufficient to make a volume of about the size we had in mind, and until we ascertain whether there is sufficient demand we do not intend to acquire the copyright of any more legends.

Yours faithfully,
ANGUS & ROBERTSON LTD.

Secretary.

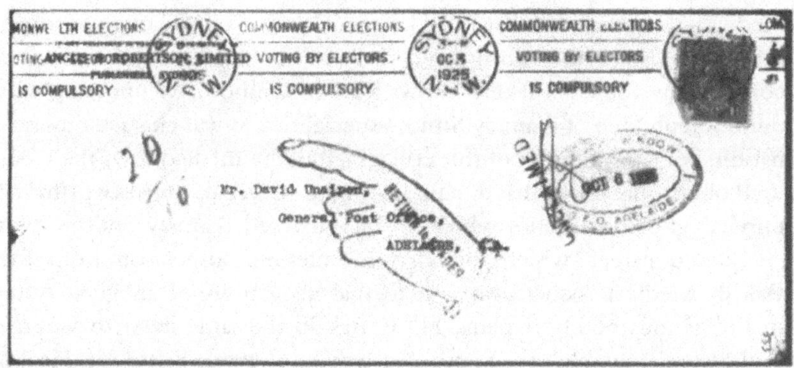

Letter and its envelope from Angus & Robertson to David Unaipon, 3 October 1925. (Courtesy State Library of New South Wales)

Australian history—and literary history—is full of accidents. In terms of twentieth-century Indigenous achievements, this has to be one of the most poignant. Had Unaipon received the letter, he could have been reinspired with enthusiasm for his project, Angus & Robertson might have completed its work on the manuscript and the first book by an Australian Aborigine could very well have been published in 1926. Instead, the evidence shows that, believing his publisher had never responded to his repeated entreaties and no longer valued his creative efforts, in October 1925 Unaipon left South Australia on a long journey to the Nullarbor Plains, gathering further legends in the company of an Indigenous translator. Meanwhile, having received no response from Unaipon, Angus & Robertson perhaps tired of the difficulty of contacting him, and the project languished for over a year until the opportunistic intervention of William Ramsay Smith in November 1926.

So it was that thirteen months later Ramsay Smith stepped into the vacuum created by the breakdown in the professional relationship between Unaipon and his publisher. Increasingly frustrated with progress towards his own Harrap publication, and on the look-out for a ready solution, Ramsay Smith seized upon the information provided by Unaipon in November 1926 that: 'he had sent you [Angus & Robertson] all the manuscript he had promised and that he had heard nothing from you for twelve months'. In the long letter to George Roberston of 5 November 1926 of which this is a part, Ramsay Smith makes obvious the fact that his 'friendship' with Unaipon is based upon a thinly-disguised version of the master/servant relationship. He confides: 'I think I led you to understand that I had known David of old. Though in some, if not most, ways he is a bad egg he is "good in parts", or rather there is corn among the chaff if one knows how to winnow.' 'Winnowing' was undoubtedly one of Ramsay Smith's specialities, as was character assassination. For, at the outset of this crucial letter, the medico sows the seeds in Robertson's mind that Unaipon might be venal, untrustworthy or unreliable; characteristics which, in fact, marked Ramsay Smith's own chequered career, which included his lifetime suspension from the British Medical Association and formal allegations of an illicit trade in Indigenous bodily remains. He writes, in the same letter to George Robertson (notably, on South Australian Central Board of Health letterhead):

> To resume a somewhat ancient story—Yesterday David Unaipon called on me. I had not seen him since 2nd October of last year. On that occasion he said that a few men who were interested in Anthropology had asked him to go 'exploring' and were 'subscribing'. He promised I should have an interest in the result and asked if I would help. From an extensive knowledge of him I did subscribe, hoping for nothing in return. He was seen a day or two after, driving in a finely outfitted motor and was 'chronicled' in the newspapers as having gone with another blackfellow who was to be interpreter among certain tribes.
>
> From that time I neither saw nor heard anything of him till he turned up yesterday. The glamour was gone; he was badly dressed, as I had never seen him before. There was no word of *quid pro quo*: I thought he was out for 'Quids for nothing'. He opened business by saying he wanted to know if I could help him to have manuscript [sic] typed. He said nothing about previous interviews, but not knowing what he might be after I raised the subject of contributions by asking him how he stood with you.

Ramsay Smith then relates the details of a pivotal conversation between himself and Unaipon (allegedly taken down in shorthand by Ramsay Smith's secretary):

> —Angus & Robertson have got all your MSS that you are going to publish?
> —Yes.
> —Do you think you can collect other legends and myths in the North and elsewhere, and if so, are you going to use them?
> —No I am not going to published (sic) what I collect. I thought that I could help you.
> —How can I help you now?
> —I want some money and expenses for the trip North. I have arranged for a motor car, but I want some money.
> —How much do you think you will need?
> —I think I will want about 10 pounds.
> —Have you thought about asking other gentleman [sic] to assist you?
> —Yes.
> —Whom were you thinking of asking?

—I was thinking of asking Dr Roger, Sir Joseph Verco, the 'Register' (Mr Burns)
—Well then call tomorrow morning and the money will be awaiting you
—Very well.
—Where are you going?
—To the Nullarbor plains, I am taking a 'medicine man' with me to interpret.
—Are you going to any of the mission stations?
—No although I may call at Point Pierce.
—Then you will let me have the legends when you return?
—Yes.
—I may make you some compensation afterwards.
—Thank you, Sir.

After the comprehensive attack on Unaipon's credibility, reliability and reputation which this letter represented, it is no surprise that—just four days later—F. S. Shenstone wrote to Ramsay Smith, offering him the rights to the collected manuscripts of David Unaipon:

G.R. 9/11/26

Dr. W. Ramsay Smith, F.R.S. (Edin.),
Central Board of Health,
Victoria Place,
ADELAIDE.

Dear Sir,
Mr. Robertson has handed me your letter of the 5th inst. re David Unaipon. By arrangement Unaipon collected and wrote up for us a number of aboriginal legends and we bought the copyright for £2/2/- per thousand words, the sum-total amounting to about £150. Quite a charming book can be made of them, and we intended asking Professor Tucker to prepare it for the press. If, however, you want them we will transfer the copyright to you for what it cost us, furnishing you with a typewritten copy and reserving the original MS. for ourselves.

Yours faithfully,
ANGUS & ROBERTSON, LTD. [Signed by F.S. Shenstone, Esq., Secretary]

To add a final insult to Unaipon, when the full typescript was 'furnished' for Ramsay Smith in 1927, Shenstone added to the package—at no cost to Ramsay Smith—the three stories which Unaipon had mailed to him in September 1925; those same tales which were the subject of the crucial letter Unaipon had never received.

Ramsay Smith's correspondence conveys a palpable sense of delight at the news that he is to be on-sold a complete manuscript of legendary tales. At the same time, there is an understated but unmistakable undertone of relief that Unaipon is no longer on the scene:

> 16th November, 1926
>
> Dear Sir,
> I have to thank you for your letter of 9th November which straightens out all matters concerning relations with my old friend David, and leaves a clear field for operations . . . I am glad to have Mr. Robertson's literary valuation of the manuscript and I shall use my best endeavour to see that it does not lose by any editing to which I may subject it.

From early January 1927 portions of Unaipon's hard-won manuscript were sent to the medical officer for his 'editing'. Ramsay Smith clearly recognises what a godsend this will prove to be for his project; the tone of his letters to Shenstone ranges from the fulsome to the unctuous. On 24 January he gushes: 'I realise that whatever place such a book may take among anthropological publications, and I shall do my best to make it worthy, almost everything may be traced to Mr. Robertson's generous action'. And again, on 11 February: 'I shall take an early opportunity of writing to Mr. Robertson and of telling him how this transaction has simplified my work of preparation of the volume of Myths, and has made it possible for me to give a view of Australian Aboriginal Myths that I take as quite new in literature'.

This is significant because, underneath all the self-deprecating ingratiation, one fact is unequivocal: William Ramsay Smith admits that he is editing someone else's work. For its part, Angus & Robertson continues to credit Unaipon as the author of the tales, right up to and including its final letter of assignment to Ramsay Smith, dated 10 March 1927. Shenstone writes: 'We have had no Board Meeting since receiving your cheque, until to-day, and I now have pleasure in sending you the original assignments of copyright of David Unaipon's Aboriginal Legends, together with one from ourselves to you'.

Yet, somehow, between March and September of the same year, a dramatic change takes place—all references to Unaipon disappear. Instead of seeing himself as simply 'preparing' the manuscript for publication, over that period Ramsay Smith appears to persuade himself that the revised work has become his, and his alone. Nowhere in the finished text is the true author acknowledged, recognised or thanked. Nowhere is the process of appropriation hinted at, in even the most oblique fashion. On the contrary, in a letter to Robertson of 16 September 1927, Ramsay Smith laments the difficulty of the task that has absorbed him for the past five months:

> Dear Mr. Robertson,
>
> By this week's English Mail I have dispatched to Mr. Harrap the MS. of "Australian Myths" complete. The book has cost an enormous amount of pains-taking work, but I think the literary result will prove that it was worth writing. You know something of the pecuniary cost: I may say that I spent a good deal more in the same line before it was finished.

Yet, despite his protestations, it is obvious that the book was prepared in record time. It is equally obvious that in March of that year Ramsay Smith was presented with what was essentially a complete second draft of nearly 80,000 words in length. For him to complain that he had to spend five months editing and polishing to completion a book of this length was as churlish as it was unrealistic.

In any event, the resultant book was published under the title *Myths & Legends of the Australian Aboriginals* by George G. Harrap in 1930. David Unaipon was totally erased from the work; the only indirect nod towards the true author appears in the preface of the Harrap edition. Though he is unnamed, there is no doubt that Unaipon is the 'narrator' in this sentence: 'The name "Teddy-bear," which was used by a narrator, would perhaps be aptly applicable descriptively, but its modernity might appear objectionable' (Ramsay Smith 1930: 9). With one oblique reference Ramsay Smith consigns Unaipon to the shadows of literary history.

Further editions were published internationally over the years. Originally, an American hard-cover release appeared under the Chambers imprint in the 1930s and subsequent facsimile copies were produced as recently as 1970 by the Johnson Reprint Corporation in New York City. Most unusually, six of the stories from the Ramsay Smith version were extracted for an illustrated Japanese edition of the tales, released in Tokyo by Oceania Press in 1985. Throughout all those years, these most Australian of stories were never published in their country of origin, nor with due acknowledgment given to their true creator.

In 1996 the book appeared in a mass-market paperback facsimile edition, published by Senate (an imprint of Random House UK), copies of which were available for sale in the UK and Australia in 1997. At the end of 1997 the entire Senate list was sold by Random House UK to Tiger Books, a British publisher/distributor specialising in older reprint and remaindered titles. In late 1998 Tiger Books released a paperback edition with a new cover, quoting increasing global interest in the title, especially in Australia. Finally, Tiger Books was itself absorbed by Senate Press in 2000, with the Middlesex publisher continuing to distribute the Ramsay Smith version worldwide.

William Ramsay Smith died in 1937. This means that the copyright in *his* published version (the 1930 Harrap book) has lapsed. But the more pertinent copyright issue is this: if—as we now know—the original author of the entire book was David Unaipon then, according to both Australian and British law in force at the time of first publication in 1930, twenty-five years after the death of the *original creator* the copyright reverts to Unaipon's heirs and successors, regardless of any assignments made during his lifetime. Since Unaipon died in 1967 the crucial date for the assertion of intellectual rights becomes 1992. Our own analysis that nearly all of the Unaipon original has been directly copied by Ramsay Smith has been corroborated by expert advice from the Australian Copyright Council. It has stated that 'a substantial portion' of Unaipon's manuscript was reproduced by Ramsay Smith and that intellectual and moral rights to the work reside with the David Unaipon Estate. Unaipon's great-niece, Melva Kropinyeri of Murray Bridge, South Australia, is the nominee of this estate, assisted by her children, one of whom, Harold [Kym], helped to prepare this new edition. Thus another road—this time an international one—may yield a return to the Ngarrindjeri three-quarters of a century later.

But what of Ramsay Smith's version? The Harrap edition of *Myths & Legends of the Australian Aboriginals* is, in its own way, a rare and beautiful publication, sometimes found in second-hand stores. It is illustrated with romantic watercolours by Alice Woodward, and has etchings and photographs of artefacts, people and sites from further afield than the origins of the stories themselves.

Most significantly, as noted above, in *Myths & Legends of the Australian Aboriginals* David Unaipon's name appears nowhere in the book; there are merely allusions to 'narrators'. Ramsay Smith outlines some of his editorial interventions on Unaipon's manuscript in a revealing way:

> It is a collection of narratives as told by pure-blooded aboriginals of various tribes who have been conversant with the subject from childhood. If some of the stories may seem to touch the verge of tediousness, they resemble in this respect the legends of other races . . . Such changes as have been made in the narratives are few and slight, and do not go beyond what were considered to be necessary in order to make clear the meaning, or to give some degree of grammatical correctness to the text without changing the 'aroma' of the story. (Ramsay Smith 1930: 7–8)

But Unaipon's preface is quite different:

> My race—the Aborigines of Australia—has a vast tradition of legends, myths, and folklore stories. These, which they delight in telling to the younger members of the tribe, have been handed down orally for thousands of years. In fact, all tribal laws and customs are, first of all, told to the children of the tribe in the form of stories, just as the white Australian mother first instructs her children with nursery stories. Of course, the mothers and the old men, in telling these stories, drag them out to a great length, putting in every detail, with much gesture and acting; but in writing them down for our white friends I have used the simplest forms of expression, in order that neither the meaning nor the 'atmosphere' may be lost. (3, this volume)

Consider also the following editorial changes effected by Ramsay Smith. We think these are the kinds of changes designed to attribute knowledge to the editor, and take it away from the 'narrator'. The first concerns one of our favourite passages from 'Narroondarie's Wives' when Narroondarie is being pursued by an enemy:

> so he looked around, hoping to see footprints which would lead to him. But there were no footprints and now he was convinced that this strange person was an enemy. A friend will always leave a footprint—this is the teaching of the Aborigines. So he thought to himself, like all wise men do, that he would be always upon the alert; and during that day he was not seen.
>
> On the second day of this event Narroondarie sat upon the peak of a high sand-hummock looking first Wolkundmia (north), then Tolkamia (west), Kolkamia (south), and Karramia (east). (127, this volume)

In *Myths & Legends* this is changed to:

> He looked round, hoping to see footprints that would lead to him, but there were no footprints, and now he was convinced that this strange person was an enemy.[1] So he thought to himself, as all wise men do, that he would always have to be on the alert.
>
> During that day he saw nothing of the enemy. On the second day Nurunderi sat upon the peak of a high sand-hummock, looking first north, then west, then south, and finally east. (Ramsay Smith 1930: 324)

The most significant change involves taking the comment on the teaching of the Aborigines out of the text and putting it in a footnote. This puts it in Ramsay Smith's voice and removes the capacity for authoritative commentary from the Indigenous narrator. It keeps that narrative at the level of 'story' while knowledge is reserved for the white editor. This is entirely consistent with the removal of authorship from Unaipon. The words 'authorship' and 'authority' have more than just an element of meaning in common. The other change involves the removal of the names for the points of the compass. Such a change is more than cosmetic; again, it diminishes the specifically Indigenous knowledge content of the text.

[1] A friend will always leave a footprint. This is the teaching of the aboriginals. (Ramsay Smith 1930: 324)

Similarly, 'The Voice of the Great Spirit' begins:

> It is interesting to learn how all races of men have wrestled with the problem of good and evil. The Australian Aborigines have a greater and deeper sense of morality and religion than is generally known . . . This is one of the many stories that is handed down from generation to generation by my people. (150, this volume)

The first comparative point is too significant for Ramsay Smith to delete, so he puts it in another footnote, and begins the text with a slightly altered version of Unaipon's second sentence:

> **The Voice of the Great Spirit**[1]
> The Australian aboriginals have a deeper and more extensive sense of morality and religion than is generally known . . . This is one of the many stories that have been handed down from generation to generation.

Again, the personal presence of the Indigenous narrator is removed with the words 'by my people', but a strong sense of intellectual authority remains even with the new first sentence ('The Australian aboriginals have a deeper and more extensive sense of morality and religion than is generally known'). Whose voice is this? The reader of Ramsay Smith tends to assume it is Ramsay Smith, but he has already taken his comment out into the footnote, as he did in the previous example we have quoted, leaving this second commentary, which seems more important since it is included in the main text. This commentary precedes the story proper that begins: 'In the beginning the Great Spirit used to speak directly'. Some residual authority—Unaipon's voice, in fact—persists, even in Ramsay Smith's edited version. Later in the same story we see once again the removal of specific cultural detail that is in Unaipon's original version: 'the tribes at last cried aloud with sorrow and regret. They cut their bodies with sharp stones and painted themselves white. They began to fear that they would never get in touch again with the Great Spirit' (151, this volume).

[1] It is interesting to learn something of the methods by which the various races of men have wrestled with the problem of good and evil. This is an aboriginal contribution to the subject. (Ramsay Smith 1930: 182)

In Ramsay Smith this becomes: 'At last the tribes cried aloud. They began to fear that they would never again get in touch with the Great Spirit' (Ramsay Smith 1930: 183).

An unfortunate change, not only because the words 'with sorrow and regret' strongly indicate the realisation of the meaning of good and evil—the *point* of the story—but also because cutting the skin and painting up are significant ritual gestures. So Ramsay Smith's version, we would argue from these examples, is poorer than Unaipon's, both as a literary text and as a cultural record.

Literary repatriation involves restoring the text to a form as close as possible to the original handwritten manuscript. But it also involves weaving the text back home to the community (or communities or family groups) where the stories were told and traded in the first place. This is why David Unaipon's descendants (especially Harold [Kym] Kropinyeri and his sisters Judy and Elaine) have been involved in checking the manuscript for anything that is inconsistent according to their knowledge, and restoring the occasional word that was lost in the transcription from Unaipon's handwritten version to the typescript.

It is our hope that this literary repatriation will point to the place-specific relevance of writing. Such works intensify their meanings if they are seen to be rooted in a series of places. This is a decolonising gesture for literature, it turns away from the imperialism and universalism of writing that is supposed to transcend place, aspire to the universal, and conquer time by becoming of permanent historical significance.

Strange now that it is David Unaipon's turn to influence history once again, partly prompted through his 'currency' on our money. With the publication of his book, the opportunity arises for everyone to restore another value to his portrait, less an iconic one, but one more related to the values of wisdom and knowledge arising from a people whose ancient occupation of place made it ecologically sustainable and profoundly social: a place where knowledge and things are shared in the spirit suggested by Unaipon, which is not a restrictive or exclusive version of copyright, but a liberal and inclusive one. As Unaipon writes in the opening sentence of 'Aboriginal Folklore': 'Perhaps some day Australian writers will use Aboriginal myths and weave literature from them, the same as other writers have done with the Roman, Greek, Norse, and Arthurian legends'.

STEPHEN MUECKE AND ADAM SHOEMAKER

Note on the Edition

In editing this work we have taken the advice of David Unaipon's descendants and have presented it as we believe 'he would have wanted'. At the same time, we have remained as faithful as possible to the style of the original manuscript, which was mostly handwritten in pencil. We have therefore normalised spellings, introduced paragraph breaks, some question marks and inverted commas, and standardised an idiosyncratic use of commas. These are gestures of writing, and while Unaipon is concerned with writing down an oral tradition, this tradition is embedded even in the author's original title: 'Legendary Tales of the Australian Aborigines *told* by David Unaipon'.

It is also clear that the manuscript is, in many sections, still a draft. At one point in 'The Mischievous Crow and the Good He Did', Unaipon writes a note to himself in brackets: 'describe the interior of the cave'. In the same legend, the animal which comes to the aid of the baby pelicans is left blank in the text until near the end of the legend. In this case, we have 'filled in' the author's blanks retrospectively. Our editorial interventions are placed within square brackets [ ]. All the round brackets ( ) in the text are Unaipon's. When in the text he glosses an Aboriginal word or phrase, we have consistently put the English second in round brackets, and very occasionally promoting the English gloss to the first occasion of the appearance of the word or name.

To add even more challenge to the textual task, Unaipon's major work is contained in two richly bound volumes in the State Library of New South Wales. The first of these—the Mitchell Library volume which is entitled 'The MS'—is actually only about 60 per cent in handwritten script. Put another way, it is not the case that volume one is entirely a manuscript and volume two is entirely a typescript. For example, in the noteworthy case of the story 'How Teddy Lost His Tail', a typeset, magazine-published version has been literally pasted into the original manuscript volume. Here, volume two actually contains a typed draft which is demonstrably prior to the published one; it is the earlier version that appears in this collection.

Unaipon's work, with very few exceptions—all of which are footnoted in the text—is not difficult to follow and little has been amended. However, some of these amendments should be mentioned. First, the text has been punctuated and paragraphed according to contemporary practice. Second, for grammatical clarity, we have aligned Unaipon's tenses when they strayed into the present having just been in the past (this, too, is a function of oral storytelling).

Third, we have altered English nouns which were in the singular in the manuscript but should logically have been in the plural. A point to note here is that the Aboriginal nouns in the manuscript are *always* in the singular, even when the context clearly refers to the plural. Another is that many of the English nouns are capitalised in the legends, whereas they are in lower case in the more 'anthropological' stories of the Ngarrindjeri written by Unaipon. We have retained these practices, but have put lower case for the second and subsequent words of composite nouns in Ngarrindjeri or other Aboriginal languages, for instance 'Goon na ghun' or 'Nulla nulla', except in titles.

Last, Unaipon's spelling of Indigenous language words changes throughout the manuscript. The most frequently cited form is used here and we have listed the alternative spellings in the glossary we have supplied at the back of the book.

Otherwise, Unaipon's unique expression remains exactly as he wrote it in his manuscript. In all cases we have tried to ensure that Unaipon's legends and other texts are presented in accordance with the aims he outlines in his preface: 'in writing them down for our white friends I have used the simplest forms of expression, in order that neither the meaning nor the "atmosphere" may be lost'.

THE EDITORS

Acknowledgements

For setting us on the path of this journey, we are very grateful to Henry and Jean Rankine and the people of Raukkan. We could not have begun the task without the support of the Kropinyeri family, especially Melva Kropinyeri and her children Judy, Elaine and Harold [Kym]. Harold has been an unstoppable researcher, co-editor and friend.

Many people assisted us in vital ways: Clare Archer-Lean, Diane Bell, Prudence Black, Isobel Bourke, Dianna Campbell, Phillip Clarke, Evelyn Dykgraaf, Rob Foster, Mary-Anne Gale, Murray Harper, Veronica Harper, Sue Hosking, Gayle Houlahan, Fiona Inglis, Michael Leigh, Andrew Lohrey, Ian McDonald, Doug Muecke, Christine Morris, Craig Munro, Maggie Nolan, David Reynolds, Luke Slattery and Christine Yates. Teresa Pitt and Gabby Lhuede at MUP, and editor Foong Ling Kong have been more than helpful.

Our most significant researcher and copy-editor, John Alexander, was totally committed to the project throughout—sincere thanks.

We are indebted to the Australian Research Council, which awarded us a three-year large grant from 1996–1998. The original research which underpins this project could not have taken place without this invaluable support. In 1998 Adam Shoemaker's six-month tenure in Canberra as a Visiting Research Fellow, Department of English, University College, Australian Defence Force Academy was crucial to the process of uncovering the complex relationship between David Unaipon and William Ramsay Smith. We would also like to recognise the financial and material backing provided by the South Australian

Museum, the University of South Australia, the University of Adelaide, the University of Technology, Sydney (especially the Transforming Cultures Key University Research Strength) and the Queensland University of Technology (Centre for Community and Cross-Cultural Studies).

Legendary Tales of the Australian Aborigines

Preface

My race—the Aborigines of Australia—has a vast tradition of legends, myths, and folklore stories. These, which they delight in telling to the younger members of the tribe, have been handed down orally for thousands of years. In fact, all tribal laws and customs are, first of all, told to the children of the tribe in the form of stories, just as the white Australian mother first instructs her children with nursery stories. Of course, the mothers and the old men, in telling these stories, drag them out to a great length, putting in every detail, with much gesture and acting; but in writing them down for our white friends I have used the simplest forms of expression, in order that neither the meaning nor the 'atmosphere' may be lost.

As a full-blooded member of my race I think I may claim to be the first—but I hope, not the last—to produce an enduring record of our customs, beliefs, and imaginings.

David Unaipon

Aboriginal Folklore

Perhaps some day Australian writers will use Aboriginal myths and weave literature from them, the same as other writers have done with the Roman, Greek, Norse, and Arthurian legends. If there is anything in the scientific theory that our Aborigines are descendants of the Dravidians (a very ancient Indian race), then Aboriginal folklore may be among the oldest in the world.

The Aborigines are great story-tellers. The Mooncumbulli (the wise old man) telling the story puts in every detail. He acts and dramatises every incident with gesture, with changed intonations, he leads his hearers from point to point in the story. A little simple legend told to the tribe under primitive conditions would take all the evening to relate. The Aborigines have a myth connected with nearly all the constellations and bright stars in the heavens.

Nearly all the tribes scattered about Australia have traditions of their flight from a land in the nor-west, beyond the sea, into Australia. That land may probably be the ancient continent of Lemuria. The traditions also relate that the Aborigines were driven into Australia by a plague of fierce ants, or by a prehistoric race as fierce and as innumerable as ants. Like the Israelites, the Aborigines seem to have had a Moses, a law-giver, a leader, who guided them in their Exodus from Lemuria. His name is Narroondarie.

This mythological Being, who now lives in the heavens, gave Aborigines their tribal laws and customs. Aboriginal myths, legends, and stories were told to laughing and open-eyed children centuries before our present-day European culture began; stories that stand today as a link between the dawn of the world and our latest civilisation.

Aborigines, Their Traditions and Customs: Where Did They Come From?

In giving an account of the traditions and customs of my race it is only logical and fitting that I should begin with the tradition of our coming to Australia. The Aborigines have always known the four points of the compass, and the four winds of the earth—Wolkund (the north), Kolkami (the south), Tolkami (the west), and Karrami (the east). The traditions say that the Aborigines came out of the north-west, the Loo loo poon cold. 'Loo loo' means a break, a severance. 'Poon cold' means a connection. The tradition implies that we arrived in Australia from another land in the north-west. The way of our coming was probably over an isthmus that has long since been sunk under the seas.

This seems to agree with science, that Australia was once part of a large and ancient continent called Lemuria. We migrated, or were forced into Australia by fierce ants, the Praid arna prodda. This may mean that my ancestors were pursued by a plague of huge, deadly ants, or by a prehistoric race as fierce and as innumerable as ants.

Since coming to Australia thousands of years ago, there has been probably little or no change in the habits and the customs of my people. They have kept the balance of Nature; for centuries they have neither advanced nor retrogressed. Our tribal laws and customs are fixed and unchangeable. Generation after generation has gone through the same rigid tribal training.

Every race has had its great traditional leader and law-giver who has given the race its first moral training, as well as its social and tribal customs. Narroondarie was our great traditional leader. The laws of

Narroondarie are taught to the children in their infancy. The hunting-grounds were given out to the different families and tribes by Narroondarie. The boundaries of the tribal hunting-grounds have been kept the same from remotest time. Whilst the children of the tribes are hearing from their elders all the traditions and legends of our race, they are learning all the knowledge and skill of bush craft and hunting, as well as undergoing the three great tests or initiations, to Kornmund (full manhood) and Meemund (full womanhood), which is generally completed at the age of eighteen.

The first test is to overcome the appetite, by doing a two-day walk or hunt without food, and then to be brought suddenly before a fire, on which is cooking some choice kangaroo steak or other native delicacy. The next test is to overcome pain. The young boys and girls submit to having their noses pierced, their bodies marked, and to lying down upon hot embers, thinly covered with boughs. The third test is to overcome fear. The young people are told fearful and hair-raising stories about ghosts and the Muldarpi (Evil Spirit or devil-devil). After all this, they are put to sleep in a lonely place or near the burial-places of the tribe. During the night the elders, made hideous with white clay and bark head-dresses, appear, making weird noises. Those who show no signs of having had a disturbed night are then admitted as fully initiated members of the tribe.

No youth or maiden is allowed to marry until he, or she, has passed through these tests. The marriage is talked over first by all the old members of the tribe, and it is always the uncle of the young man who finally selects the wife. The uncle on the mother's side is the most important relative. The actual marriage ceremony takes place during the time of festivals. The husband does not look or speak at his mother-in-law, although he is husband in name to all his sisters-in-law. Under native conditions, the sex-laws are very strict.

A fully developed Aboriginal has, in his own way, a vast amount of knowledge. Although it may not be strictly scientific learning, still it is a very exact knowledge, and his powers of physical observation are developed to the utmost. For instance, an Aboriginal living under primitive life knows the habits and the anatomy and the haunts of every animal in the bush. He knows all the birds, their habits, and even their love, or mating, notes. He knows the approach of the different seasons of the year from various signs, as well as from the positions of the stars in the heavens. He has developed the art of tracking the human footprint to the highest degree. There is a whole science in footprints. Footprints are the same evidence to a bush native as finger-prints are in a court of law.

He knows the track of every individual member of the tribe. There is as much difference and individuality in footprints as in fingerprints. Of course, it will be readily understood that the Aboriginal language and customs vary a great deal according to the nature of the country the tribes are living in, although there is a great common understanding running through us all. Our legends and traditions are all the same tales, or myths, told slightly differently, with local colouring, etc.

For instance, all the tribes in South Australia (my native State) agree that we originally came out of the north-west, struck the Darling River, and followed it down to Lake Alexandrina. We did not all come at once, but came in waves, and we have preserved the names of the tribes and the order in which they came. The first tribe was the Par oung de kuld. The meaning of this name is that they were the leaders, probably the most war-like and venturesome. The second tribe was the Yar rald de kuld, meaning the back people. There is not the slightest hint in any of our traditions that there were any other previous inhabitants in Australia.

The greatest time of the year, to my people, is the Par bar rarrie (springtime). It is then that all the great traditional corroborees take place. All our sacred traditions are then chanted and told.

All the stars and constellations in the heavens, the Milky Way, the Southern Cross, Orion's Belt, the Magellan Cloud, etc., have a meaning. There are legends connected with them all. We call the heavens the Wyerriewarr, and the ruler of the heavens Nebalee.

From time immemorial we have understood the subtle art of hypnotic suggestion. Our medicine men (the Mooncumbulli) have used charms, etc., to drive out pain.

It will be seen from the foregoing account, and from other sources, that my race, living under native and tribal conditions, has a very strict and efficacious code of laws that keeps the race pure. It is only when the Aborigines come in contact with white civilisation that they leave their tribal laws, and take nothing in place of these old and well-established customs. It is then that disease and deterioration set in.

Some Stories about My Race: What the Aborigines' Carvings Near Sydney Mean

In various parts of Australia, and within ten to twenty minutes' drive from Sydney in a car, are evidences of the existence of a primitive race which has passed on to the western sky, the land of mystery. Many of these evidences consist of figures cut in the surface of vertical or horizontal rocks, with the aid of a stone axe.

For instance, at Manly there exists a carving of Aborigines representing a male figure with both arms outstretched and one hand holding a karnark (waddy), also another human figure and a form to represent a shark. There are other carved objects hewn into the flat surface of the rock. At one spot there are four male figures, with a boomerang over the head of one, and a fish between the legs of another.

There are also two figures nearly oval in shape, and one of the figures has smaller circles cut around the edge. All these forms and figures have a meaning. An animal, bird, reptile, or fish represents the totem of a tribe.

Tribe Totems

As in the instance of the Manly figure, where a fish is placed between the legs of a person, it is the totem of the tribe living in that locality. Before a tribe can occupy a hunting-ground it must select a totem—a fish, animal, bird, or reptile, or something that exists. It may be sun, moon, wind, lightning, or thunder. Thus in some instances you will see a figure representing the sun or half-moon. Sometimes you notice figures of a kangaroo and an emu, or two other forms. The kangaroo might be the totem belonging to the Chief of the tribe, and the emu that of his wife, showing that she comes of a tribe with the emu totem.

Totems have an important part in the social life of my race. If a person has committed an offence, or broken a tribal law, he becomes a fugitive, travelling to some distant part of the country. Perhaps he comes from the Gulf of Carpentaria, and finds himself wandering down the banks of the Parramatta, creeping along stealthily, winding, listening intently, scanning through the dense foliage of every bay or cove to see whether his path is clear of the owner of that country—to be seen would be death—noticing every footprint on the way, reading every marking on the trunks of large trees, and the perpendicular and flat rock surfaces, reading every form or figure to see whether there is hope of protection and friendship.

Key to Safety

Presently the keen eye of the fugitive sees the figure of his mother's totem. Casting aside all fear, he walks boldly into the beaten track that leads to the camp and presents himself. Producing a string of kangaroo teeth made in bead fashion and a bunch of emu feathers, he holds them up to the sight of the Chief without uttering a word. That is a sign that he belongs to the Kangaroo totem, and his mother likewise belongs to the Emu totem tribe. He is then received into that tribe and becomes one of them, participating in all their privileges.

Then again, you will notice other forms or figures, a wallaby and a kangaroo with a man figure and weapon. The weapon may be a boomerang or Nulla nulla. This represents that the Wallaby totem tribe once occupied that country, and that the Kangaroo totem tribe came, did battle with the Wallaby tribe, drove them away, and took possession of the country. Or perhaps the Chief of the Emu totem is not content; he would like to change his hunting-ground. He likewise has put to flight the Kangaroo totem tribe and dispossessed them of stolen country. The Chief then orders that his totem be carved upon the same rock, and so it goes on. As there are various figures carved on the surface of one rock, it shows that the tribes of the different totems shown have occupied that locality.

ASTRONOMY

There are other forms and figures hewn into the rock at Manly. The oval line may represent the Sun on its course, or to be more exact, my race has the knowledge of the earth's motion. There are old men in each tribe who study the stars and their positions in the heavens at night, at certain times of the year. At intervals during the night they give a call: 'Kee eel all icth rervu wee (the earth has already turned).' It may be to instil that knowledge in the minds of the young.

There are other carvings that deal with their sacred ceremonies and traditions that I will describe later.

Belief of the Aborigine in a Great Spirit

The belief in a Supreme Being and the religious instruction, as well as religious ceremonies and worship, are not the experiences of the Jew and Mohammedan alone. Neither did it belong to one particular age or place, but it is universal and belongs to every age. This wonderful experience of a longing for something beautiful and noble, something spiritually Divine, lives within the bosom of the nations of the past as it does today.

Wonderful is the soul of man. A capacity for the Great Spirit of the Eternal God. Go back into those ancient civilisations and review the wonders. Those sensational discoveries in the valley of the Nile or in the jungles of Indo-China, or let your mind be carried away to far-off Peru or Yucatan, or think of the grandeur that once was Rome's, the glories that once belonged to Greece. Amongst these ruins are monuments and fragments of magnificent temples erected to their gods. These are evidences that go to prove that man is a worshipping creature irrespective of colour, language, or clime. The only difference is, as a nation's conception of the Great Spirit, so is their form of worship.

The Jews have their synagogue, where they find delight and satisfaction in the offering of sacrifice and the singing of psalms to God Jehovah. The Mohammedans have their mosque, where they love to bow in reverent attitude praying to Allah, their God, and to Mahomet the prophet. The Christian churches of today, churches of various denominations, people worshipping, some within humble buildings, some worshipping in beautiful churches and cathedrals with towers and spires, artistic windows, decorated ceilings and walls, sculptured pulpits, altars and fonts, with the genius of a Raphael and Michelangelo—as it was in the past, so is it today. People in every clime still bowing and worshipping their gods, material gods hewn and fashioned in rock and clay and wood. God's animals, birds, and reptiles—these they believe possess the spirit of the Deity.

Not so with the Aborigines of Australia. We build no place of worship, neither do we erect altars for the offering of sacrifice, but, notwithstanding this lack of religious ceremonies, we believe in a Great Spirit and the Son of the Great Spirit. There arose among the Aborigines a great teacher, Narroondarie; he was an elect of the Great Spirit.

And he spoke to our forefathers thus: 'Children, there is a Great Spirit above whose dwelling-place is Wyerriewarr. It is His will that you should know Him as Hyarrinumb; I am the Whole Spirit and ye are part of the whole, I am your Provider and Protector. It has been my pleasure to give you the privilege to sojourn awhile in the flesh state to fulfil my great plan. Remember (porun) children (nukone illawin), your life is like unto a day, and during this short period on earth you are to educate yourself by your conduct to yourself as a part of Myself and your conduct to others, with the knowledge that they are part of Myself. Live as children of your Great Father. Nol kal undutch me wee (control your appetites and desires). Remember never allow yourself to become slave to your appetite or desire, never allow your mind to suffer pain or fear, lest you become selfish, and selfishness causes misery to yourself, your wife and children and relations, and those with whom you come into contact. Selfishness is not of the Great Spirit. Cultivate everything good, moderation in food and pleasure, be generous to others, develop a healthy state of mind and body. Body and mind governed by good and pure morals with kindness for others, remembering that they are a part of that Great Spirit from whence you came.'

This knowledge develops the soul, which is a part of Whole Spirit, to a state fit to become a companion to the Great Spirit. To this end the little boys and girls are placed in the hands of the elders and their wives to be educated. The children's first education is the control of their appetites. During this training they travel from one hunting-ground to another for years.

The children endeavour day by day to control their appetites by their moderation in taking food and their conduct to those who may be weaker in body or mind, and their moral behaviour to either sex. The children also submit themselves for the testing whether they are able to control pain. The first test may be the knocking out of their front teeth by a blow from a stone axe, and the cutting of their bodies with flint knives and the sprinkling of ashes into the wound (ashes burned from a particular shrub or tree), which intensifies the pain, but also has a healing effect.

The lying upon live fire coals or heated stone red hot for a moment; the youths submitting themselves to have the beard plucked like you would a dead fowl or turkey; or sitting in a bull-ants' bed; all kinds of cruel methods are adopted to test and train the children to experience what pain is like and how to control it.

There are stages of inflicting great pain every day, and the mind and body develop accordingly. The last training is that of the control of fear. Night after night men are selected to make up some terrible story of great and ugly monsters. Monsters like the mythological Bunyip and the Muldarpie, a demon that disguises itself in all kinds of form like a kangaroo or wombat or waterfowl to trap the hunter, or a butterfly with beautiful colouring such that children like to capture. And at night during a thunderstorm they relate ghost stories, and the children sit and listen. After the story, the elders will lead them to their camp selected during the day.

'Children, you are to sleep in the burying ground of your forefathers.'

They spend the night in the cemetery, and at sunrise present themselves to the elder, showing no sign of a disturbed night. By this act they prove to the elder the control of fear.

Then on a particular day all members of the tribe meet upon a sacred spot set aside for the purpose, and an elder, in the presence of the congregation, will declare that the boys and girls are men and women. And all men of the congregation stand and the female portion will sit with head bowed, the men alone with faces turned and with spears and Nulla nulla pointing to the setting sun shout: 'Kay kay, kay kay,' meaning: 'Well done children, you have already fought the battle of life and have conquered. Manhood and womanhood is complete in you. The Great Spirit is pleased. He is now awaiting your presence in Wyerriewarr, the Home of the Spirits.'

Confusion of Tongue

Kule thou oo (in the long ago) uoo goo nook (when) the coming of the many dawns and many sunrises, the sun shone on sea and land, kuk koo loon distributing its life and energy to Animal, Bird, Reptile, and Insect, Noop eel itch nungee, the sun continued its journey across the trackless sky over to Tolkami (the mysterious west) there was never a cloud of disappointment or sorrow, but eternal sunshine. Creation smiled, and Animal, Bird, Reptile, and Insect were linked up by one common language. For instance, the Kangaroo and Goanna were able to converse and exchange ideas; so would the Eagle Hawk and Platypus; and the Wombat and Dragon-fly. Each endeavoured to please and entertain and instruct the other, whilst following their individual vocations.

The food of the Animals, Birds, and Reptiles consisted of vegetable and fish. Once every year they would congregate and have great feasting and corroborees, and there would be giving in marriage. But on this occasion they were going to do something which would change the whole condition of affairs of the race. Some were desirous that they should give away in marriage the Kangaroo and Emu, the Dingo and Goanna, the Koala (Teddy Bear) and Lyre Bird. Whilst some were in favour of it, others were strongly opposed. Those in favour were strongly represented by the Kangaroos, Emus, Dingos, Goannas, Carpet Snakes, Koalas, Pelicans, Cockatoos, and Lyre Birds. Against them were the Tortoises, Frogs, and Crows.

These three stood out against the whole of the tribes. The majority felt within themselves that they had a great and cunning antagonist in the Crow, for they knew that his wit and cunning would be sufficient to overcome their brute force.

Those in favour of the proposition set to work to consider what tactics they should adopt. The Dingo enquired of the Tontick nub bie (Tortoise), but he would not tell how or when the Crow would begin his campaign.

The Frog was next approached, but he too refused to give information.

Whilst they were preparing bann ka gee (boomerangs), yar na barrie (throwing waddies for killing animals or to do battle), key key (reed spears used in warfare) and other weapons, the three confederates, the Crow, Tortoise, and Frog, whose weapon was their mind, used to meet on top of a mountain or in the open country, on a great plain where there were no trees or shrubs, and they would sit and plan out a method of attack. The three were of one mind that if their opponents could be caused to have a great hunger, and to become angry with each other, they would be able to dispose of all their silly ideas.

Now there were three things which the whole of the tribes admired. First, the Crow was a great composer of native songs and an active dancer and impersonator; the Frog was one of the greatest dancers —more so than the Crow—and he was an artist and painted designs on his body that were unique with colouring that was much sought after and he was the possessor of a wonderful bass voice which could be heard for miles, and what was most remarkable, he was a ventriloquist. The Tortoise possessed neither voice nor agility.

The first act announced was a dance by the Tortoise in imitation of the Kangaroo. This aroused intense curiosity and wonder. Every Animal, Bird, Reptile, and Insect of the tribes turned out to see the Tortoise dance. They were asked to sit in a semicircle, and no one was allowed to cross, because the Crow reserved the remainder of the circle for his performance. The Tortoise and Frog retired behind the scenes and Crow began to sing the song of the Kangaroo. Presently a figure approached the footlights. There was great shouting as the Tortoise came creeping slowly towards the audience, and at a sign from the Crow commenced leaping and bounding here and there just like a Kangaroo. They whispered amongst themselves how wonderful it was to see the slow-moving Tortoise acting the Kangaroo dance.

'Kay hey (Hurrah, hurrah),' they shouted.

The figure dancing was that of the Frog, wearing on his back a coolamon with a shield in front. The second dance, the Swan dance, was announced, and also that the Tortoise would sing the Swan song. Taking his stand in front of the audience, the Tortoise commenced singing, whilst the Crow danced to the song. The Animals, Birds, and Reptiles could not understand how it could be the voice of the Tortoise singing. Really it was the cunning Frog ventriloquist.

The audience was carried away with enthusiasm by the marvellous performance of the slow-moving, voiceless Tortoise.

'Kay hey, kay hey! Mumgung! (Hurrah! Again! Encore)' they shouted, and for three days and three nights the performance lasted.

On the fourth morning everyone began to feel hungry, and the Kangaroo called out: 'Get the net, bring the net, and go fishing. The people are famishing with hunger.'

The Pelican set out and caught a number of fish, and the Crow was unanimously appointed by the various tribes to take charge of the distribution of them.

'Come, let us go to yonder point and cook the fish,' he said. 'You know it is against the rules of the tribe to cook fish where they are caught. But there is not sufficient, try and get some more in yonder bay.'

And they dragged with their net and caught some.

'Come to yonder point, it is unlawful to make a fire and cook here,' he kept repeating, until the whole tribe became impatient.

They began abusing the Crow, and the cunning Frog threw his voice, making it appear that it came from the Kangaroo in support of the Crow.

Presently it appeared that the voice of the Kangaroo was insulting the Emu, then the Goanna commenced to insult the Koo ka ku, and the Wombat and the Dingo. They all grew angry with one another.

The Frog saw his opportunity and called: 'To battle! To battle!'

They were so angry that they all commenced calling and shouting and calling each other ugly names. Each challenged the other to battle, and there was hurling of spear and boomerang. There was a terrible pandemonium of sound.

The only tribe which stood aloof and took no part in using insulting words, and which strove to bring about a reconciliation, was the Lyre Bird, and no one would listen to his entreaties. That is why Animal, Bird, Reptile, and Insect tribes have adopted a language of their own, and that the Lyre Bird is able to imitate them all.

Fishing

Just as my race has made the study of animal, bird, and reptile life, so it is with the same proficiency they have made a study of fish life. To possess a knowledge of animal, bird, or fish life makes one more competent to snare and capture. That is why you can never come across or hear of an Aboriginal dying of thirst or starvation. He is well informed about where and how to procure water and food. These are the two principles that constitute the means of existence for an Aboriginal. Every boy and even girl, especially those living by the river or lake, is taught to study the life and habits of the fish, to know and watch them in the shallow water among the weeds and rocks and hollow logs lying beneath the surface of the waters of rivers, lakes, and billabongs.

Now I am speaking more about the fish found in the great river Murray and its tributaries, the Darling, Murrumbidgee, the Wagga, the Seymour, and other streams that flow into the Murray. These waters contain or abound with the wonderful fish the Pondi (Murray cod) and lesser fish such as the Murray perch and bream, the silver bream, which is very bony, the cat fish and peang-ee. To the Australian Aborigine the Murray cod is *the* fish. None like it in freshwater lake or river, or salt lake, or sea. According to a legend there was a great earth shock or earth tremor at the source of the Murray. This continued for days, and suddenly the earth was rent right along where the Murray now flows, but there was only a small amount of water, just trickling and winding its way to the Southern Ocean. Presently another earth tremor, more severe than the first one, when suddenly there burst forth from the depth of the earth a huge fish, a Pondi, and as it came out of the earth it was followed by a great flow of water, the cod struggling along this narrow stream, acting like those great steam shovels, digging with its head, making the river deep and swinging its powerful tail, causing all the bends in the river until it reached what is known as Lake Alexandrina. Then Nebalee, the great prophet, caught it and cut it in pieces and threw the small fragments into the river and named them Tcherie, Thookerri, Pummerrie, Pil lul kie, Ploongie, which are the fishes caught in the Murray and its tributaries.

The freshwater fish are more easily obtained than those that live in the sea. All the fish mentioned above live in the lagoons and billabongs as well as the Murray. When there is a flood in the Murray and it overflows its banks, the water lays in the low country covering perhaps a mile or more, and frequently the Pondi, Tcherie, Thookerri, and other fish are living in this water, and after a while, through evaporation and soakage, the waters become less. Perhaps there was at flood time about five or six feet of water, in about a month's time there is only about three to eighteen inches of it, and the fish are caught without any difficulty. This is an occasion when the women, girls and boys enjoy themselves. They wade into the shallow water with baskets made specially for the purpose, and scoop the fish into them. They are made somewhat after the construction of a fisherman's net, that is fishing with a line only minus the handle. Some of the boys take their little spears and try their skill. When the water falls low, say about a foot deep, some of the fish die because there is not sufficient to live in.

The falling of the water in the Murray drains the lagoons and billabongs very considerably at times, and sometimes to such an extent that they become quite dry, and the fishes, and turtles, and yabbies seek the main stream of the Murray, and now we adopt another form of hunting in canoes, floating down with the stream, sometimes tying the canoe to a gum tree and waiting patiently until a fish swims by. Our eyes are watching intently, and presently there is a ripple, and swish, the spear is sent with the speed of lightning into the midst of the ripple. As soon as the spear strikes the fish it struggles to free itself, it becomes exhausted and then it rises to the top and is captured and placed in the canoe.

The most interesting and exciting, and one that requires a great deal of skill, is what we call the Kreel thool lin. A person gets in his canoe, with a long spear about nine feet in length. One end of it is a plain tapered point, whilst on the other end are two prongs made of hard wood with very sharp points. These two pointed sticks that form the prongs are tied or wound on to the spear with string made of rush or the fibre of the mallee tree called Thul lung ee kreel thool lin.

He thrusts the prong end of the spear suddenly into the water, which must have a depth of at least four to five feet. When this thrust is made it carries a quantity of air right to the end of its travel, and the air being compressed and lighter, seeks to rise which it does, and so comes to the surface with a report that can be heard fifty or sixty yards away. This noise created startles any fish that may be near and causes them to move; that gives the hunter an opportunity to spear the fish. This method of fishing mostly takes place near the shores of Lakes Alexandrina and Albert, in the lower Murray in South Australia. There are shallow waters having a depth of from three to five feet extending from the banks of the lakes for about two or four hundred yards, and in these shallow waters is a growth of water weed, ribbon shaped. They grow from the bottom of the water to the top, with a foot or more of their length lying upon the surface of the water. These weeds sometimes grow very densely, and make it difficult for one to pass through them in a canoe. There are other water weeds as well. Then there are growths of bullrush and reeds. And it is here that the fish find their food and rest, or, if I may use the phrase, 'where they have a nap'. It is in these growths that the catfish spawns—lays its eggs.

Often a tribe will challenge another tribe to compete in skill and in number of speared fish. The Prillthinyeri tribe, whose hunting ground is on the banks of the southern shores of Lake Alexandrina, will challenge the Thooree tribe of the western shores of Lake Albert. And this challenge is made known to all other adjoining tribes, which may extend hundreds of miles, and people will come even further, say two hundred miles. The place chosen for the competition is Wee cherr warr, a place between Point Malcolm and the homestead of Mr Bowman Poltollock's estate on the southern shore of Lake Alexandrina. Now, when this challenge is issued with the instruction of the locality chosen and on what days or weeks it will take place, the two parties are out every day on their respective hunting grounds, training and making spears for the occasion. And a week before the event, people arrive from all points of the compass at Wee cherr warr, and the evening before the day on which the two tribes introduce their picked men, the Ranijeri tribe give a corroboree, imitating the competitors in their canoes on the water, spearing fish. Perhaps they go so far as to personify the Prillthinyeri man making an attempt to spear a fish and missing the object. Then the others will laugh and jeer, telling him that he should be better occupied at home, going into the bush and assisting the old women in digging roots and gathering herbs. The Prillthinyeri are sitting quietly, never expressing their feelings, but on the other hand the Thooree are enjoying the joke. They laugh and shout 'Kay hey', which is equivalent to the European 'Hurrah' or 'Encore'.

Now before the sun rises both parties are astir, looking to see whether their spears and canoes are in order, examining them to see that no one has tampered with them during the night. Now all the camp is awake; the tribes have come to witness and encourage each competitor and speak words of cheer and hope to embolden them for the trial. After the sun rises to about nine o'clock each of the selected men of the Prillthinyeri and the Thooree take their place in the prow of their respective canoes. Then one of their men belonging to the tribe will push the canoe from the shore and they will get in at the stern of the canoe, using their pole to propel them through the weeds and they make a bee-line direct to the fishing ground. And just before they begin spearing the fish, the referee in another canoe calls the competitors to halt, to await the arrival of the onlookers who come in their canoes, perhaps there may be three or four persons in one canoe. And there may be two to three hundred canoes, and they form a large circle around where the competition will take place. This circle may be three hundred yards in diameter.

Perhaps the Prillthinyeri, being the challengers, will enter the arena from the eastern side and a canoe darts forward with a single occupant whose duty it is to arouse the fish from their lair. He is equipped with a spear as already described, he thrusts it into the water and the startled fish swim away and he shouts aloud so that everyone around the circle hears him and he tells them that it is a Tcherie (fresh water bream). Now this is taking place among the weeds. As the fish is passing in its flight, the disturbed weeds will indicate the kind of fish. The Tcherie has a small head and narrowly touches the weeds in a way that is so fine that you are unable to notice the weeds moving, only by a trained observer. Suddenly the Tcherie stops and the Prillthinyeri takes up a reed spear, places it upon a Thy rall ghie, and stands at the prow of the canoe, raising the spear in a position to throw.

Again, for the second time, the man appointed to rouse the fish from their lair thrusts his spear into the water to set the Tcherie moving. Like lightning the Kykie (spear) is sent from the Thy rall ghie straight into the fin or through the body of the fish. The referee goes forward, picks up the fish and holding the spear, raises the fish to view. Then as with one voice a shout goes up for either side: 'Kay hey, kay hey.'

The Prillthinyeri retires, taking his place in the circle and the Thooree enters the arena. The referee, the single occupant of a canoe, startles another fish called a Pummerrie (cat fish). The Thooree man rises in the prow of his canoe holding in his hand a Yundi, a long wooden spear about seven feet long and an inch in diameter. This is a spear thrown from the hand without a Thy rall ghie (this throwing stick is better known as a wommera). Another fish falls prey to the hunter, this time to a Thooree tribe. The referee goes forward, takes up the Yundi and holds the fish to view. Again the cry is raised: 'Kay hey, kay hey.' All the women and children who have congregated on the banks of the lake respond 'Kay hey', and the representatives of the tribes take their place alternately in the arena until midday, then they go ashore and partake of the spoil for their dinner.

Perhaps they have speared between them a hundred. This is given to the elders of each tribe. After resting awhile and listening to a person whose duty it is to entertain them with a legendary story to while away the time, the referee tells them it is time to begin. The competitors get into their canoes and go through the same performance. Perhaps two Tcherie are seen swimming through the weeds and the Thooree tribe is in the arena. He takes up his first reed spear and throws it with unerring aim and strikes the fish which is swimming about fifteen yards away. Then with all speed he takes up another spear and strikes the other fish through the body before it has gone twenty-five yards. This performance causes a great deal of shouting and Kay heying on both sides. Even the opponent gives the Thooree man a hearty cheer. He becomes a hero for such a wonderful display of spearing two Tcherie so quickly within such a short space. I suppose the time between the spearing of the first and the second fish would be two seconds.

All the canoes set out for the homeward journey, and when they reach the shore the competitors go quietly to their whalie (a camp made of boughs of shrubs and reeds or rushes), and sit without uttering a word to their wives, and when bedtime comes, they retire with one thought, of spearing fish. And in their sleep and dreams they are still in the arena with the Tcherie, Pummerrie, and Pillulkie.

Then everybody is astir. On each fire you will see fish being roasted for breakfast. Again the fish hunters get into their canoes, but this time they are alone and armed with a spear that is made of young pine and well dried and greased, and has two prongs made from the she-oak tree. This spear is from seven to eight feet long and an inch in thickness, one end with a sharp point and the other end having two prongs tied with kangaroo sinews, the prongs being half an inch in diameter with sharp points.

Instead of going to the same hunting ground among the weeds, they go along near the bank of the lake where the reeds and bullrushes and several other rush species grow. Amongst this growth fish are also found, not in the midst of the growth, but along the edge of it. They propel their canoes, and the noise of their canoes passing through the water startles the fish, and they rush through the reeds or bull rushes out into the open water. When the hunter sees the reeds moving caused by the flight of the fish, he thrusts his prong spear into the line in which the fish is travelling, with the result that the fish is caught with the prongs of the spear firmly embedded in its flesh. Then the fisherman raises his spear and fish to the vision of the referee and the onlookers for their approval.

Then one of the Prillthinyeri men, eager to score a point, keenly watches for an opportunity and presently two Pummerrie (catfish), startled by the splashing of the paddling pole, rush from within the reeds for an open space of water to safety, and the hunter with the agility of his race and as a trained and skilled Kreel thool lin yeri (a fish-spearing expert), with lightning speed thrusts his spear into the first fish and in less than two seconds takes up another spear and drives it into the second fish. It is done so quickly that the referee and witnesses were unable to follow the movements of the Prillthinyeri man and were therefore not aware that two fish had been speared, until he lifts both spears with a fish attached. Suddenly and simultaneously a shout goes up from the onlookers. Then without any outward show of emotion the Prillthinyeri competitor sits in his canoe and allows the others to tow him to the camping ground, where he is met and received as a hero, satisfied that he is equal to the Thooree man. Every individual male among the tribes congregated come along to congratulate him for what they consider a wonderful achievement. Even the Thooree tribe will come and express themselves of having the pleasure to be eyewitnesses to his ability as a fish-spearing expert.

One thing that is very noticeable is that each competitor who has taken part in the competition is not allowed to eat or partake of fish that he, himself, or any other competitor has speared. There is always an elder who was an expert in his younger days, and he will provide the fish for them and it is wife who will do the cooking. The competitors are not allowed to eat their food hot. When the fish or bird or animal food is cooked, it is put aside and placed upon the bough of a tree to cool. Sometimes the food is cooked a day before and wrapped in herbs that are also eaten with the fish.

Another custom is that the competitors are not allowed to camp near their wives. They have a camping ground set apart for them, and no female member of either tribe is allowed to come within speaking distance of such ground. The females are not even allowed to go near their path in which they go to their canoes, and not to touch their canoes or spears.

A gathering of this nature usually takes place during the summer months, from November to April. Sometimes if the climate and weather is favourable, it would take place earlier, in September.

This way of fishing requires a great deal of knowledge, or to be more correct, mathematical knowledge. I am not attempting to claim that my race are mathematicians from the civilised standpoint. But let us review them standing in their canoes, with a spear seven or eight feet long with prongs made of wood bound on to the end of the spear, the depth of the water four to six feet with weed and reeds as described in the earlier part of this article. The water is of a chalky colour or milky, and the fisherman is not able to see an object more than four inches below the surface. Among those weeds the fish is something resting on the ground. They mostly swim or rest halfway from the ground to the surface, where the depth of the water is from three to four feet. When a fish is disturbed it sometimes rises towards the surface, or supposing I disturb a fish in six feet of water, it rises about three feet. Supposing I thrust my prong spear into the water and strike the ground, the fish rises to within two feet of the surface. And then I strike the water about it without touching the ground the fish will go towards the bottom. This experiment must be done with a prong spear to cause a large bubble which explodes and causes the fish to rise or fall.

Now the fisherman in his canoe thrusts his pronged spear into the water and touches the ground with a force which causes a slight vibration; a fish is startled about ten yards away from the canoe, and in its movements it causes the reeds to quiver. He knows that it is a Tcherie and he takes up his spear, he knows the depth of the water and the size of the fish. All this is done in a moment of time, ten yards away the fish is racing for life, and the speed at which it is travelling and the depth at which it is swimming has to be allowed for, and also the speed and depth of the fish at a distance of fifteen yards away, and the spear is thrown unerringly and strikes the fish. This is often done by an expert, who will make six shoots and two misses.

Now to tell a Tcherie or Pillulkie swimming through the reeds, these fish divide the weeds neatly, causing a quivering motion. A Pondi, with its large head, carries the weed towards its line of travel as does a Pummerrie (cat fish).

In low-lying country, trenches are made two or three hundred yards long and four to five feet deep. During great floods or rises in the river and lakes, the water extends to these trenches carrying various kinds of fish, the Tcherie, Pummerrie, and Pondi, and when the waters abate, some of the fish are left in the trenches and the people come every day and collect sufficient for a day's meal until the supply is exhausted.

THE FLOOD AND ITS RESULT

Bernwerina Tribe, Darling River

There was a time when the Animals, Birds, and Reptiles multiplied so greatly in number that the country in which they lived was not large enough to accommodate them in comfort. So it was decided among themselves that something must be done, some understanding arrived at, which would benefit them all and to avoid bloodshed, as they were continually bumping or treading upon each other's toes, with the result that some ugly words were spoken. So the Animals decided that they would send along the Kangaroo as their Chief and that he (the Kangaroo) should be accompanied by the wise Teddy Bear as their advocate and adviser to the Kangaroo. The Bird tribes agreed to send their Chief the Eagle Hawk, with the Crow as their advocate and adviser to the Eagle Hawk. The Reptile tribe was represented by their Chief the Goanna, with the Tiger Snake as their advocate and adviser to the Goanna.

When the Chiefs and the advocates and advisers first met they agreed that the conference should take place on the Blue Mountain. The first meeting held was to arrange which of them should be given the first opportunity of stating their grievances and claims with suggestions to overcome the difficulty. So the Animals and Birds with one consent gave the preference to the Reptile representative.

Now the Goanna and Tiger Snake were given the order to proceed, so the Goanna rose addressing the Kangaroo and the Eagle Hawk and their advisers, saying: 'The only way out of the difficulty would be if only the Bird tribes would consent to a suggestion that my adviser will make, that I shall leave for him to do so now.'

Then, turning to the Tiger Snake: 'Will you kindly proceed and make your statement, remember you are supported by the whole tribe of your race which we are proud to recognise.'

So the Tiger Snake rose and began his speech. 'Animal and Bird representatives, I have been thinking deeply upon the whole situation, and I would ask you both, that one or both of you should take yourselves into some other country. First, because you are both in a better position or fitted to travel, as you the Animal have two legs whilst the majority of you have four legs that support your belly from dragging upon the earth. These legs that you are blessed with are able or fitted to carry you with great speed as well as to great distances; you are able to leap over obstacles, across creeks. Now Kangaroo and Teddy Bear, does not this suggestion appeal to you, may I have the honour of your approval to this end; or shall I leave it to your consideration?'

Then the Tiger Snake, turning to the Eagle Hawk and the Crow, said: 'Oh, Chief of the Bird tribe, to you and your family is given the blessing of the God of Thul lang (the power of speech and language), the gift of expressing your thoughts and the exchanging of thoughts and ideas. With this gift you are not only a blessing to your family, but you are a blessing to the Animals; and to my family you have delighted us with your song in the morning as well as your love songs at twilight. Then again, Oko pul garrin, you and your families are blessed with the God's Nhar ull lin (Gods of Flight). You are able to change your abode in a moment of time. You delight yourselves in your speed, you travel like the wind, you can rise above the storm. But we poor Reptile family are unable to change our abode as quickly as the Animals, still less quickly as you. Consider us, and may I ask that you should take your flight to some other clime. I am sure you will agree with me that you will not entertain the idea of a battle for mastery, let us not rely upon strength. You are aware that we are gifted with the sting of Death. We are willing to avoid any clash of hatred between the tribes represented here today. I leave it to you, Phull lie (in the by and by, or till we meet again). This is a solution when persons are leaving a question to be considered. Remember, let us refrain from force of arms.'

The Kangaroo rose at this stage to introduce the Platypus. 'Friend, representatives of the Bird and Reptile families, I have much pleasure in introducing the Platypus. His presence here this day is because he belongs to a tribe that has a majority. His family is more than the whole of my race and your family, oh Bird tribe, and placing your family with ours, oh Reptile tribe, still this gentleman with us outnumbers us still. Now, oh Reptiles, cannot you suggest that we should deal with him or ask that tribe that something should be done to prevent them increasing so rapidly. Just look on either side of this range of mountains, Platypuses everywhere in great numbers.'

The Crow, the advocate of the Bird tribe and adviser to the Eagle Hawk, rose without permission from his Chief, asking that the conference should rise and adjourn till tomorrow. So they with one consent rose, and the meeting closed for the day.

Now the Platypus represented a great family. They were so numerous that they were continually getting in the way of the Kangaroo, Emu, Wombat, and Dingo, hindering their progress, or something would cause the Kangaroo to trip and fall and perhaps hurt the poor little Platypus, and then the Wombat would tax the Kangaroo for his clumsiness in treading on the harmless Platypus. And sometimes the Koo ka ka (the kookaburras), sitting on the limb of a gum tree resting themselves, would witness scenes like this, and they too would join in in ridiculing the Kangaroo, and when he would answer their unkind remarks they would simply laugh him to scorn and call him: 'Clumsy feet, your feet take up as much room that would contain a dozen Lizards,' and these remarks would cause the Kangaroo shame.

He did not know what to do. He had such a kindly nature that he did not like to retaliate, fearing that his remarks would result in warfare. So rather than cause further ill-feeling, he would bear his cross with a good spirit. So when they met upon the second day the Kangaroo gave instructions to the Teddy Bear not to think too much about the animal's thoughts upon how to meet this great question of the day, but also to think out such means that would help to benefit the Platypus family.

So on the next day the Chief of the Animal tribe, Whingammie (Kangaroo) and the Koala (Teddy Bear); the Chief of the Birds, Pee wing ie (Eagle Hawk) and the Marrungarie (Crow); and the Chief of the Reptiles, Thooyoungie (Goanna) and the Kry yie (Tiger Snake), met. The Kry yie rose, and requested that before going any farther he would like to have a definite reply as to whether the Bird tribe would be willing to accept his suggestion.

The Crow leapt forward and in his croaking voice said that they considered that the Animals should be made to take the journey to some other country. 'Was it not the adventurous spirit of the Koala that brought us from the sea where there exists a thousand isles? Why is it that such a great mind is not able to grasp this problem and find a way? Have they lost the spirit of their father and become weak in mind and body?'

Then the Crow, working himself up to a mischievous mood and looking the Koala in the eyes, tauntingly made the remark: 'Oh Koala inda, great was thy mind in the long long past. Thy all powerful mind, it bridged the mighty ocean. Hast thou not brought us from homes far across the sea? Oh, where is that mind? Where is that mind? Come think a way out of this difficulty. Was thy thinking power in thy tail which has since become food and an inspiration for sharks?' (Readers will encounter the story of the Koala in another chapter.)

These remarks stung the Koala, and he rose to his feet and was about to say some unpleasant word to the Crow, but through the kindly interference of the Kangaroo a row was prevented. The Kry yie spoke, saying: 'We have not come here to stir up strife. I would like to ask the Crow to take back the unkind words spoken to the Koala. We are all thankful that the Koala brought us from lands far away. To him we owe this great family of brotherhood. Come, let us not quarrel.'

Whilst this conference was progressing, there was a tribe or family connected with the Reptiles that possessed the knowledge of rain-making, or whose Totems were the elements Lightning, Thunder, Rain, Hail, and Wind. They were becoming important. They resolved that they would not consult anyone, but act as they pleased. This selfish family was the Frilled Lizard. They sent representatives to various parts of the country with the instruction: 'On days and evenings of the week preceding the new moon, let every Thunk cum bulli (Lizard) begin the singing of the Storm Song.'

And when the time arrived, they took their flint knives and cut the body, causing the blood, and then they smeared the body with fat and red ochre and daubed the face with pipe clay, and then began chanting their prayer song, pleading that the Great Spirit of the Lightning, Thunder, Rain, Hail, and Wind should grant this their humble request:

'Come oh Thildarrin (Lightning), come oh Rroararund (Thunder), Pa noondi and Miyundi, come with all thy force and destroy the Platypus family, they have become too numerous and they are more easily overtaken in the flood than any other tribe.'

And they sang and sang their Song of the Storm until the last few days and evenings before the appearing of the new moon. Then great dark clouds began to mantle the clear sky, and out of the black cloud the lightning flashed and rent the darkened sky and earth, and struck terror into the hearts of the Animals, Birds, and Reptiles. And the thunder roared its reply to the angry lightning flash, and the winds came hurrying, all in response to the thunder's voice, tearing the limbs from the huge towering gum trees, uprooting smaller trees and shrubs, strewing them along its path, driving the rain and hail into every hiding-place of Animal, Bird, and Reptile.

When the Bird tribe saw what was coming, they took to their wings, and mounted upon the wind, up and up, until they were far beyond cloud and storm, into lands beyond the sea. The Animals struggled into the blinding storm, seeking shelter up and up, dodging behind the trees and rock boulders of the mountain-side, until they reached the summit, seeking a place of safety. Thus ended the conference with no satisfaction but desolation and death.

It rained and rained. The valleys and low-lying countries were deluged, all life living therein was nearly all destroyed in the great flood. But whilst the cunning Frilled Lizards (the Thunk cum bulli) were singing their Storm Song, they were seeking the mountain tops, and they built homes to protect themselves against the storm.

When the storm ceased and the flood abated and the sun shone, the Kangaroo, looking about him, called the others of his tribe, the Wombat, Possum, and Koala, instructing them to scour the country. 'Go in haste and find out whether the Platypus family are safe, or how many of them have survived the awful storm.'

The Wombat, Possum, and Koala ran down the mountain-sides into the valleys, visiting water-holes, billabongs, creeks, and rivers, to see and find out whether the Platypuses were safe. But an awful and distressing sight met their vision. There upon the broken branches of the gum trees and among the rocks on the hill-sides and in the valleys were the mangled and dead bodies of the poor platypuses, not a living one could they discover.

So they came back to the Kangaroo and told him of the sad news, that the Platypuses were no more. And the Kangaroo and his tribe began to wail the loss of the Platypus. And the Reptile tribes that were hidden among the rock ledges and caves heard the cry, and came out to see what all this noise was about. And the Frilled Lizards that were hidden away comfortably upon the mountain top came out of their snug homes and inquired: 'Why weep, oh Kangaroo, have you suffered great loss amongst your family and tribe?'

'No,' said the Kangaroo, 'I would not feel it so much had some of my tribe and family been lost in this flood. I am so sorrowful because the Platypus family is no more.'

And the Frilled Lizard said: 'Don't be so silly, Kangaroo. He is no relation of yours and he is no relation to us Reptiles, neither can he claim relationship to the Bird tribe. Come, Kangaroo, do not let the thought of the loss of the Platypus trouble you.'

The Kangaroo, who is always of a loving nature to all tribes of other peoples, said: 'I love all Birds and Reptiles and Insects. The Kangaroo shows it in not eating flesh food, always herbs as food.'

After three years had passed, the Bird tribe returned to their home. Some came to live upon the lakes, rivers, lagoons, and billabongs; others made their home in dense forest, and some went into the desert country. Sometimes the Emu would become sad, thinking of the poor Platypus, and he would come on a long journey seeking the Yoldie (Cormorant) to inquire of him if he heard or saw anything that would lead to some knowledge of a talk that some had heard, that there were a number of Platypuses seen somewhere.

The Yoldie said: 'Yes. That reminds me, I and my wife were living for a while beyond the Blue Mountains; halfway between the mountain and the sea, there is a stream winding and flowing on to Karramia, the eastern sea. I have noticed the tracks of several Platypuses on the bank of the stream, and during the night I was lying down and thinking where I should go fishing to provide food for my wife, who was at that time looking after the children. Just beneath the tree in which we lodged was a large pool of water, and presently, in the little stream I heard the sucking noise like unto that of the Platypuses when they are feeding. I rose from my perch and flew to the pool to see whether I could come across the Platypus. I saw none, but what I did see made my heart jump. There along the bank was the impression of the beak of a Platypus. I rose and flew back and watched the stream, thinking that perhaps he or they would come out again to feed. But no one came out, since perhaps they had gone to some other stream.'

With this little information gathered, the Emu went home, thinking seriously, lying in bed and tossing his head from side to side all through the night. In the early hours of the morning he rose and made his way to the Kangaroo. When the Kangaroo saw the Emu coming, he went out to meet him. With the usual salutation the Kangaroo, placing his right hand across his stomach and closing his fingers as if gripping his bowel, placed with closed fingers his hand upon the stomach of the Emu, which is a sign of: 'With all good feelings of pity and love I receive you to my home. All my food and comfort of my home is yours.'

The Emu nodded his head and said: 'Hick ka (Is that so?),' and accompanied the Kangaroo to his home, and sitting down, partook of the food that was offered him. After enjoying the meal, the Emu began relating the incident gathered from the Yoldie, and it seemed that there must be some truth because there were others who had seen the footprints and the impression of the Platypus around the same locality. So the kindly Kangaroo sat silently for a few moments as if in a prayer-offering to the Spirit of their Being.

None of the tribes could understand why the Platypuses would not reveal themselves. The Platypuses were under the impression that the Animals, Birds, and Reptiles had become their enemies. They thought that this great flood was caused by them to destroy their race from the face of the earth. So that is why they moved about at night. So the Kangaroo asked the Emu if he would be so kind as to summon the various tribes to a meeting to organise a select party to explore all rivers and lakes or water-holes and billabongs, to try and discover these few remaining Platypuses. The Emu said that he would gladly do anything to help to find and get in touch with them (the Platypuses). The Emu took his departure and asked every tribe—Animal, Bird, and Reptile—to meet the Kangaroo at such a spot on a certain day.

In the meantime the Carpet Snake had made up his mind that he would discover the whereabouts of the Platypus. So one day he wandered along the steep valley, up until he came to the stream where it was said the Platypuses had been seen. So he went to sleep all that afternoon about a few yards away from this pool that the Yoldie had described to them.

After sunset, when darkness covered the valley, the Carpet Snake crept stealthily to the bank and peered into the pool all that night, but he saw no Platypus. Then in the morning after the sun rose he made his way farther down the stream, and came to a pool of water, and went to sleep a few yards from the water. He arose and crawled to the edge of the pool; peering into the water again, he met with disappointment and saw no Platypuses, and then in disgust and disappointment he made up his mind that he would return home. Crawling his way through a dense valley, he came to an ideal spot. Among the fern and convolvulus was a pool of water, clear as crystal, and in the middle of this pool was an island covered with ferns. As the Carpet Snake was admiring this little island, thinking what a beautiful home it would be for the Platypus, his keen eyes noticed a hole beneath the surface of the clear water. He leapt from the ground and ran as fast as he could through the dense undergrowth of plant and fern, up over the mountain-top, down the other side, on westward away from the mountain, into the plain country of the west, until he arrived at the home of the Emu. He threw himself down at the door of the mia mia of the Emu, exhausted, and lay there as if dead.

The Emu and his family rushed out to see what this visitor was doing there, and when they came out they saw the almost dead body of the Carpet Snake. They lifted him up and took him into one of the spare mia mia, gave him water to drink, and waited until he was over his exhaustion.

Then the Emu inquired: 'What is your mission?'

The Carpet Snake said: 'Oh, I have made a great discovery. I have found the home of the Platypus. Now will you hasten as fast as you can and tell the kindly Kangaroo he need not worry much longer, the lost ones are found. I saw their home. I shall wait here and rest awhile until you return with the Kangaroo. Then I shall take him to the home of the Platypus.'

So the Emu selected one of the young men of his family who was a great runner. He was told to run and run—not to stop until he found the Kangaroo. So the Emu ran with great speed and travelled over a great deal of country. He ran around in a circle, round and round, ever wider, until the circle was one hundred miles in diameter and he came nearer to the home of the Kangaroo, and with ever-increasing speed hastened on with the thought that he was the chosen one to convey a message of great importance to the kindly and expectant Kangaroo, of the discovery of the long-lost Platypus. Suddenly he arrived at the camping-ground of the Kangaroo family, and without delay he inquired of the Chief. He was taken to the Chief, who was anxiously awaiting news of the Platypus.

'Oh, Kangaroo, I have such pleasant news for you. The Platypuses are found. The Carpet Snake has brought us this tiding, and I was instructed by my Chief to inform you, and to be at your service should you require it.'

The Kangaroo became so overjoyed that he shed tears of gladness. Oh, it was a great burden taken from his mind. He said: 'Wait my child Emu, until I am over my excitement. I've been thinking and thinking of the Platypuses, fearing that they had been completely swept off the face of the earth and were to be no more. And I have been fretting a great deal over them. Now, rest awhile and take food to renew your strength for your journey. And in the meantime I shall think out some plan, and go and meet the other tribes, the Birds and Reptiles.'

So the Emu sat down and enjoyed a hearty meal of berries and sweet tender grasses that were fresh picked from a glade especially set aside for the use of the elders of the Kangaroo tribe.

The Emu could not help exclaiming: 'What lovely berries and what tender grasses, and how sweet and appetising; I feel tempted to eat and eat until I have gorged myself. I should like to be always sent by my Chief to carry messages to you, so that I may partake of such nice food.'

After his meal the Emu said, as was their custom, without further talking: 'I am ready to do thy bidding, oh Kangaroo, what is thy order?'

Then the Kangaroo gave the Emu a stick on which were marked out curves and angles representing words and localities, and the sign of the Kangaroo to all peoples of the Bird and Reptile tribes that he would like to meet them in conference to discuss the future of the Platypus.

'I am afraid that we shall have a difficult problem to deal with when we come into touch with the Platypus. I feel it—there is something within me that tells me.'

After expressing himself thus to the Emu, he said: 'Go, my son, and prepare the Bird and Reptile tribes to meet me in conference.'

With that the Emu leapt forward on his mission. Again he ran in a spiral ever-widening, meeting the various tribes until he completed his duty. Then he returned to his tribe. Instead of running in a spiral, he ran with great speed in a straight line until he reached his home and delivered his last message to his tribe. All tribes had agreed to meet and to arrange and decide upon some definite steps to assist and encourage the Platypuses to take [their] stand once more, with their social and traditional rights. In the meantime no one was allowed to go near the home of the Platypuses, lest they should think that the Animals or Birds [or] Reptiles were spying to do them further injury.

The time elapsed between the instruction issued by the Kangaroo and the conference was twelve moons. The beginning of the first week of the new moon, preparations were being made for the conference. Every tribe with its respective family journeyed to the Blue Mountains. There was one huge Wail lar roo mundi (a camping-hut, made of boughs and grass, better known as a mia mia). The Kangaroo family, the Wallabies, the tree or climbing Kangaroos, and the Possums, had their mia mia on the north side; the Bird family, Emu, Eagle Hawk, Marrungarie (Crow) and other members of that family stood on the west side; the Reptile family occupied the south side; the Insect tribes camped on the eastern side.

I may say here that the other larger tribes did not recognise the Insect tribe, they looked upon them as a very inferior race and did not consult them or invite them to any of their great meetings. But upon this occasion, the Kangaroo had of late since the flood thought otherwise, that all life, whether Animal, Bird, Reptile, or Insect, were one in life and death, although they differed greatly in form and fashion and living. Yet the mystery of life and death was common to both. Some lived to a great age, others with only a short duration, so that all were bound or united with the same trouble, and who can tell (thought the Kangaroo) that the Insect tribe may solve, or help us to understand, Life and Death, or any other problems. So the Insect tribe was invited to this important gathering.

The Kangaroo gave notice to the others that in the first week of the new moon the conference should or shall begin. In the meantime all the tribes must consult their family tree and the stock or race from which they sprang, and so gather sufficient knowledge to find how near they may be related to the Platypus, so that they may be more inclined to assist the Platypus. The Emu, Pelican, Swan, Eagle Hawk, Parrot, Lyre Bird, and the various kinds of duck were all busily looking into their tradition, consulting the drawings and carvings on rocks and trees. The Reptile tribe were doing the same, consulting their family tree to see what relation existed between themselves and the Platypus. So were the Animal tribes, who were in earnest to find the relationship between themselves and the Platypus.

The first to discover a trace of relationship [was] the Bird tribe.

'Why,' said the Black Duck, 'why is it that the Platypus has the beak of a bird which resembles so closely that of our cousin the Cul par rie, a duck that has a beak with comb-like teeth along the edge, which the duck uses to suck and divide the food and refuse. I think the bird is called a Widgeon Duck.'

So the Birds swore allegiance to help and protect the Platypus.

'Still farther,' said the solemn-looking Pelican, 'he must be truly our relation because he lays eggs.'

'So he does,' joined in the Cockatoo and Koo ka ka. 'The only difference is that it is more like the eggs of the Reptile family.'

'That does not matter,' said the Native Companion, 'it's an egg all the same.'

The Koo ka ka was in a mischievous mood when he heard that the dull Native Companion was making himself heard. He said to him:

'Oh, just fancy the Native Companion, him with the bald and small head and thin wiry, long legs.'

'Koo, ka, ka, ka, koo, koo,' laughed the other Koo ka ka burras.

'Shut up,' said the snappy Magpie (Muldarie). 'We are not here to make jokes and say funny things at each other, we're here for something more serious than that.'

'Come now,' said the Crow, 'on with our business.'

'It is a pity,' said the Emu, 'that the Platypus does not dress himself in feathers. I am sure that he would make a nice bird.'

'Koo, koo, ka, ka,' said the Koo ka ka, 'what a ridiculous bird he would make with those short and funny web feet of his. Just fancy your grandson and granddaughter, Oh Emu, with four short clumsy feet and that funny tail, jogging along beside you. Oh, what a funny relation. You would become the joke of the whole tribe. Animals and Reptiles would laugh you to scorn.'

'Now,' said the Muldarie, 'if you do not stop your impudent talk I shall have to put you out, or drive you away from the meeting.'

No doubt some of you have noticed sometimes that the Wagtail and Magpie often peck at the Kookaburra, well it is for this often repeated attempt to make fun at the relationship of the Platypus. The Emu gave orders that they should not discuss the subject now, but wait until the general meeting took place.

Away yonder on the southern portion of the great camping-ground, the Reptiles were earnestly looking over the traditions of their race to find out what relationship they held with the Platypus family.

'Well, I must admit,' said the Carpet Snake, 'that he resembles more of the Animal and Bird race than a Reptile.'

'There is no likeness whatever with us, only their laying of eggs. And that is not much to rely upon, is it?' said the Goanna, addressing the sleepy Lizard, who was at this time yawning, showing his blue tongue.

Just at this moment the cheeky Frilled Lizard threw a pebble right into the open mouth of the sleeping Lizard, who began coughing and coughing until he removed the pebble from his throat. The Goanna ordered the Frilled Lizard to retire, and if he began his nonsense any more he would instruct the Tiger Snake to take action to destroy the whole of the Frilled Lizard family, as they had already caused a great flood in which many families perished and that he (the Goanna) and others of the Reptile family would see that it would not occur again. So the Frilled Lizard left the meeting and wandered away and would not take any interest in tracing his relationship to that of the Platypus. So he sulked and sulked and he brooded over being ordered away from the others, and caused the hatred to fill his whole being, and he bears the ugly frown of anger today with the spiky frill on either side of his face like whiskers. The more he thinks of the humiliation imposed upon him by the Goanna, the uglier he looks. The Goanna instructed other members of his tribe to keep an eye upon the wicked Frilled Lizard to prevent him causing further trouble.

The Animal tribe [was] decided upon this one thing, that they were a decided relation to the Platypus family. The Kangaroo advised the Koala, Possum, and Rat not to push forward any suggestion, but let the others make their claim and see how far back and how much resemblance could be found between themselves and the Platypus. A day before the moon night, the Kangaroo called a general meeting. When they all assembled, the Kangaroo asked the audience that there should be no speaking out of their turn, no reflection made against any tribe or person, that each should consider the interest that was at stake—the building up of a race that was at its decline.

And further continuing, the Kangaroo said: 'The Platypus comes of a very ancient race, not only so, but of a very learned and cultured people. I feel sure that although he has not made himself heard upon this question before, I know that he will be able to enlighten us upon the subject. Now I would like to ask that the Carpet Snake shall go and ask the remaining Platypuses that are to be found at Par, rack, pack, Par ran mar, the waterhole at the foot of this mountain. And tonight being full moon, we shall discuss the question, and hear what the Platypus has to say.'

Amidst great Kay heying the Carpet Snake rose and went on his journey to ask the Platypus to attend the meeting. The Carpet Snake, wending his way down the mountain-side until he arrived at the foot of the mountain, rested awhile, lying down to take a little nap and to wait until the sun was well over western mountain. The darkness gradually approaching, he hastened to the waterhole in which he saw the home of the Platypus, and eagerly waited, intensely gazing into the clear water for a sign of life. But nothing revealed itself.

Presently he could hear the voice of someone speaking, as if addressing a great audience. It was the elder of the Platypuses addressing the younger members of his race, advising them that they must each make up their minds to travel north, south, east, and west, in search of their people or tribe.

'It will be a great calamity if we fail to discover some of our race.'

The Carpet Snake, without waiting to hear further, glided across the clear stream and on to the island, and with such a soft sweet voice said: 'Brother Platypuses, I have been sent by the great nation, the Animal, Bird, and Reptile families, also the Insect tribe, that you are asked to stay and enjoy yourselves among us till such time as you see fit to leave us. We are all anxious to have you. Come, Par ruch el how (rise and follow me).'

Without questioning the Carpet Snake, the Platypuses rose and followed the Carpet Snake until they arrived at the top of the Blue Mountains.

'Rest here awhile until I return. I shall go forward to prepare the tribes to receive you.'

So the Carpet Snake came to the Wail lar roo mundi. Every tribe gathered around in a large circle, waiting to receive the Platypuses.

The Carpet Snake returned to them. 'Come friends, all are ready to receive you.'

The Platypuses followed the Carpet Snake, who led them towards the gathering. The Owl announced their arrival, all heads were bowed, and each tribe placed upon its head the pipe-clay caps used in mourning. All eyes were closed and a pathway was made leading into the centre of the large gathering, and a circle formed inside this gathering to leave a clear open space for the visitors. When they took their seats they also bowed their heads and clay caps were placed on their heads by Wombats. That was a sign that all were sharing in the great loss suffered by the Platypuses. They remained thus until midnight, then all the tribes rose to their feet and went to their homes, whilst the Platypuses remained where they were, surrounded by the elders of the Animal, Bird, and Reptile families who had provided them with rugs made from the fibre of barks of trees. The Platypuses slept soundly until the morning and a mia mia was built around them to protect them against the heat of the sun.

In the late afternoon the Kangaroo came to see the Platypuses alone. He placed his arm around the neck of the elder Platypus and wept bitterly.

'I am sorry, oh Platypus, that you have suffered. I am your friend. We have met that you shall choose the most beautiful daughter of our race—either the Bird from the Emu girls or the Swan, Pelican, or some of the beautiful daughters of the Parrot or Cockatoo. Or the Reptile girls, the Snakes or Lizards. Or you may choose from my family. You are willing, for we give you the opportunity to choose?'

So the Kangaroo left them to consider the question.

Just after sunset, everybody, instead of retiring to rest as was their custom, to give every encouragement to the Platypuses, attended the conference at night, which would be more to their (the Platypuses') advantage, because they come out at night, not being accustomed to daylight. So they gathered in a large circle about the Platypuses.

When all were seated and silence reigned, the elder Platypus arose and addressed the audience. 'Animals, Birds, Reptiles, there was a time in the long, long ago, I was closely akin to the Reptile family, and then as the years went on I became related to the Animal, and later to the Bird family. But those times are a very long while ago. I can still claim relationship with my great friend the Kangaroo, in fact I can call him brother without fear of contradiction. We are one flesh—Marri (hairy or fur family). I do not wish to say much until I have heard the Bird and Reptile families give their opinion.'

So with these few remarks the Platypus sat down, and called on the Emu.

'Theen who ween,' that is the name that the Platypus called the Emu by.

Every one of the tribes became amazed at this name that sounded so ancient. The Crow looked at the Magpie, all turned their eyes to the Owl, who looked as if trying to recall some carving and painting in a cave somewhere in the mountain which recalled to memory the name he heard. Then he looked upon the Platypus, and, turning to his friend the Nightjar, said: 'We are in the presence of a learned man. He speaks a dead language belonging to the Kule thou oo, a language belonging to past generations. That name is not in our records, neither in the Animals' nor Reptiles'. It just shows how far back the Platypus can go.'

The Emu rose at the request of the Platypus and addressed himself first to the Animals and Reptiles, expressing his pleasure to be able to meet and converse with the remaining few of what were considered a great race in number as well as in knowledge and wisdom. He was rather startled when the Platypus addressed him, calling him by such an ancient name. He was always called by the name Peen jul lie, or When gum mie, but this morning he was called 'Theen who wheen'.

'This shows that we shall be helped and enlightened by the great knowledge that he (the Platypus) possesses. I will not say much, only I am pleased that on an occasion like this, which is considered sacred to our race, the Broo parr or Kullee em been, and it is only on these occasions in which tribes are allowed to enquire of the relation.'

So the Emu availed himself of this opportunity to inquire directly of the Platypus: 'What is your totem, or flesh, or friend?'

The Platypus replied: 'Go-rool (Bandicoot), this is the tribe to which I should be allied. For a moment, Theen who wheen, allow me to ask to whom do you belong, to what tribe are you allied, who is your flesh?'

'Thoo roo (snake) family,' replied the Emu.

Then the Platypus said to the Emu: 'Once upon a time your family was my brother, or we were brothers. But since, you have embraced another belief and religion.'

'Yes,' said the Emu, 'we have or are following another religion and belief, because it will suit your purpose and mine.'

'What benefit do we Platypuses gain by your change of religion?'

Then the Theen who wheen replied: 'It makes it possible that you can marry into my family.'

This point of law quoted by the Theen who wheen placed the Platypus into a trap. There was no way out of it.

Then the Platypus said: 'Give me time to consider your proposition, and after Broo parr I shall give you a reply.'

The Platypus said again to the Theen who wheen: 'I shall interview my uncle the Poop pill la (Water Rat), and see what he thinks of it.'

'That is not the case,' said the Theen who Wheen. 'Poop pill la is my uncle, and no longer a relation of yours.'

'Then,' said the Platypus, 'if things have so changed since the flood I do not wish to become a relation of either of you. Let us ask the audience whether it is possible to make an appointment to bring this matter at the next Bun boon (sacred meeting-ground). And I should like to have there all the Mourn bour (fur tribes), and all the Thar na wun (Snake and lizard tribes), and you, feather tribes, must go together.'

Through the obstinacy of the Platypus, the Emu became angry, and would have forced the Platypus to accept his terms, but for the kindly Kangaroo who intervened and advised him to sneak away at night and make away to the Wolkundmia (the north). The daughter of the Bandicoot heard the Kangaroo advise the Platypus to go away unseen by anyone, so the Bandicoots waited in the way where they should pass. The uncle accompanied their niece Bandicoot. When they saw the Platypuses passing, they called out: 'Will you come with us to the home of the Bandicoot? We of the hairy tribe sympathise with you. Come and spend a few moons with us. We are living away down near the water-pool from which you came.'

The Platypuses agreed and made their home with the Bandicoot and made love to the Misses Bandicoot and were bound in the bonds of matrimony, and took their young wives with them to the north. When they arrived at their adopted country they lived happily.

But there was one of the hairy tribe, the Water Rat, who became jealous of the Platypus for taking the girls that should by the law of their country become their wives. So the young Water Rats followed in the trail of the Platypuses until they came to their home. And when at night the Platypuses came in search of food, the Water Rats attacked; then there was a great battle.

While they fought in the water, grappling with each other, the Platypuses called out to their wives: 'Bring our spears, we are in danger.'

So the girl Bandicoots ran with haste to the rescue of their husbands. Each had a spear in her hands, which she used with fatal effect upon the jealous Water Rats. So the Platypuses with their wives returned to their home on the bank of the river.

So the Platypus, although he tried to break away from the Bird tribe, is ever reminded that his wife lays eggs and still retains the bird or duck's bill. He has tried hard to separate himself and family from the Birds. He has succeeded in getting rid of the feathers that the Emu reminded him of, that he wore long, long ago, and he tried to sever his connection with the Animals. But in this he has also failed. He still belongs to the Kangaroo and Possum tribe. He is making a desperate effort to cause a great gulf between himself and the kindly Kangaroo who looks upon him with pity. The more he tries the greater becomes the difficulty. So he makes no more effort, but simply contents himself to be neither Bird, Reptile, nor Kangaroo, but a plain Platypus. He no longer seeks the companionship of the Animal, Bird, and Reptile families, but lives affectionately with his wife in the rivers and billabongs.

In songs he petitions the God of Food: 'Cup poona garle garle malle e charle Weri guli doo gal gool la ween doo Dalli wa la loon aa we coon da we.'

'Give me more grubs as the water ripples
And make for me bread of the Nardoo seed
Do this often and often as the sun does rise; And I shall gather in the shade of night
The food thou shalt throw into the water, hunting place of mine
Because I am hiding all day, fearing that someone may call up the Lightning, Thunder and Rain.'

The Gherawhar (Goanna)

This is a story belonging to the Murrumbidgee River tribe, and they associate this locality as the first settled home of the Gherawhar (Goanna family) after leaving their temporary home at Shoalhaven, and before migrating to other parts of Australia. When they occupied this country there was no flowing Murrumbidgee River. The only river then was the Murray, which was formed by the ancient Pondi, a fish commonly called the Murray cod.

Now one of the laws agreed to by the Animals, Birds, and Reptiles, was that each tribe should marry not into their own tribe, but some other. For instance in the case of the Gherawhar, he would have to marry into the Muldarie family (the Magpie), so the wife of the Gherawhar was a Teal Teal, a little bird like the Magpie family in appearance, but a smaller type. At this time of the occupation of the Murrumbidgee district there lived on the Wolkundmia (north side) of the Gherawhar a great hunting family known as the Wandhillie (Porcupine) tribe, and at the Tolkamia (west side) lived another well known family, the Peenjullie (Emu) tribe. They too were hunters, but they did not attain to that perfection in bush craft as the Wandhillie.

After the landing of these Beings from their home in the sea of the birth of day, the change of place and climate and environment caused a change in each life, more so in the Gherawhar family. They were in their native land a very industrious family; they tilled and cultivated the soil, and grew vegetables and fruit. But since coming to Australia the climate had caused them to dislike vegetable food, and an uncontrollable craving for flesh food took possession of them. They became cannibals, and would slay and devour the smaller lizards of their species, and sometimes when it would happen that a young Wandhillie would wander from the care of his parents and become lost, and like little children would begin crying, perhaps a Gherawhar would hear the noise and would know at once that it was a cry of distress of a little Wandhillie, and he would hurry on towards the sound and pounce upon the helpless thing and devour it.

One thing noticeable when the Gherawhar changed their diet was that they became very lazy, indolent, and dishonest. They would steal food from their neighbours, the Wandhillie and Peenjullie, and it seemed strange that for many years the Wandhillie and Peenjullie could not find out the culprit. The Gherawhar were so cunning that they were able to cover up all clues leading to their discovery. Every surrounding tribe knew that the Gherawhar were lazy, and they also had a suspicion that they did steal their food, but were not able to sheath home the charge, until it came about in an unexpected way. One day the Wandhillie organised a hunting expedition and the Gherawhar heard of it, and on that day they went along and met the Wandhillie all prepared with their spears and Nulla nulla.

The Chief hunter of the Wandhillie was giving instructions. 'Ten shall go Wolkundmia (north), ten to Kolkamia (south), ten to Karramia (east), ten to Tolkamia (west). And you shall all walk straight along until you reach parties consisting of another who shall join, and then all shall spread out and walk in a circle, gradually coming towards the centre which you are now about to leave.'

And just as they were starting forth the Gherawhar, who were in hiding and listening to all that was said, suddenly made their appearance, looking as if they were surprised, and were sorry to interrupt them.

'Oh, that's all right, we are just going to hunt for food.'

'Oh,' said a Gherawhar, 'will you allow us to accompany your party?'

'Will you pardon me,' said a Wandhillie, 'but we think that you cannot help us in this matter, as you will admit that you are not competent to hunt the game, and in that case you may be a hindrance.'

'Yes, we are no hunters of game, we are aware of that, but supposing you allow us to come with you. There is no doubt we shall find honey. I am sure some of you know where there is some to be got;

admitting that we are unable to hunt, you will also admit you are no tree climbers. Now you all are very very fond of honey. Come, let us accompany you.'

The Wandhillie were fond of honey. They would give anything that was in their possession for honey, and now here was an offer made to them by the Gherawhar, who were looked upon as expert climbers. The suggestion was such a tempting one that the Wandhillie would not let it pass, accepted the offer, and gave their consent that they should follow. Now they began the drive, and they were very successful. Those who were in front would come upon the game first and slay the Possums and hang them up in the limb of a tree, and those following would come and take them down and carry them to the centre. In the meantime the Gherawhar were busy; wherever they saw a bee, they would follow it until they discovered the hive. And they would climb the tree, and with their stone axes would chop and chop, just so that the Wandhillie were under the impression that it must be hard work for the Gherawhar to climb the tree, chopping footsteps as they climbed. But this chopping was only a sham, the Gherawhar were able to climb without steps cut into the bark of the tree.

Now when the Wandhillie and Gherawhar arrived at the starting point with their spoil, the Wandhillie were very tired and exhausted with running and chasing and carrying the game. Before resting, they made a large fire and began shearing the Possums before cooking them. After completing this first process the Gherawhar gave the hunters some honey to eat, so they sat down and enjoyed a good sweet meal. Then the Gherawhar suggested that they should lie down and have a sleep, and they would cook the food and wake them when it was done.

The Wandhillie agreed that it would just suit them and so they all lay down to sleep. One of the members of the Gherawhar went away to a large gum standing just on the boundary-line of the Gherawhar and Wandhillie hunting ground. This large gum tree was used as a place of refuge or vantage point, where the Gherawhar could take view of the doings of the Wandhillie.

Whilst the Wandhillie were sleeping one Gherawhar was removing all obstacles that were in the way leading to this tree, and the others were attending to the cooking of the Possums. Now the cook would place the head of the Possum into the midst of the fire with the tail out, the idea was that the tail would serve as a handle. Sometimes a Wandhillie would drowsily half-raise himself into a sitting position and enquire: 'Are they cooked?'

The Gherawhar would answer: 'No, a little while longer,' and the Wandhillie would lie down again. Then another would do the same and enquire: 'Are they cooked?' and the Gherawhar would reply, 'No, a little while longer.'

Now this was repeated by each Wandhillie, and they had the feeling that something was going to happen.

Now number two Gherawhar, who had climbed to the topmost limb of the gum tree, saw that everything was ready, and that there were no other Wandhillie about, and gave the signal. And the cook Gherawhar waited. Half-rising from his sleep a Wandhillie enquired: 'Are they cooked?'

'No,' said the Gherawhar. He waited a moment as the Wandhillie lay down to sleep, then suddenly rose to his feet and taking the Possums by the tail, made a dash for the gum. But when he did this a coal of fire fell upon the belly of a Wandhillie and burnt him so much that he jumped up with pain and trod upon a firestick, and scattered fire upon the other sleeping Wandhillie, who were burnt, some on the leg and other parts of their bodies. They rose, shrieking with pain. The first who rose came to himself, and looking into the fire, saw that the Possums as well as the cook were not there.

Turning sharply round he saw the Gherawhar running as fast as he could with the cooked Possums, and shouted: 'Look, there goes the Gherawhar.'

Seizing a firestick, which the others did also, he gave chase, and just caught up to the Gherawhar as he was about ten yards from the foot of the gum tree. A Wandhillie raised a firestick, and down it came swiftly upon the back of the Gherawhar, who ran around the gum tree. Just as the Gherawhar turned, out flashed a blaze of fire and it came into contact with his body. Round and round like a merry-go-round, with streaks of blazing stick, blow after blow was delivered at the body of the Gherawhar. One of the Wandhillie suddenly stopped and waited as the Gherawhar came round the tree. A flash of fire-light, and a blow upon his head, but still the Gherawhar clung to his prize. Then in desperation the Gherawhar made an upward move on the trunk of the gum tree, and climbed and climbed until he reached the hollow which was the resting-place, and with the assistance of the other members of his race, packed the cooked Possums safely away and then sat down and enjoyed a meal.

Down below the Wandhillie were shouting threat after threat, and strange to say it did not occur to them to burn the tree, but they attempted to throw a firestick into the hollow. They tried time after time, but met with failure, and in disgust as well as sadness, they went home, vowing to be avenged.

The Gherawhar who stole the Possums became very ill indeed. His body was covered with the marks caused by the blazing firesticks and these marks have been handed down ever since that day to all the Gherawhar as a reminder of their theft in the days long ago.

Now after some months of illness and suffering the Gherawhar became well, and they joined the great Waillarroomundi; that is, they went back to the great camping-ground, or what the modern boys and girls would say went back into town or city. Now, after this event a great drought visited the country; there was no rain and all the dams and rock-holes became dry, and the Wandhillie and Peenjullie tribes did not know what to do. Because there were among members of their tribes many aged and infirm, some were sick, and a great many had little children, it was rather a difficult proposition. They had no means of taking them down to the River Murray. The drought did not affect the Gherawhar tribe, as they were in possession of a large reservoir which would last them for many, many years.

The cries of the little children and the distress of the aged and sick touched the hearts of the wives of the Gherawhar, and they would secretly go among them and do all they could to relieve their want and suffering. One day they enquired of their husbands the whereabouts of this great rock-hole, as they were anxious to go and get a supply to give to the aged and the sick and the children of the Wandhillie and Peenjullie. But the selfish Gherawhar refused to tell them, and what was more, they said to their wives: 'Since you are taking such an interest in the need of other Beings, we will not give you much water, but just sufficient to slake your thirst.'

And the Teal Teal, wives of the Gherawhar, found it useless to plead with their obstinate husbands. But they were determined that although they had given way to many objections before, and had willingly suffered the indignity of their refusals, they would not let this insult go by.

So they began their search, unknown to their husbands. They would take up their yam-sticks and make their husbands believe that they were going to dig yams and other roots of plants and shrubs, and they would track the footprints of their husbands, which led them into the mountains, but at the foot of the mountains they lost all trace of the footprints, so they returned to the valley and gathered a few yams and herbs, and went straight home to their mia mia. They would cook the yams in the hot ashes and then sit down with their husbands and family to a meal.

And the Gherawhar would ask questions where they had been so long, which was unusual.

'I noticed a speck of dirt that comes from the mountain. Have you been there?'

And the wives would say: 'What do you think you silly, we go hunting yams on the mountain top? We find and dig yams in the low flat country, not on rocky mountains. Now why do you ask such questions?'

The Gherawhar without another word would lie down upon the Possum skins.

In the morning, just as the sun rose over the eastern range of the mountain, the Gherawhar were out looking for food. Their wives were up too, and gathered together and held a conference as to what steps to adopt to try and wrest the secret of the reservoir, and one more thoughtful than the others suggested that it would be a wise plan to go upon the mountain and make a mia mia and camp there, taking observations.

'Now who has courage among you? Let us sit awhile and think who will go.'

So they sat in silence a few moments, then up rose a figure, and all eyes were fixed on her. She was the wife of the Chief, and she spoke: 'Karroonnoo, Sister, I will take the responsibility. I volunteer to go. I consider it my duty as the wife of a Chief, and I am convinced within me that it is the wife of a Chief's duty. Who will come and assist me to take my Now wondie (Camp, belongings, rug, etc.)?'

Up rose two young wives. 'We go with you.'

So they made haste and rolled up the belongings of the Chief's wife, and hurried away to the mountain before the Chief and the other Gherawhar returned from their hunting expedition. Halfway up the side of the mountain was a spot which gave a good view of the surrounding valley, especially the Gherawhar camping-ground. After making the mia mia the two returned home, leaving the Chief's wife.

In the evening the young Chief summoned the Gherawhar to come before his mia mia and to give information whether anyone had seen his wife, or knew of any suspicious character that would lead to her disappearance. They were all ignorant about the matter, and expressed sorrow that they did not know of any reason that would cause her to leave the camp. They would do all in their power to assist him to try and recover her if she were taken captive to some other home.

And then the Chief summoned the Teal Teal, the female members and wives of the Gherawhar. They were closely questioned by the Chief and the elders, but they would not make any statement, and remained standing with their heads bowed. And the Gherawhar tried by threat to make them speak, but they shook their heads and remained silent. Then the Chief of the Gherawhar ordered that they should return to their mia mia. When the Teal Teal were safely home, the Chief spoke unto his people thus: 'I have a suspicion that the Peenjullie have come to our home whilst we were out hunting and taken my wife and given her to the young Chief of their tribe. So tomorrow before the sun rises beyond the mountain peak, every one that is able to fight, equip yourselves with three Kykie, four Rarrabarr, and four Pankuggee, and a Nulla nulla, and we will march into their land and seek my wife. Then, if she be not there, we shall return and march into the land of the Wandhillie. So tonight every one to their mia mia, so you shall hear the cry "Par ruch ool low (Rise at once)".'

So every Gherawhar went straight home to bed and slept the sleep of the just, and they rose early and marched into the Peenjullie land.

Now as soon as the Gherawhar left home, the Teal Teal rose and met in conference as to what they should do, and one thought it would be wise that the two young ones that accompanied the Chief's wife should hurry away and tell her that her absence had caused a stir. And as the Chief with his army was marching into the Peenjullie land, thinking that they had captured his wife and made her the wife of the young Peenjullie Chief, the young Teal Teal girls ran away to the mountain to tell the Chief's wife all that was taking place.

And she sat quietly listening to what they had to tell, and then in reply she said: 'Now is our deliverance; we have been given in marriage to these Beings who are not of our race and kind. I have made a discovery. At the dawn of day I was fast asleep, and one Tuckoonie (little men that live in thickly timbered country), came into the mia mia and sat beside the fire warming himself, and suddenly I awoke and saw him comfortably seated there. And I became so alarmed that I shrieked with fear, and he turned his eyes upon me and said: "Thou pulthook (Don't be afraid)", I am your friend, and the friend of all that are in trouble and distress. I with my companions saw you and the other two come up from the plain and some members of our Beings have visited your camping-ground and know all about you.' (I may say here that the Aborigines believe and are told very often of these queer little people, that they visit the camping-ground and become acquainted with all our ways.) 'You are in search of the water-hole of your husband, and you have been guided by the Mee well lum (the mind of my tribe), right to the spot. You slept upon it. If you will follow me I will show you the opening on top of this mountain.'

The wife of the Chief Gherawhar rose and followed the Tuckoonie up to the mountain and she was asked to sit down and rest herself. And the little man went a few paces away and gave a call somewhat like a 'Coo ee', and like a flash somewhere out of space came many little men Tuckoonie, their bodies painted with stripes of red ochre and white pipe clay, with white Cockatoo feathers decorating their heads and tied round their wrists like bracelets, and holding in their hands small spears about the thickness of an ordinary lead pencil, about two feet long, and each wore a belt made of Possum skin round their waist, and into this belt were placed three tiny boomerangs and rarrabarr. They circled round their leader, eager to receive his instructions.

After a little palaver they made way, and he came from their midst to the Teal Teal, wife of the Gherawhar. They followed, and standing beside her he addressed his bodyguard thus: 'Hear, oh my Being, we have been appointed by the unseen forces that are about, the Spirit of the Good, the Spirit of Water, the Spirit of Food, the Spirit of Pleasure, the Spirit of Lightning and Thunder and Wind and Rainstorm, and lastly the Spirit of Sunshine: it is with their displeasure that the Gherawhar have withheld from the tribes that inhabit the country the long-needed water that is locked up in this mountain, and have used this gift for their selfish needs and have refused to give to the aged and infirm and children of other tribes. And what is more, they have refused to give and supply to their wives. Give this Meminie (woman) the help she requires to let loose from this mountain the water that there be within.'

The Tuckoonie turned to the Chief's wife and took her a few spaces father to a basin-like rock and commanded her to look in it, and she saw the sparkling water clear as crystal.

'Drink,' and she drank until her thirst was satisfied.

'Now you must descend, and when you reach the bottom of this mountain you shall meet the two young Meminan (women) and you must ask them to hurry back to their camp with this instruction to give to the others, that they must all stand on the Wolkundmurr (northern side) of the valley towards the Wandhillie boundary, and must await your coming.'

So she went and did as she was told. And the two young Meminan hurried back to give this strange order. But the other Teal Teal did just what they were asked to do, they stood on the Wolkundmurr of the valley. And the Chief's wife stood at the base of the mountain waiting for further instructions.

Presently the Tuckoonie stood beside her and said: 'Oh Meminie (woman), it is given to you by these good and great Spirits the privilege to let loose the waters that are anxious to be freed from the bonds that hold them prisoner these many, many years. Thou shalt be a blessing to all Beings, Animal, Bird, Reptile, and Insect life. And thou must keep in remembrance this great event. Teach thy children of the privilege the spirit of Pronhookie (Water) gave you. Take this.'

He handed her a grass-tree stick, and said: 'At a given signal thrust it to the mountain-side, and the water shall be let loose.'

Again the Tuckoonie disappeared, and she stood there alone, thinking of this strange happening; and she would pinch her arm and strike herself on the leg to see whether she was asleep and in a somnambulistic state. Yes, she felt the pinch and the blow.

'I am very much awake. What a wonderful experience.'

Then without warning a voice said: 'Thrust the stick into the mountain.'

She placed the stick to the mountain-side and pushed hard. It gradually went farther and farther, until its length was gone. Then the voice of the Tuckoonie said: 'Now flee for your life to where your sisters are.'

She sped away down into the valley as fast as her feet could carry; when she was gone half the distance, a loud noise broke the still air as if of a mighty wind. It was the water that leaped forth out of its prison and came thundering down the valley with a speed like that of a mighty wind.

And now the Chief's wife arrived among her Teal Teal sisters and breathlessly told them that the water from yonder mountain would be flowing down the valley, and before she finished her sentence they saw the dust rising on the hillside in the valley and the water tearing its way through the valley, and huge trees were uprooted and carried along. And they looked with amazement as the water came by them onward to join the Murray. And when it reached the Murray it settled down to be a flowing river. And the Teal Teal came down to its bank and sat down in the shade of the trees, watching their children sporting and splashing in the water.

On the next day the Gherawhar returned and were making their way to the camp, and beheld with wonder that a river separated them from their wives and children. They were greatly annoyed. The Chief called across the river, asking where this flowing stream of water came from, and he was answered by the familiar voice of his wife: 'From the rock-hole that you and your Beings, the Gherawhar, have kept a secret from us and the other tribes. But I, oh Chief, your wife, have discovered your secret and have let loose the water that you have kept for your selfish purposes, this great gift and blessing that belongs to all Beings. So we who were your wives have decided that we shall no longer belong to you, we shall henceforth make our home in the trees. And we do not wish, or will not be your wives.'

So the separation of the husbands came about by the selfishness of the Gherawhar. Since that time the Teal Teal refuse to become the wives of the Gherawhar, and to keep in memory that long, long ago event, they make their homes in limbs and branches of the gum trees, and they construct their homes or nests with mud or clay designed after the shape of the mountain that contained the water. And in the miniature mountain-shaped homes they lay their eggs and when these are hatched and the little bird comes to see light and home, the mother in bird language tells them of the long, long ago time when another was in distress seeking water to quench their thirst, how a little man helped them and showed them where it was to be found, with the promise that they should ever throughout the generations of their kind, have a home and rear their children [in] such a memorial.

As for the Gherawhar, through their rough natures, stealing from others who endured the difficulties and hardships of hunting with its dangers so, they carry upon their bodies the mark received as a punishment for their misdoing; and also a much more grevious punishment, for their selfishness to all the surrounding Beings and more especially to their wives the Teal Teal, they have lost the great pride of their heart, the wonderful rock-hole which kept a lasting supply of beautiful refreshing and clear water. And what was more, that pride of theirs, their strictly guarded prize, now became a great barrier separating them from their wives and children for ever. And now in sorrow they have wandered to all parts of Australia, and in certain seasons of the year they dig a hole into the ground and bury themselves, with sorrow, and weep and weep during the dark cold wintery nights, until they fall into a deep sleep until the coming of Parr bar rarrie calls them forth again to start their lives over once more. And in revenge for losing their wives the Teal Teal, they rob all their nests of their eggs, thinking that by devouring the eggs they may annihilate the existence of their former wives.

Gool Lun Naga (Green Frog)

This is one of the many stories of a strange Being that came into existence. No doubt somewhere in the many stories that I have written I think I have mentioned that to the Aborigine's primitive mind there are many Spirits which exist in the elements—Myeyea (Wind Spirit); Pa nee (Rain Spirit); Kallitthie (Hail Spirit); Sunlight Spirit; Cloud Spirit. Then there are Spirits that take the form of Trees, Bush Shrubs, Plants, and Rocks. Everything that exists has some life apart from itself.

Now in this story of the Gool lun naga, a Green Frog came into existence from the Spirit of Water. Water Spirit or the Spirit of Water is the most multiple Spirit of all, because from it and into it there is a continual change of organism taking place from one form to another; life coming from it may be in plant form or weed. A life goes into it and comes out a quite different body. So that is how in this story the Gool lun naga came to be with us. There was a stream of pure liquid water flowing down the mountain-side on the western side of the Blue Mountains that now forms a tributary to the great Murray River.

Now some of you little readers will or have noticed some water-courses that have the water-flow murmuring and gurgling songs of these Water Spirits. They form into tiny bubbles clinging closely together and make the limpid pool white as snow. In these clustering tiny bubbles dwelt a Spirit peeping out of its many watery windows that were clear as glass. Thinking that it would be nice to free itself of its invisibleness and come in the freedom of some form and shape and be of some use and help, to become part of the many lives that now live, the Bubble

Spirit sat and watched the little fishes sporting and swimming, darting here and there in the clear waters of the pool. It would watch some strange tiny objects wiggling in the water, then burst forth and take wing and fly out over the water and away to the reeds and rushes and then among the flowers that grew upon the bank. Oh, what a wonderful life to live, to go where you will and come back in your own appointed time.

Then the Spirit began to think how nice it would be to leap forth and feel the cold refreshing stream, or to touch the tender leaves of the water-lily, or to ride upon the swaying stem of the reed as it is rocked by the gentle breeze blowing from the Karramia, the warm breath of the Sun God. Then it would sing and become enthralled in the song of the little water-bird, and would sit in wonderment at the merry laughter of the Kookaburras, their forms reflected in the clear water as they sat upon the overhanging branch of a large gum tree. Oh, what wonderful realisation to be able to become part of the material world.

And as the bright sun shone in the clear sky above, sending beams of light that gave warmth, vigour, and strength, suddenly the Bubble, behold by a wish of a Spirit, materialised into a living Being. The process was slow, but it gradually developed into a Green Frog, and began to experience a new life.

The first thing that he did was to try and produce sound, and began to imitate the various sounds that he had heard in the Spirit Land. By and by he became adept. He lived in this water-course for a while when the Birds would come in the hot summer days to drink of the clear, cool, and refreshing stream. They would fly upon the branches of nearby trees and pour forth their song of gratitude; or perhaps in the early hours of a summer morning all the feathered tribes would sing their morning anthems, sending forth notes of various tone yet blending in harmony.

'Oh, could I join in such wondrous melody,' said the Green Frog, who by this time was known by the Bird and Reptile and Animal tribes as Gool lun naga, a son of the clear running stream of water.

'Because,' said the Lyre Bird, 'I saw a froth of water in the pool, the place of our watering-place. I was just a few paces away from it and I saw this bubble floating upon the water, and I was attracted towards it. There seemed to be a Spirit from within it calling me to release it. But I would not. As I sat upon the bank resting I began to sing; I sang the song of the Crow and Teal Teal, and then I sang the song of the Magpie, and imitated in between the liquid notes of the song of a running stream, all the while keeping my eyes upon the Bubble, lying peacefully upon the clear limpid water. And a Spirit from the unknown whispered into my ears, "Sing on, a wonderful song doth give life to a Being within a form." So I still sang the same song, repeating it again and again. And the hot sun gave forth a glow of health and strength to all life upon the water, as well as beneath it; the little fishes darted swiftly here and there.

'And behold the bubble was no more, and nothing of importance was seen, until a little time after I was amazed to see a strange living form, and it looked straight at me and I came towards it and stood upon the bank bewildered. I could not recall any shape like it before. And then I sang to it. I cast my voice to the opposite side of the bank and it turned, looking in that direction. Then I cast it quickly all round the bank, and it turned quickly round and then stopped as if puzzled. I became very interested in this strange Being. I would pay him a visit after the sun rose high in the Wyerriewarr and I would stand upon the bank and sing to it the songs of our tribes and imitate the flowing stream running down the hillside. He became a good student and was able to make a deep guttural sound, and by and by he was able to make distinct sounds. And then I began to ask him questions about where he came from so quietly. "No one has spoken of your coming. Tell me, from whence are you." And he answered me: "From the Running Streams I live and move and have Being." And I said: "Then I shall call you Gool lun naga." So he is known today as Gool lun naga.'

The Gool lun naga expressed a wish that he would like to be able to sing like the Magpie and laugh like the Kookaburra. And the Lyre Bird consented that he would do all he could to educate him. So the Lyre Bird came every morning and gave the eager Gool lun naga a course of lessons.

After a while he was able to sing a few songs to the Lyre Bird. Then the Lyre Bird did not come so often to see his pupil until several moons had come and gone; then he thought that he would once more pay him a visit. And just as he was coming down the valley he could hear the song of his brother as he thought, so he wondered what his brother was doing there at the pool, so he came cautiously down, dodging round the shrubs and bushes, so that his brother would not see him, until he came right upon him. When he got to the edge of the bank of the pool he looked about but saw no brother of his. Then he wondered, 'Perhaps it is my brother that is playing a joke upon me.'

And presently the thought struck him, 'Perhaps it is the cunning Gool lun naga that is playing a joke on me.'

So he called: 'Gool lun naga,' and the answer came from away down the gully from whence the Lyre Bird came, and he called again: 'Gool lun naga,' and the voice answered: 'I am coming, I am coming,' and the voice came nearer and nearer until it sounded right down in the pool of water.

The Lyre Bird looked very much amazed, and stood, pleased that he had been able to educate the Gool lun naga.

'And now,' said the Lyre Bird, 'I want to know how many songs of individuals can you imitate?'

So the Gool lun naga sang like the Magpie and the Butcher-bird, laughed like the Kookaburra, and imitated the sound of the running stream as it gurgled over pebbles, and the splash of the Water Rats as they sported chasing each other. And the Lyre Bird complimented him on his wonderful achievement, and said that he was better in the art of ventriloquism than he himself. And this statement caused the Gool lun naga to swell with pride, and he thought within himself that he would seek others.

Before he did this he settled down and began in earnest. And he became a hypnotist. He would make the sound of a Magpie at a certain spot and would speak to his audience in such a manner that they would imagine the sound and were sure they saw him settling there. And then he made the sound of water being disturbed by the sporting Water Rats, and the soft north wind rustling among the gum leaves and moaning through the She-Oak's long wiry leaves. And presently the sound of a mighty storm was heard with rumbling thunder and breaking boughs, as if the wind was tearing up the huge gum trees, and then came the rain and hail, as if lashed by the furious wind. All this the Gool lun naga was able to do.

Then the Gool lun naga thought that he would go and gain the experience of the outside world, and he expressed this to the Lyre Bird, who told him that the world was large and that there were many, many kinds of Beings with strange habits and strange languages. But during this time, unknown to the Gool lun naga, there came to this pool of water to rest and refresh their wearied bodies a Swift and a Falcon. They sat there enthralled by the wonderful song that came from the silent nowhere. It was by an accident that they made the discovery that all this beautiful song came from a stranger lying in the leaf of a water-lily. When they saw and heard it speaking to the Lyre Bird who had just arrived, they leapt from their perches, and as if carried on the mighty wings of the storm, sped throughout the country, telling the various tribes of a great man who did wonderful things. And the Animal, Bird, Reptile, and Insect tribes became very curious, and asked if they could be allowed to pay him a visit.

So the Falcon and Swift returned and came and perched upon the same limbs they had occupied a few days previous, waiting for the Lyre Bird to appear. Presently he arrived and they spoke to him, telling him of the wishes of the various tribes, that they would like to come and be entertained by the strange Being.

'Well,' said the Lyre Bird, 'if you shall wait a moment I will speak to him. But I think he may be at rest among the reeds yonder.'

So the Lyre Bird, Swift, and Falcon sat down on the bank of the pool and patiently waited for the Gool lun naga.

Now the Gool lun naga was in deep sleep and in this state he was enjoying himself with the people of his race in the Spirit Land, and when he awoke he was greatly disappointed, and came out of the reeds and went to his usual spot. And there he saw the Lyre Bird with two strangers, the Swift and Falcon. Then the Lyre Bird spoke and told him that a great many people, great in number as the reeds that grow in the water of that pool in which he lived, had heard of his wonderful accomplishments, and were anxious to see and hear him. There would be the Animal, Bird, Lizard, Snake, and Insect tribes. Would he be pleased to give them an invitation?

'Oh, yes, I would like to meet them. Will you ask them to come next full moon?'

When the Swift and Falcon heard the answer they were eager to be off with the message. But the Lyre Bird asked them to think how they would carry out the delivery of the message. So it was arranged that the Swift would fly Wolkundmia, twenty miles, then travel in a spiral, widening outwards, and the Falcon should fly forty miles, and begin from there, and when the Swift had reached the forty miles he should fly Tolkamia, sixty miles; by that time the Falcon would arrive there on that line somewhere; then the Falcon would fly Kolkamia for twenty miles, and so forth until during this travel they informed every tribe of the invitation of the Gool lun naga.

As soon as the instructions were given the Swift was off like lightning, wending the air as he went with the speed of a hurricane, and when he reached the twenty miles in a straight line he began to fly in a spiral towards Wolkundmia, dropping a word of the approval of the Gool lun naga as he went. Then the Falcon leapt, as is his custom, straight into the air, until he was invisible. Then he shot forth like a arrow from the pull of a bow aimed by a mighty archer, away into Tolkamia (west) until he came to the limit of the straight line. By this time the Swift arrived at this point, then it rose upward in a small circle till it reached a certain height and shot forward towards Tolkamia in a straight line. They both kept this up until they completed their journey, giving the message of the goodness of the Gool lun naga's approval to grant their request and to be there next full moon.

Their duty fulfilled, they came back to where the Gool lun naga lived, and became his servant to carry any messages that he desired to be delivered, until the great entertainment was over. And on the appointed time the great army of Beings—the Kangaroo with all his family, the Animal tribe, the Eagle Hawk and family with his tribe, Snake, Reptile, and Insect tribes—all came to see this strange Being who could sing their song when heard once, and could mimic any peculiar movement of an individual or tribe.

So when the night-time approached they were all seated on the bank, and the Beings heard some very wonderful songs all round, and when the sun rose the Gool lun naga still performed his wonderful feats; in the still air they imagined the noise of a mighty wind, in the clear sky they fancied they saw the flash of lightning and heard the thunder roar, the sound of rain and hail lashed by the fury of a mighty wind. They all scattered and ran to seek shelter. Suddenly the storm ceased and they all looked about themselves and saw a clear sky, which had been there all the while; they looked at the trees and saw that they were not disturbed. Then he caused sound to be heard that came from a cataract. They looked about but saw no waterfall and were greatly bewildered. And they all shouted: 'Kay hey, kay hey.'

Now, after a few days' entertainment, the Beings all went away to their homes, and for many days afterwards they spoke to each other of the wonderful thing they had seen. And then the Gool lun naga settled down and by this time the Spirit of the Running Stream gave forth a beautiful wife to the Gool lun naga, and one day the Gool lun naga was entertaining his wife, Yohon keeng, with his wonderful voice. And he sang and sang, and his pride became greater, and with his conceit he strained his voice. And today he is only heard to Croak-Croak, never more to sing the song of the Birds.

Hunting

I may say with confidence that in bushcraft and hunting the Aborigines excel, and are undoubtedly second to no other of the primitive races in this respect. And as to observation, I think we may claim to stand alone and have no equal, because we are trained from early childhood to make a careful and thorough study of forest, scrub and plain countries as well as rivers, lakes, lagoons and billabongs, with their vegetation. These are environments of animal, bird, reptile, insect, and fish life, and with our little brain capacity we know that environment has a wonderful effect upon all living organisms; that the animal, bird, reptile, fish, or insect is able to imitate or adapt itself to the colouring that offers itself from tree shrubs, plant, and water vegetation, or even water or ground colour.

Now we shall begin our hunting expedition. An experienced hunter would not begin haphazardly, but would, according to the animal or bird's nature, seek it within that environment. For instance, hunting a pheasant, he would not enter a plain country where there may be a few scattered shrubs, or down by a river's bank void of shrubs. Nor would he venture to hunt the teal or black duck and swan in a running stream near its source, wending its way down between the steep rocky mountain-side; or where the stream finds itself in the deep valley where the huge gum tree pushes itself up skyward, and sending its branches across the stream, shuts out the sunlight; and where the dense undergrowth and wild clinging creepers and convolvulus hides the running stream from view. Nor would he think of waiting the approach of the thirsty kangaroo or emu at this spot. This is not their environment: this little stream further down the valley may be an ideal spot for Mr and Mrs Platypus to live and rear a family.

Nor would I find the wombat; this is not the kind of country that he would seek to live in, the low-lying scrub and limestone country; no high mountain with steep rocky valley and dense undergrowth would entice him to make it a home. Perhaps the lyre bird would love to be in an enchanting place as this, but not so the eagle hawk or the graceful swan; neither is this their environment.

Supposing he seeks the swan as food. He goes to the Murray River, or some other large river where there may be low-lying land in which the water during a flood overflows its bank and forms a lagoon. This is where I would expect to find the various kinds of water-fowl, black duck, teal and swan; some on the bank basking in the sunlight, whilst others may be washing themselves, dipping themselves into the water and ruffling their feathers, and flapping their wings, and others thrusting their heads under the surface of the water in search of weed and gravel.

From among the bush about thirty to fifty yards away the hunter allows his vision to take in every detail of the ducks, swans, and other water-fowl. Presently his eyes rest upon something he was looking for. Away yonder, well-trained eyes see standing just where he was to enter the water, a plover on duty as a sentinel; he, too, is taking in every moving object to see whether an enemy is hiding in ambush awaiting an opportunity to pounce upon the birds. But the keen eye of the Aboriginal, with the cunning of his race, outdoes the plover. Then the hunter, after planning the attack, and satisfied of the position of the sentinel, begins with the alertness of a cat, slides from bush to bush; presently he throws himself upon his belly and wriggles his way to the water's edge through rushes and water shrubs. He halts and plucks some rushes and reeds and water-flags, and whilst upon his belly he constructs a hat by tying the ends of the rushes and reed about eighteen inches apart; then places that upon his head and pulls it down over his eyes, and begins wriggling his way until he is clear of the rushes and reeds.

The eye of the plover catching sight of the object makes a warning cry, and all birds, swans, ducks, and water-fowls fly from the bank into the lagoon about fifty yards away. There is an instinct which tells all animal, bird, and reptile life that there is danger, hence the warning note of the plover. Then the birds look about to see from where the danger comes. They see nothing. But the plover who was on duty, reasoning in his bird mind that that object now floating toward the ducks and swans is not an accident, but must be an enemy, rises upon its wing and flies toward the floating object, circles around several times, still giving the warning cry of danger, then returns to the bank and settles, satisfied that it is only a floating rush or weed.

Then the hunter is peering through the rushes and looking for an opportunity, and sees that the ducks are among the weeds; then he eagerly approaches nearer and nearer until he is within a measured length from a duck, then the arm goes out beneath the water and through the weeds and takes the duck by a leg and suddenly pulls it beneath the surface and takes the duck by its neck; a twist and a pull, the duck has a broken neck.

The hunter is wearing a rush belt and he places the head of the duck between the belt and his body; the duck is kept there secure, and he, counting, capturing duck after duck until he thinks he has sufficient, swims on to the opposite bank from which he entered the water to give the bird mind the impression of a floating object. After relieving himself of his burden, which he does still lying upon his belly, he returns to the hunt and captures a few more ducks and will swim on the side of the lagoon from which he first entered the water, and will relieve himself of the second amount of ducks captured. He may continue this until he has captured sufficient to supply the whole need, which may consist of three or four people. Then he will be still until in disguise he creeps into cover of the shrubs, and makes a bee-line straight for home, and will tell them of his great capture and instruct to the whereabouts of the ducks, and some of the young men will go to the lagoon. In this case they walk without sneaking to give the bird mind the impression that it is different to coming upon them without being seen, which makes it easier for the hunter the next time.

Now the hunting and capturing of the swan are done in three different ways. First perhaps the hunter would go to the same lagoon in which I captured the duck. I would creep along as I did for the ducks, until I arrived at a spot upon the edge of the reeds or rushes that grow in the water about five or ten yards from the bank.

The hunter takes his place, say, in a bunch of reeds and he has a wing of a dead swan with feathers upon it; we shall say that the swans are feeding in the middle of the lagoon. The hunter begins to flap the wing in the water, imitating a swan in distress. (That is what we call: 'my a min'.) The swans in mid-stream hear the water being struck and they see the wing of one belonging to their kind and they swim to the supposed swan in distress. The hunter stops for a while and prepares his rod made of ti tree and the root of ponie oo lunkie (a shrub that grows on the bank of the lagoon and bears red berries in the months of December and January). He takes its roots and treats with water first, and after gives them a certain temper by heating in the blaze of a fire, but mostly in hot ashes. This is then tied to the end of a ti tree rod made after the fashion of a fishing rod. At the end is tied a noose made of the sinews of the kangaroo tail or made of rushes twisted like string. He places this rod in readiness.

As the swans approach nearer he strikes the water with the wing. The swans do not suspect the danger, but draw closer until they are within reach of the rod, when the hunter places the noose over the head of one of the swans and draws it towards him. Then the swan begins to struggle, and the hunter takes the swan by the head. This is done so quickly that the other swans do not follow to see what has taken place. The hunter then twists its neck, throws it behind quickly and, deftly placing the noose upon another swan, deals with it in the same manner. An expert in this way will capture half a dozen swans before the others will swim away suspecting danger.

Here is also another way in which they capture the swans. A hunter will get into his canoe and with a pole propel it in and around the lagoon until he arrives at a spot where the swans have a passage through the reeds or bullrushes for travelling from one clear spot to another. The hunter will make that passage of reeds or bullrushes so narrow and so low that it will just be large enough to allow one swan at a time. Two to four passages may be made in this fashion, side by side, and a noose is set in each passage so that when the swan stretches its head and neck forward, it places it right into the noose, and upon finding that it is hindered from further progress, it begins to struggle, with the result that the noose tightens on accounts of its being tied firmly to two poles which have been placed into the ground under the water. When the hunter returns in his canoe on the following morning, he releases the dead swans from the snare and returns home, perhaps taking the snare with him, only setting such snares when he requires food. Other small birds are caught in the same fashion.

Now, let us return to the capture of the duck—black duck, teal, or other birds of the same species. Now let us suppose that it is midwinter, the water is very cold and the hunter does not feel inclined to risk his life, thinking that possibly the sudden cold may cause a cramp which may result in drowning, so he thinks of another idea practised by his ancestors. He has in hand his waddy, or probably a boomerang and spear. He holds something else, it is the flower top of a reed. Perhaps he has three of these tied together. He silently sneaks under cover to the river bank and begins waving the flower-topped reeds so that the duck can see it. Then they become curious, they swim towards him and when within striking distance about ten to fifteen yards away, he rises suddenly and the ducks meet with a surprise, leaping into the air in a commotion. The hunter hurls his spear first, then the boomerang into their midst.

The object of throwing the spear is that when the birds rise it is in their midst, perhaps it strikes half a dozen birds, and the force with which the birds have risen carries the spear along with them and it becomes an obstacle, other birds strike it, perhaps another half-dozen. Then when the boomerang is thrown with such force that it cuts through the air making a sound similar to that of a hawk, the birds hesitate, not knowing whether to continue their flight or swoop back into the water. They decide to settle on the water, more afraid of the supposed hawk than the human hunter. The boomerang returns to the thrower. He takes the now returning boomerang and he throws it so that it skims close upon the surface of the water, and if there is a head which happens to be in the way it is cut clean off its body, and sometimes three or four heads are severed from the bodies of the ducks.

Another way of procuring ducks is to closely watch their habits of flying from one lagoon to another, or from the river to a lagoon, or from a lake to a lagoon. The hunter has a special net constructed from the rushes that grow along the river bank. These nets are made like European fishing nets, thirty to fifty yards long and ten to twelve feet wide. This net is stretched across and hung or suspended from tree to tree in the line of flight of the ducks from lake to lagoon. The net is tied sufficiently to bear its own weight. The hunter awaits the ducks. He allows the first lot to pass unmolested and presently the second swarm of ducks flies in the same course as the first.

There is in this method two or three taking part in the catch. The third man stands about forty yards away in front of the net toward which the ducks are flying. As they pass him he whistles, imitating the whistle of the falcon, loud enough for the ducks to hear, then suddenly he hurls the boomerang with great force and the whirr as it cuts the air is like the sound of the wing of a falcon. The birds, thinking it is a falcon rising to attack them, swoop down in a body right into the middle of the net, striking it, and with their momentum, carry it with them, and eventually they become tangled in the mesh. The two men who are standing each side of the net rush forward and draw the net so that all the birds that are in the net are captured. At times a hundred or two are caught thus.

This is the most effective and advantageous, in that the hunter simply awaits the approach of a swarm of ducks, and they are caught in great numbers at once and near to their camping ground. Sometimes the boys will amuse themselves awaiting the approach of the ducks, and as they fly by, they will throw a stick like a spear into their midst. The ducks flying at a great speed strike the stick and some fall to the ground with broken wings, or broken necks, and some with their heads smashed.

Hunting the kangaroo requires a great deal of skill and patience because there is something that is almost [like] human reasoning in some animal life. The kangaroo always takes shelter at midday in a scrub which may be low mallee and ti tree country. It will dig an oblong hole under the shrub just by the root, the hole is just large enough to take in the body and legs. The forearms and head rest on the surface out of the hole, whilst the body is hidden from view. This is where the kangaroo[s] spend their midday rest. There are always one or two who keep watch for the approach of an enemy. It is very difficult to come upon the kangaroos when resting in this state. It seems that the sound of the footsteps is conveyed upon the earth—I suppose the kangaroos have some knowledge of sound and medium, hence the hole with its head resting on the surface of the earth.

Kangaroos are like human beings, they choose to live in one locality and frequent one particular feeding ground regularly.

The hunter, when in search of kangaroos, does not hunt at it the camping-ground, but before the kangaroos go to their feeding ground. The hunter is already equipped with a spear and Rarrabarr but just before the arrival of the kangaroos, the hunter has cunningly constructed a shield made of the boughs from the shrubs that are growing around and in the feeding ground. This shield is made sufficiently large to conceal the body of the hunter. As the kangaroos are feeding he gradually comes nearer and nearer. The kangaroos will cease feeding and look around as if expecting an enemy. It is the animals' instinct that warns them of danger. As they look around, scanning every shrub, grass or tree, and fail to see the enemy, they continue feeding.

'After all,' the kangaroos think, 'why be afraid, we only see shrub, and bush, and grass, no enemy,' little dreaming that behind one of the shrubs that appears to be real, an Aboriginal is drawing closer.

He has in his right hand a spear made of ti tree with a keen tempered point. When the hunter is within striking distance he thrusts the spear into the vital spot of the kangaroo. One captured, he then moves on to the next; the second is speared in the same fashion. An expert hunter will always spear a kangaroo when it is stooping and feeding, in doing this, there is less danger of the kangaroo warning the others by its struggling.

Another way in which we hunt the kangaroo demands great skill in throwing the spear or Rarrabarr (a small throwing waddy about fourteen or eighteen inches long with a knot at one end). This weapon requires a strong and skilled hunter. It is not any person. All members of the tribe volunteer to take part in this hunt. Some are told to go to the bush and disturb the kangaroos, which rush out with great speed. There are people set at intervals and when the kangaroos come in sight they make a great noise by shouting, the kangaroos are excited, and they race straight ahead. The picked men with the Rarrabarr, say about two dozen or more, stand in a line along which the kangaroos are driven. Presently a hunter hurls his weapon at the head of the prey and the kangaroo falls with its skull smashed. The other animals are still racing along to safety and another Rarrabarr is sent on its mission by number two hunter. This is done by selected hunters, and perhaps all have scored a kangaroo.

Sometimes when the weather is unfavourable to the hunter with spear or Rarrabarr, a party of young men is sent out to a spot where the kangaroos are numerous and they dig large pits about five feet deep and many feet wide, not necessarily round, or square, or oblong, and they are cunningly covered over with small boughs and sand. The pits are made right in the beaten track of the kangaroos. These hunts take place when two or three tribes meet to discuss tribal matters, and the members of each tribe are represented. There are men standing at intervals of fifty yards, more or less; the distance does not matter much, on both sides of the animals' track. Others are sent into the bush to arouse the kangaroos from their lair or resting ground. They rush along this laneway, they see no danger. Suddenly some fall into the pit, the others continue their flight and fall into number two pit; perhaps half a dozen pits have been prepared, so these contain four or five kangaroos each, which is a good day's sport.

There is little difficulty in hunting the possum—he is an easy prey. A few scratches on the gum tree will tell us that he is having his day's rest within the hollow trunk of the tree, or in the thick bough of a tree. A few furs among the rocks leading to a hole, if the hole has a smooth surface around its entrance, indicates that Mr and Mrs Possum are having their daily nap.

The emu is hunted in the same way as the kangaroo, with bough shields, or digging a hole which is concealed with boughs and rushes.

The wombat is another animal that is an easy prey. Although they live in holes like rabbits, when they come out late in the afternoon, the hunter will be watching their movements from a nearby bush. When he thinks that he will be able to get to the hole he cautiously approaches it, and when he arrives he blocks the hole about two or three feet inside from the entrance. Then he sneaks back to his ambush, takes his Nulla nulla in his hand, and boldly goes towards the wombat. Presently the wombat sees the enemy and with haste he seeks shelter, making a bee-line for the hole. When he arrives he only has his head three feet from the entrance in safety. The hunter takes it by the hind legs and then there is a tug of war. The wombat is a very obstinate customer, especially when asked to leave home and to become a meal for the other fellow.

There is not much difficulty in capturing an emu. The hunter is acquainted with its ways and usually waits along its path leading to the riverside or waterhole. The hunter conceals himself inside a thick bush just within arm's length of the path. When the late afternoon approaches the emus wend their way, unconscious of the danger awaiting them, looking about at the bushes and shrubs. As they come close to the shrub in which the hunter is hiding, the hunter thrusts out a hand and grasps a leg; at the same time he rises from the ground, still clinging to the leg of the emu, and with a Nulla nulla strikes the bird on the head.

The poor unsuspecting emu lays dying, and is carried away to the camping-ground, cut up in pieces and distributed to the members of the tribe, or it may be cooked whole. A hole is made in the earth, a little larger than the emu, and a fire is made within this hole. The ground in the hole becomes hot with live coals, then boughs of shrubs and grass are placed in the hole, and the emu is laid on the grass and hot coals. It is then covered with some more boughs and grass and covered with earth and a fire is made on the top. The head and portion of the neck is left uncovered. This is left alone until steam issues from the mouth of the emu, which is a sign that it is cooked, then it is then taken out of the hole and allowed to cool for half a day, or perhaps a day.

How the Tortoise Got His Shell

Long, long ago, all the bush Birds and Animals lived in a big deep valley that was hemmed in on all sides by rough high hills. Food had become very scarce, and all the Birds and Animals held a great Yun mundi (conference) to discuss the problem of food.

All the Birds and Animals talked and talked, and yet they came to no decision as to how to obtain more food. At last the Tortoise arose to speak, and all the Animals laughed. Everybody laughed at the Tortoise for he was so slow and ungainly; and everybody looked upon him as a fool, because he was always asleep.

However, the Tortoise proposed that the big Eagle Hawk, the fierce King of Birds, who was a great hunter, should fly over the ranges and find some food.

'Oh yes,' said the big Eagle Hawk, and away he flew over the ranges.

When the Eagle Hawk reached a long way over the other side of the ranges, he saw a beautiful country full of all kinds of food. But he saw there were no Birds or Animals there, except one little Willy Wagtail.

So the Eagle Hawk said to the little Willy Wagtail: 'May I fetch my brothers and sisters who are starving into this beautiful country of yours?'

'Oh yes,' said the Wagtail, 'but you must wrestle with me first.'

Of course the big strong Eagle Hawk thought this was easy, but the cunning little Wagtail had placed some sharp fish-bone-like spikes in the ground where they were to wrestle. When they began to wrestle the Wagtail was very quick and nimble, and hopped and jumped about as he does today. Suddenly the Wagtail tripped the Eagle Hawk, who fell among the sharp spikes, and was pinned to the ground. Then he was at the mercy of the Wagtail, who at once pecked him to death.

All the other Birds and Animals over the ranges waited and waited for the Eagle Hawk to return. At last they became tired of waiting, and they sent out the Kite Hawk. But the Kite Hawk met the same fate as the Eagle Hawk. Then the Magpie, the Wombat, the Dingo, and others went. But the wicked little Wagtail tripped them all onto his spikes and then pecked them to death. All the Birds and Animals became very much afraid at none returning. Things became serious—food had to be found somewhere.

At last the old Tortoise volunteered to go. Away he went, crawling painfully slowly over the ranges, and into the land of the Wagtail. As usual, the Wagtail invited the Tortoise to wrestle.

'Oh yes,' replied the Tortoise, 'but just wait a while.'

The Tortoise went into the bush, and cut a coolamon (a long wooden dish for carrying water) out of a gum tree, and a thick strip of bark. The Tortoise placed the coolamon on his back, and he tied on a thick sheet of bark as a breastplate. Then away he went to wrestle the Wagtail.

The lively, quick Wagtail soon hopped around and tripped up the slow old Tortoise, but when he fell on the spikes the coolamon protected him. Again and again the Wagtail threw the Tortoise, but either the coolamon on his back, or his bark breastplate, always saved him. After a while the Wagtail became exhausted, and the Tortoise fell upon him and killed him.

Of course, the Tortoise let all the Birds and Animals know as quickly as he could where there was plenty of food.

Now, what the Eagle Hawk, and the Dingo, and the Kangaroo failed to accomplish with brute force, the slow-moving old Tortoise achieved with wisdom, and, as a memorial of a great victory in overcoming a cunning and wicked enemy, he is to be seen through the long years of his lifetime seeking no applause, but humbly bearing his shield.

Immortality

My race has a legend to explain every natural phenomenon. The same as in the legends of other races, we must not ask too many questions. We have to take it for granted that all these wonderful events took place in 'the long, long ago'—before the race of men came on the earth, and when the Animals could talk to each other. In those delightful days when any unusual event occurred, the Animals were able to call together a great meeting to discuss the matter.

One day a young Cockatoo fell from a high tree and broke his neck. There he lay, Pon el itch (dead). All the Animals gathered around to try and wake him. They touched him with a spear, but he could not feel. They opened his eyes, but he could not see. The Animals were completely mystified, for they did not understand death. Then all the Medicine Men tried to awaken the Kuthuwarr (Cockatoo), but they failed.

A great meeting was called to discuss the mystery of the dead Cockatoo. First of all, the Owl, who with his great big eyes was supposed to be very wise, was called upon to explain this mystery. But the Kroult-humie (Owl) was silent.

Then the Eagle Hawk, the great Chief of the Birds, was asked to explain this great mystery of death. The Eagle Hawk took a pebble and threw it out into the river, and all the huge gathering saw the pebble strike the water and sink out of sight. Turning to the tribes, the Eagle Hawk cried: 'There is the explanation of the mystery; as that pebble has entered another existence, so has the Cockatoo.'

However, this answer did not satisfy the gathering; so they next asked the Crow to explain. Although everyone knew the Crow was very wicked, they also knew he had great knowledge. The Crow stepped forward and took up a Whit whit (small egg-shaped hunting weapon) and threw it out into the river. The Whit whit sank, and then gradually returned to the surface again.

'There,' said the Crow, 'is the great mystery explained. We all go through another world of experience, and then return again.'

This explanation impressed all the tribes, and the great Eagle Hawk asked: 'Who will volunteer to go through this other experience to test it, and see if it is possible to return again?'

Certain hibernating animals offered to go and test the experience.

'Very well,' said the Eagle Hawk, 'but you must go through the experience of not being sensible to sight, taste, smell, touch, or hearing, and then return to us in another form.'

When it became winter time, away went all those Animals—the Goanna, the Possum, the Wombat, and the Snake—who crawl into holes and hollow logs to sleep during the winter months.

Next Par bar rarrie (the springtime of the year) the tribes gathered together again to wait the return of those who were trying to solve the great mystery. At last the Wombat, the Goanna, the Possum, and the Snake returned, all looking half-starved.

When they showed themselves to the gathering, the Eagle Hawk said: 'You have all returned in the same form as you went out, although the Snake has half changed his skin; you have failed to solve the mystery.'

Still, the gathering was anxious to solve the great mystery of death.

At last the Insect tribes—the Moths, the Grubs, and the Caterpillars—volunteered to solve the experience and mystery of death. All the other tribes—especially the Kookaburra—laughed at this, because the Insects had always been looked upon as ignorant and inferior. The Insects, however, persisted, so the Eagle Hawk gave them permission to try. But the Insects did not of their own volition crawl away out of sight. The Water Grubs asked to be wrapped in a very fine bark and thrown into the river; some asked to be placed in the bark of trees and others asked to be placed under the ground.

'Now,' said the different Moths, Grubs, and Caterpillars, 'we will return at the springtime of the year in another form, and we will meet you at Parram pairrie, a place away from the river surrounded by high hills, a deep valley with only one entrance.'

The tribes then dispersed until the following spring.

When springtime approached again all the Animals knew that the season was nearing by the position of the stars at night, and because all the trees and shrubs were beginning to put forth their buds. As the time drew near there was great excitement everywhere. All the Animals felt the mystery would be solved this time.

The day before the time fixed for the return of the Insects, the Eagle Hawk had sent out notice, and all the Animals had gathered in Parram pairrie to await the great event. That night the Dragon-flies, the Chilli (Gnats), and Kroo wulthee (Fireflies) came round the campfires as heralds of the great pageant that was to take place on the morrow. Already the trees, the shrubs, and the flowers had consented to lend themselves for the great occasion. The Dragon-fly went from camp to camp, from tribe to tribe, telling all what a great sight it was going to be, to see all the Insects returning from death in their new bodies.

At daybreak all the Animals were out to witness the pageant of new forms arrive. The wattle put forth all its wonderful yellow, the waratah its brilliant red, and all the other flowers their glorious shades. Just as the sun rose over the tops of the hills the Dragon-flies came up through the entrance of Parram pairrie, leading an army of gorgeous-coloured Butterflies. Each colour and species of Butterfly came in order. First the yellow came up and showed themselves to everybody. They flew about and rested upon the trees, the wattle, and the flowers. Then came the red, the blue, the green, and right on through all the families of the Butterflies.

The Animals were delighted. They gave great cries of praise and admiration. The Birds were so pleased that for the first time they broke forth into song. All Nature looked its best.

When the last of the Butterflies had entered Parram pairrie they asked the great gathering: 'Have we solved the mystery of death? Have we returned in another form?'

All Nature answered back: 'You have!'

Thus it was left to the little, despised Insect tribes to demonstrate to all other Animal tribes the possibility of overcoming death and gaining immortality.

Love Story of the Mar Rallang

There were two sisters living at Pool loo we wuld, an isthmus between Lake Alexandrina and Lake Albert, on the Lower Murray River. They had been well educated in all the tribal customs and also in all forms of bush craft. It is the custom of the Aborigines to name their young people after some particular characteristic or peculiarity the children may have.

These girls had not been given individual names, because they were so alike and attached to each other that, although there was a slight difference in their ages, they were the same as one girl. So their elders called them Mar rallang, meaning two in one.

There was also a fine young man called Wy young gurrie. Wy young gurrie was a gift from the great leader Narroondarie. Years before, about the time the two sisters were born, a widow was mourning the loss of her husband. The widow had plastered her hair with white clay and had cut great gashes in her body to express her intense grief.

In her distress she cried to the great spirit, Narroondarie: 'Oh, why did you take my husband? Oh, why have I not a son?'

Narroondarie heard her and placed a young baby boy in the bush nearby. When the baby cried the widow went and discovered him. She was delighted. She took the boy and reared him, and her brother also helped her to educate him, as it is the tribal custom for a brother to always take a great interest in his sister's children.

They called the boy Wy young gurrie, which means 'He who returns to the stars', and, because the boy sooner or later had to return to the stars, great care was taken with his bushcraft and knowledge of the birds and animals.

The uncle also sent a messenger around to all the families, saying: 'No girls are to be given to Wy young gurrie in marriage, and I have also set aside a narrow strip of hunting ground by the lake for Wy young gurrie to live upon, and nobody else must trespass upon that ground.'

The families of the tribe answered: 'Kutchle kutchle (True, let it be as you say)'.

Par bar rarrie (the springtime of the year) is a great time in the training of the young people of the tribe. They are taught to become quick and observant in detecting the different love notes of the wooing birds and the mating impulses of the animals. One springtime, when all Nature had become alive again around the lake, the two sisters caught the spirit of the season, and felt a great urge to meet the young Wy young gurrie. So early one morning the elder sister hid herself in the bush near the camp of Wy young gurrie, and imitated the cry of an Emu. Instantly Wy young gurrie sprang up to hunt the supposed Emu, but when the girl saw him she revealed herself and asked Wy young gurrie to help her to find her lost sister. Of course, this was only a trick to meet Wy young gurrie and tempt him to love. Later on the younger sister played the same trick by giving the love note of the Swan. The end of all this was that the two sisters married Wy young gurrie.

When the uncle heard Wy young gurrie was married he was very wrathful, and off he went to Nebalee (the great man of the heavens) to ask him what he should do.

Nebalee answered: 'You will have to separate them.'

The uncle then took some ashes and, wrapping them in paper bark, placed them near the camp of Wy young gurrie, thinking that a fire would separate Wy young gurrie and the two girls (to the Aborigines fire symbolises the truth and inexorable law). During the night the ashes burst into flame and set fire to the bush. Gradually a huge bush fire encircled the camp. At last Wy young gurrie was awakened, but in the danger and excitement of the burning flames and the blinding smoke he did not lose his presence of mind. He seized both of his wives and, with one under each arm, made for safety to the lake. To escape the flames he dived again and again under the water. But the fire came and began to burn all the dry reeds around the lake. So Wy young gurrie took his spear, to which was attached a coil of rope made of rushes.

Then, calling to Naboolea (the great God of the Stars), he uttered a prayer: 'O Father of the Kom nu kalda (mankind), hear me, not for my sake, but for the sake of these my wives. Take hold of this spear until they have climbed into safety. Then in thy pleasure do unto me what to thou seems best.'

Naboolea heard the cry, and he held the spear as the wives of Wy young gurrie climbed into heaven.

Then Naboolea called to Wy young gurrie: 'Come, my son, take thy place in heaven and shine forth thy mission, reminding the children of earth this lesson—that thou didst think more for the safety of thy wives than of thine own life.'

The Aborigines still point to the three stars in the eastern sky that represent Wy young gurrie and his two wives.

THE MAR KAR REE (MOON)

The Mar kar ree at one time was a queer man. He was a happy-go-lucky chap, always whistling and singing and laughing, but there were times when he would have very despondent moods. The reason of this was that he was unable to win the affection of any one of the beautiful girls with whom he came into contact. In spite of his bright disposition he failed to attract the Yartookas (girls), who would only laugh and make jokes about him, because he was a very fat man, and very dense. Every night he would travel from place to place seeking a wife.

The tribe would send the message: 'Mesap ell Mar kar alk (Look out, the Moon is on his way seeking a wife. Inform the girls).'

During one of his night-walks on a clear, cloudless night, when Wy young gurrie, Jeir ell ang, Mungingee, Now warrie, and Naboolea were shining brightly, sending the message of plenty in food, plenty of enjoyment, and plenty of strength to fight the Evil Spirit, the Moon was singing merrily along the banks of a river and attracted the daughters of a widowed mother.

They sat quietly awaiting his approach, full of excitement. They thought: 'This person who is in possession of such a lovely voice must be handsome.'

Presently he came before their vision, and they saw a palpullae—a very fat man, small, with short legs and arms that were very thin, and a big head with shining eyes.

'What a funny man,' laughed the girls, running to the riverside and leaping into one of the canoes which were paddling across the stream.

The Mar kar ree shouted and called piteously, begging to be taken across the stream. The girls stopped paddling midstream, and called to him: 'We have heard of you, that you are a min kerrie (flirt). We were all warned not to have anything to do with you. Swim across the stream.'

'Oh,' said the Mar kar ree, 'I am hungry and weary, have pity on me. Mungungad (oh, for the sake of the Pleiades), who has set all girls an example to think of others, look at yonder sky. How disappointed they must be to see you treating me thus.'

Then the girls remembered the beautiful story of how all the Aboriginal girls are striving to imitate the beautiful character of those lovely girls who are now shining to remind them to do good to friend and foe alike. They pondered awhile, and, responding to the spirit call of Mungingee, as they reached the bank of the river, they both leaped ashore. They invited the Mar kar ree to board the canoe, and he stepped into it.

They said: 'We will lend you the canoe, but you must row yourself across the stream.'

He said: 'I am unable to row.'

'All right,' said the good girls, 'we will take you across.'

So they grasped the sides of the canoe in which the Moon sat, and towed it across, swimming beside it. Before they had gone a quarter of the distance the Moon began tickling the girls under the arms, and they became angry and told him to stop this rude behaviour. He stopped for a while, but just as they arrived in midstream he once more commenced to tickle them, and this time without warning they tipped the Moon into the deep clear river and watched him sinking into the depths, where they could see his shining face looking up at them. The further he sank the smaller he grew, until only one part of his face was visible, and that too gradually diminished until there was only a small crescent visible. Eventually that quite disappeared.

The girls went home and told the story to their mother and the whole tribe, telling of the fate of the flirting Mar kar ree, and how he sank to the bottom of the river. The news was spread all over the country by smoke signals, and when the Crow heard the news he sent his messenger forth.

'Mar kar ree is not to go forever. You will see him coming out of the Land of Spirits, part of his face visible, peeping round the coming night, until the whole of his face is seen, then he will gradually disappear into the west. He will not be seen for a season, then he will rise and go.'

Thus Mar kar ree every month comes out of the west, peeping expectantly, then becomes wholly visible, sinking in the eastern sky, endeavouring with a silvery smile to win the affection of a Yartookie; passing into the west, to rise in the eastern sky, disappointed, gradually passing behind the night shadow, sinking, waning, and disappearing.

Marriage Customs of the Australian Aborigines

When the youth or maiden arrives at an age which is considered marriageable, sixteen to eighteen years, the uncle, who is brother to the mother of the young folks concerned will summon the members of the family to discuss the all important subject of matrimony at his Mundi (home) on a particular night.

Before the meeting takes place, the mother of the young man or maiden will seek a private interview with her brother, and will express her wish that her child should be married into such-and-such a tribe. The brother will take a spear into his hand, which is a sign to his sister that he will enforce her wish at the cost of his life. The mother departs to her home, awaiting the appointed night. When it arrives, the family are gathered together at the mundi of the uncle. The family consists of the father and mother, the elder sons and daughters, the parents' brothers and sisters (with their elder sons and daughters), and the grandfathers and grandmothers of the young folk concerned.

Now, each of the relations will speak of certain tribes and whom they consider would make a good husband or family. Usually the father and mother of these young folk will sit silently, taking no part in the exchange of their wishes. Now, this important personage (this uncle), he sits patiently until every one of the family have had their say in the matter, then all eyes are to him awaiting his approval or disapproval. Without any sign of excitement he takes his spear and Thy rall ghie (a throwing stick), rises to his feet and stands in an offensive attitude, with the spear in a position ready [to] throw with lightning speed into the body of anyone who objects to his decision, which is the will of his sister, the mother of the young folk discussed. And he will say to them that at dawn tomorrow he will ask the Pree ghee (a messenger whose privilege it is to travel through the hunting ground of each tribe without being questioned).

In the early hours of the morning the uncle (who is in search of a wife or husband for his nephew or niece), accompanied by the Preeg ghee, begin their journey. At midday they arrive at the home of a strange tribe. The Preeg ghee explains their mission to the Chief of that tribe, who will ask them to rest awhile and kindly accept the hospitality extended. They sit, and the Preeg ghee will tell them of any important or interesting news, because each tribe would like to know what is taking place around them. For it is only in this way they are able to receive news, when a Preeg ghee is passing through on duty a day before their destination is reached. They make a fire and place the green boughs of shrubs or trees and a dark smoke ascends into the clear sky, followed by a white smoke column.

The surrounding tribes read the meaning: Kliee holo napparook key (someone is in search of a wife). I wonder whether we shall have his company; so each tribe is expectantly waiting. As near as possible they arrive at their destination at the time they saw the smoke the day previous. Now this tribe feels greatly honoured by a visit of this nature. All members of this tribe are full of excitement they are willing to minister to the Won oo wee's (uncle's) needs. One family will bring along a swan baked in the earth with various herbs. Another will bring fish rolled in clay, preferably pipe clay placed in hot ashes. Others will bring bits of the select flesh portion of the Kangaroo, Wombat and Emu or mussel cockle, and each are seeking to be favoured by being asked for a wife or a husband.

Now Won oo wee spends a week with this tribe visiting each individual family, studying the disposition of the youths and maidens, looking for one who has the likes and dislikes of his nephew or niece. Now when he makes a discovery, Won oo wee approaches his or her Won oo wee, giving him an invitation to visit him and giving him a privilege that he received, to come and enjoy his hospitality and the acquaintance of his nephew or niece, to which number two Won oo wee expresses himself to the honour offered him and his tribe. So number one Won oo wee returns home and tells his tribe of a successful mission and to be prepared for the visit of number two Won oo wee, who arrives a week later. On the first visit, number one Won oo wee introduces him to his brother-in-law and sister and he stays with him for a week and then number one and two Won oo wee fix a date and place where the marriage is to take place.

Now, the place of marriage does not necessarily take place at the bridegroom or bride tribe's hunting ground; sometimes it takes place at her grandmother on the mother's side's hunting-ground or at some friendly tribe at a distance. They are at an appointed place, the bridegroom and bride's tribe camping about half a mile distant. All Aboriginal marriages take place at midnight, usually when there is a full moon. Just before sunset, the younger members will bring bundles of sticks to the camps of the families of the bride and bridegroom. As the night gradually becomes midnight there is a stir. A person who is appointed to announce the ceremony, camping between these two parties, makes a huge fire so that the Wail lar roo mundi (the surrounding camp), can see where he is stationed. And all the camp do likewise.

Presently his voice rents the clear and still night: 'Narparrooka nar ulge pun thun (Behold the bridegroom comes, behold the marriage party to join).'

Each member of the family that represents both tribes carries a fire stick and from each starting point they move in a line to form the figure V; they place their fire sticks together and the number one and number two Won oo wee address the bridegroom and bride. 'Children, the fire is symbolic of the severity of the law, neither of you must make light nor abuse this privilege of becoming husband and wife, and father and mother. It is the will of the Great Spirit that you shall honour and respect the bond of marriage. As the fire consumes, so will the law of your father destroy all who dishonour the marriage law.'

There are various ways in which the young parties are joined together as man and wife. Away in the south-east of South Australia in the Coorong are the Punbarlie tribe. They belong to the Seagull totem. A girl is born and in the lower Murray live a tribe known as the Warrawaldie tribe of the Black Swan totem. There is a boy just entering into their tribal custom of training to become a man and to be educated to the law and tradition of his race.

At some time in one of the Munmundi (great festivals), the Seagull totem tribe made the acquaintance of the Black Swan totem tribe. The uncle of the girl recently born allows his mind to seriously review the various tribes met and all the boys and youth comes before his vision;

presently, one boy stands out more conspicuously than the others. It is the Black Swan totem boy of the Warrawaldie tribe. He calls his sister and her husband and they discuss the matter, he tells them of this boy, son of Yoṇginjerr, the son of the Warrawaldie and expresses his intention that the girl should be pledged in marriage to this tribe as the wife of Rim mill limp pin jerri, the boy of the Black Swan totem.

The mother and father of the infant girl are pleased with the selection. And now the uncle of the infant girl of the Seagull totem sends a Pree ghee to the Warrawaldie tribe to inform them that they (the Seagull totem tribe) are pleased to offer Nar ra meer jerri, the infant girl who is already twelve moons old, as a wife. Would they kindly accept the offer and send a reply?

The father and mother receive the message and the mother summons and in haste sends a message to her second elder brother of the Dingo totem tribe, and he comes to his sister and she tells her brother that the Seagull totem of the Punbarlie offer their child daughter as wife to Rim mill limp pin jerri. And Won oo wee, that brother of the woman, wife of the Seagull totem man, is very pleased and advises his sister to accept the offer.

Now when the girl is seven or eight years of age, her mother will every week relate stories of this wonderful young man; that he is a great hunter, a fierce warrior or a Mooncumbulli, or such stories that will arouse interest and admiration, so that the girl in her tender years is looking forward of taking a glimpse of this her hero. And when she has undergone the training or educating the mind of overcoming pain, fear and endurance, she becomes more anxious, and she approaches her parent.

'Oh, mother, when shall I see this young man?'

The mother sends for Won oo wee and he comes and he whispers to her that at next Munmundi (which will take place two moons hence) she will have the privilege of seeing him.

And the Munmundi takes place and [he] arrives at a certain sporting ground on Lake Alexandrina, an ideal spot, plenty of fish, wild fowl, Kangaroo and Wallabies. I may state here that the Munmundi offers a splendid opportunity for the youths and maidens of seeing each other, but they are never allowed to speak.

Another form of marriage is in the case of a husband's death or a wife's. In the case of a husband's death the widow goes into mourning for twelve months. Every morning and evening she wails in a loud tone: 'Mack umb indum nemung, narpume (Why did you leave me, O husband of mine)?'

The first day of her wailing, she beats her head with a Nulla nulla, and cuts her arm with a flint knife and causes the blood to flow from head and arms. She takes the ashes from an old disused fire-place and covers her head with them and smears the body with them. After a month's wailing in this fashion, she prepares pipe clay and places it upon her head which forms a cap, and she wears it for twelve months or more, removing it at night when retiring to bed. After completing the twelve months of mourning she removes the clay cap and washes the pipe clay from her face and breasts. She leaves her parents' home and seeks the protection and hospitality of her late husband's brother's home.

Perhaps there may be four brothers in the family and they all minister to her wants. Then she stays with her mother-in-law for three months, she speaks to her and says: 'Kerning (mother of my husband and my mother), I want to be thy daughter-in-law until I die and meet my husband in the happy hunting ground. To which of these sons shall I carry my belongings and become a wife?'

The mother-in-law will say: 'My daughter, I would like that you should become the wife of Kuljarroo, the eldest of the four. But, my child, choose for yourself and it shall please me and the whole tribe.'

And the widow makes her choice. She tells her mother-in-law that she would like to marry the young man next to the eldest. At night when everyone is preparing to go to bed, the widow enters the home of this young man and he is lying in bed. She goes and lies at his feet so that the letter T is formed. She repeats this for some time, say about a fortnight; this is a sign that she is willing to become his wife, and he accepts her. This is the only case where a woman is allowed the privilege to choose her husband.

A widow is the only case in which a woman or girl is privileged to choose a husband. And when a woman dies the husband goes into mourning, takes his children to his late wife's mother and his sister-in-law and leaves them awhile, say for twelve months, and when he returns, one of the sisters volunteers to become his wife, and takes the children and makes a bed for herself and children at the foot of her brother-in-law's bed. This is a sign that she is desirous to be a mother to her sister's children, and they become man and wife.

The Mischievous Crow and the Good He Did

I suppose our ancestors in those times immemorial have always experienced the ruling forces of Good and Evil. According to the Bible story, there was a time when our first parents were only conscious of all Good, and that Evil was foreign to their nature, which was perfect in all ways. Their eyes beheld visions of beauty. They heard sounds of harmony that were pleasing to the ear. They ate of the good of the garden, luscious fruits and herbs that were appetising to the taste and gave strength to the body, and were void of bitterness. The whole surrounding atmosphere was [enlivening]. They walked with the elasticity of perpetual youth. It was eternal days of perfection, with glorious sunshine sending rays of light and life to all creation. The Great Author of life and creation was pleased with his work, that he declared it was good. And it was his delight to come into the Garden of Eden in the cool of the evening and converse with Adam and Eve, and to inform him that he, Adam, shall be lord of the beasts and fowls of the air, and that all creatures shall obey him. And further, that he shall eat of all the fruit of the garden, except the one in the midst of the garden: 'Thou shalt not eat thereof lest thou shalt surely die.' We do well just to imagine the Lion and the Lamb lying side by side or drinking by the river together.

But somewhere out of space there arrived in that beautiful and happy home a visitant. From whence came he? Yander puntre, Nhum dom wimming (Where didst thou come from? Who wast thy creator, oh stranger)? Per ruch unda, Nhin tie (Art thou self-existing, didst thou call up thyself into being? Art thou of thyself)?

The visitant did not tell from whence he came or what his mission was, but simply looked on with envy upon the beautiful work of the Good Spirit. Then one day he took upon himself the form of a Serpent, and waited by the forbidden tree. Presently Eve came along, happy to be enjoying life. She arrived at the tree. Presently she admired the fruit hanging upon its branches; they looked so beautiful. A voice from within told her that they were not to pluck the fruit thereof, because they would surely die and would become Gods. The Serpent, at this time causing himself to be unseen to the vision of the woman, fixed his fascinating gaze upon her.

Presently an invisible presence was felt, and a voice whispered within her bosom: 'Take a fruit and taste its sweetness.'

'No,' said the woman, gazing with astonishment at the Serpent upon the tree, 'nay, boldly we may eat of all the fruit except this one, lest we die.'

Now the cunning Serpent, continuing, said, 'You shall not surely die, but if you eat your eyes shall be opened, you shall know not only good but evil as well. Ye shall be as Gods. Eat, oh woman, and thou shalt be blessed.'

So she took of the fruit and ate thereof, and gave to her companion, Adam, and he also ate thereof. And behold their eyes were opened. And since this allegorical teaching, we inherit not only the voice of the Good Spirit, but the evil whispering of the Serpent today.

Now, to an enlightened age, Evil still presents himself as the Serpent. He comes to us with that fascinating power and cunning of the Snake. Sometimes he comes as an angel. To each nationality he comes in all kinds of forms. But to the Aborigines he comes as a Crow, or, in other words, he is personified to us in the bird body of the Crow.

Now, the Crow plays an important part in the tradition and legends of my race. Although he is an embodiment of all that is mischievous and evil, yet there are some very good and great things he has taught us, and one of the greatest teachings of the Crow was the immortality of the soul. Readers will remember this in another issue or in another chapter. Or still further, the Reverend J. Mathew has written a book on the Eagle Hawk and the Crow; I may also add that from an historical point this Reverend Gentleman has a greater knowledge about the Crow than I have. I am only dealing with the Crow as a legend or a nursery story.

There are many stories told of the Crow by different tribes. I shall attempt to deal with him from the Ngarrindjeri tribe's standpoint.

According to our rendering of his doings and travels, he began in the north of Queensland and struck the Darling and followed the river up towards Albury, then to its source, and returned on his way back until he reached the Murray from the Darling. After living there for some time, he made the acquaintance of the Eagle Hawk. There was one outstanding tendency of the Crow to address every person (we shall use the term person for convenience, as it is customary—my race speaks of Animals, Birds, and Reptiles as persons): 'Rhonghund un, Oh my brother-in-law.'

Now, to become a brother-in-law to a man by marrying his sister, you are assured and guaranteed hospitality and protection. Or shall we say, I am travelling and I have met a tribe and one of the members of that tribe has married my sister; I am entitled to claim hospitality and protection, that is an unwritten law. So that when the Crow arrived at the home of the Eagle Hawk he called him brother-in-law. Then the Eagle Hawk questioned the Crow how it came that he was his Rhongee.

The Crow made an explanation: 'Far away back in the past ages, long before any of the present members were in existence, a Miss Crow married into the Eagle Hawk tribe.'

'Oh,' said the Eagle Hawk, 'come, stay with me, and thou shall take thy journey after you have slept and eaten sufficient to strengthen thy body for your journey.'

With this invitation the Crow made his home with the Eagle Hawk. After spending two weeks with the Eagle Hawk, the Crow said: 'Rhonghund un Nap pa prakin (Oh my brother-in-law, I rise to you and shall continue my journey).'

In response the Eagle Hawk said: 'Ghee ill ourwar, Rhonghund shun ellen itch Murrill lup Nungee (Go on thy way, brother-in-law of mine, whilst the sun is young and only just begun).'

Then the Crow began limping on his way. The Eagle Hawk watched him as he gradually disappeared in the distance. When the Crow was satisfied that he was out of their vision, he ceased his limping—it was only a sham or make-believe that something was the matter with his leg and caused a defect in walking. He was now endowed with the spirit of Evil and was carried on the dark wing of the Devil.

In a moment he was at Lake Victoria. The speed which he travelled was so great that when he arrived at his destination, it was so sudden that he stood for a moment to allow himself to collect his thoughts. As he stood thus awhile dazed from the shock, one of the elders of the Pelicans, who was sitting by himself meditating, was startled by the noise as of a mighty wind. Jumping to his feet and staring around with wide staring eyes to see from whence the noise came, he saw the Crow standing not more than ten paces away. The Pelican in bewilderment did not know whether to run away from this awful monster.

Just as he was about to flee the Crow spoke: 'Rhonghund un, I am exceedingly sorry that I came to you so suddenly. Will you forgive me?'

The Pelican was staring with wide-open mouth, thinking here was a stranger addressing him as brother-in-law. For the moment the Pelican was unable to speak.

When he got over his surprise, he said to the Crow: 'Oh stranger, why dost thou, in addressing me, call me Rhongee? I have not seen thee before, neither have I heard my elders speak of thee. Thou hast not seen me before.'

The Crow in reply said: 'Rhonghund, before thy great-grandfather was born, my brother married one of thy sisters, Larlailin marrowie. Thy sister became the wife of my brother. In the land Loo loo who itch es Phunculd, I have in my race Marra kun arculdar. The race who speaks my language has a tradition that the Pelican tribes are my Rhongee. Here read for thyself a record of our relationship.'

The Crow held out a message-stick that by its appearance seemed ancient. The Pelican was not likely to show his ignorance, and did not take the message-stick because he was not able to read the various curves and angles and dots. So he said: 'Oh Rhonghund un, Ek kutch thum kung in (Oh brother-in-law, I accept what you say), and believe that we are brothers-in-law. Come follow me and I will take you Nhow wundahung (my home and the camping-ground of my race).'

So the Pelican led the way, followed by the Crow, who began to limp behind, and made a noise as if in pain. The Pelican turned around and saw the poor old Crow limping, and inquired: 'What is the matter, Rhongee, when did you hurt yourself?'

The Crow then related an imaginary incident. 'Oh Rhonghund un (oh my brother-in-law), I was coming down from the great mountain yonder, and walking in the plain country, and met the Peenjullie tribe. They would not accept me to their home, but began to show that they were no relation of mine, by taking up the Key keys (reed spears with wooden points) and Rarrabarr and Pankuggee (boomerangs), and challenged me to do battle. I responded, taking hold of my shield to defend myself. The Emu threw a spear, and I caught it upon my shield. Then he threw a boomerang, and it struck the shield and broke in halves; one piece fell away from me, the half struck me in the ankle. That is why I limp. And when I threw my spear, behold I saw the tribe of Emus coming out to do battle with me. Of course I thought the best thing for me to do was to run away and try to escape that way. So I ran and ran. That is why I came upon you so suddenly.'

'But,' said the Pelican, 'where were the Emus? I did not see them.'

'I don't suppose you would, for I ran so fast like the wind that they were not able to be near me.'

'Come, only a little way now and you will be at our Mundi. Then you shall have food and then you can lie down and have a rest. And we shall attend to your wounds. Now will you sit here; my Mundi is there beside the bank of the lagoon. I will go before and explain to my people that our Rhongee comes from Loo loo who phoonculd.'

The Crow sat down and the Pelican went to his camp and summoned the elders of his tribe and told them that a stranger had arrived, and had made himself known by claiming a relationship with them. The elders were curious to meet this stranger who claimed to be their Rhongee.

'Go and ask him to partake of our hospitality and we shall do all to make him happy and well to continue his journey.'

So the Pelican went out and asked the Crow to come now for all things were ready. When they arrived at the camp, all the elders of the Pelican tribe came forward and gave their salutation: 'Rhonghun ahun la whon eenda (Thou shall rest awhile with us).'

The Crow sat down just outside a mia mia that one of the Pelicans gave up for the purpose of his accommodation during his stay. And to show their appreciation of his visit, other members of the tribe were offering him as food select portions of Murray cod (Pondi in the Ngarrindjeri tribe), and Pil lull kie (perch), Pummerrie (catfish), Meyokkey (lobster), and yabbies. These bits of delicacies were placed upon gum tree bark, which were the plates used in those times.

The Crow was so hungry that he ate all the food that was placed before him, and turning to his host he addressed him thus: 'Rhonghra, Thun tul up weerinalg un reewar (Brother-in-law, with your permission

I shall lie down to rest and sleep). My body is feeling tired with the long journey.'

The Pelican rose and took him into the Mundi, showing him the bed clothes, and bidding him: 'Thun tul how (Sleep thou must),' and with this last remark the Pelican left the Crow to himself.

The Crow slept the sleep of the just, and when he arose the next morning the sun was well up in the Wyerriewarr (heaven), somewhere about ten o'clock. Now, sleeping so long and sound and waking so late was unusual to the Crow. He sat upon his bed, looking around him wondering why he had made such a mistake to sleep soundly and so long. This worried him greatly. Then he began to allow those evil thoughts that so often came to him.

'Perhaps the old Pelican, my host, has used witchcraft, or must have placed around this Mundi a thoo ee (charmed human hair rope). Now these are the only things that will cause a deep or sound sleep.'

The more the Crow thought of these things, the more real his thoughts became.

Now, overcome with this evil thought uppermost in his mind, he vowed that he would be revenged. Bear in mind that the Crow was always doing something wrong, that when anything unusual happened to him he arrived at the conclusion that someone was trying to do him an injury. So he came out of the Mundi, and just by the doorway, about three yards away, was a fire, and by the fireside were various portions of food placed in bark plates. He sat down and broke his fast, and continued sitting beside the fire, brooding over the cause of his sleeping late. Then he rose to his feet, looking about him to see whether there was anyone at home. The Mundi were all empty, not a Pelican about. Then he began walking around the camping-ground in a circle several times, widening out in the form of a spiral, and each time he met the tracks of the Pelicans leading in one direction, and that was towards a large lagoon. He followed the track until he came upon them all sitting there.

Up the bank were the old Pelicans with their wives and the youths and maidens and younger male and female Pelicans, enjoying themselves in the water, whilst the elders were making and mending their nets, preparing to go a-fishing. The Crow sat in ambush, watching and taking in everything they did, and planning to do them some wrong for the imagined wrong done to him. Suddenly there came before his vision one solitary Pelican running so fast from the opposite side of the lagoon, coming towards the other Pelicans that were busily engaged with their nets. When the Pelicans saw their companion running towards them, they rose to their feet with their nets in their hands, and hurried towards him; the younger Pelicans did the same, ceased their sporting in the water and followed their elders. Then this one Pelican led the others to the opposite side of the lagoon; then they waded into the water and spread their nets and captured the fishes: Pondi, Pillulkie, Pummerrie, Thookerri, etc.

Presently there came the sound of babies crying. The Crow, leaving his hiding-place, came seeking the cause of the noise, looking into every bush, no sign, he peeped into hollow logs, thinking perhaps their mothers would place them there, no sign. Again he heard the crying, the sound seemed to come from all around him. Then he ran around in a circle until he came to his starting-point. Again he ran, now in a spiral ever widening. Suddenly he stopped. The voices of the crying babies seemed to be above his head. He looked up, and away, just above his reach, were the baby Pelicans, softly placed between the forks or branches of a huge gum tree; and around the limbs of this gum tree was tied a net, so as to prevent the babies from falling.

The Crow stood awhile, thinking deeply. 'Now is my opportunity. I shall steal the babies and give them to the Pee wing ie (a species of the Hawk family that frequents rivers and lagoons and Lake Alexandrina and other large lakes or sea coast). I am sure he will be glad to have these young Pelicans. What a nice tender meal they would make for him.' Such were the wicked thoughts passing through the evil Crow.

He made an effort to take the young Pelicans down, but he failed in every attempt. And then he decided to cut the tree down, so he hastened away to the camp and found an axe and hurried back and began to cut the tree. But the axe belonged to the Pelicans and refused to cut the tree on which the young baby Pelicans were. He tried again and again, so he cursed the axe and said: 'Oh, you useless axe, good for nothing axe, you have the resemblance of an axe but you are deceiving.'

'Oh, oh,' said the axe, 'do you think that I am going to obey your wicked command and respond to every stroke you give me to cut the tree on which are the babies of my masters, whom I obey? I am not your servant, Werruninda Murrunanni. Oh, you cruel wicked old Crow, I will not obey you. I am only the servant of the Pelican, whom I obey.'

So he threw the axe to the ground, and cursing it, said: 'I can do very well without you. I shall use some other means. I shall set fire to the tree so that it shall fall to the ground.'

Again the Crow ran to the camping-ground and brought along a firestick and placed a huge heap of dry sticks around the trunk of the gum tree, and placed some dry grass amongst the wood and applied the fire to it. But the firestick refused to burn the dry grass and wood. So the Crow blew and blew the firestick to cause a flame. Still the firestick refused to do what it was intended to do.

The Crow grew angry, saying: 'And you, too, oh firestick, like the axe, refuse to do your mission?'

'Yes,' said the firestick, 'I am the servant of the good and inoffensive Pelicans. They seek to do no one harm. They have given you hospitality and now for the good they have done you, you seek to do them an injury by stealing their babies to give to the nasty old Pee wing ie. I am the servant of the Pelican and take my orders from them.'

And the heat of fire left the stick and it was only a dead black coal in his hands. So the Crow did not know what to do. The axe refused to cut the tree and the firestick would not burn the wood.

'Now let me think awhile. Oh, I have it, I shall sing the Tuckoonie Tree Song. It is one of those Magic Songs that belong to the people of the Forest, where they sing the little trees to become big trees. It is a song foreign to the Pelican.'

So the Crow began singing the Tree Song. Suddenly from out of somewhere the little Tuckoonie appeared, each with a tiny boomerang. They stood around dancing to the singing of the Crow: 'Wirrinda, Oh thou tree of all trees, kringal (grow) lawrawal (up and upward), ever skyward.'

And every time the Crow came to the word 'lawrawal', the little Tuckoonie would leap upward and act as if they were pulling up an imaginary something and pushing it upward. Every time this was done the tree as it were leapt skyward. The tree grew and grew until the Pelican babies looked so small that one was unable to distinguish them. The Crow was laughing to himself and feeling pleased that he had accomplished something great. He had placed the babies far beyond the reach of their parents. He said to himself: 'What I was unable to do with the axe and the firestick I was able to do with the Song of the Forest, assisted by the Tuckoonie.'

The Crow thought, or was thinking, that he was able to pay back for what was only an imaginary wrong, little dreaming that he had rendered the Pelican a great kindness, for just on that day there arrived in a canoe made from the trunk of a tree, Narpange krye (Mr and Mrs Carpet Snake). They had just been sunning themselves on the bank of the river, and feeling a bit hungry, the Carpet Snake went in search of food, and, wending his way through the bush, came to the camping-ground of the Pelican. He began searching among or in each camp, thinking he would find at least a young baby Pelican, but the wise mothers had taken their children with them, fearing that they would be visited by their enemies, the Carpet Snake. That is why the two sister Pelican mothers had placed their babies upon the Wirri (gum tree), whose surface was smooth, but they had not noticed that at the base of the tree was a hole leading into the trunk and up to halfway, where the babies were placed.

When the Carpet Snake came to the tree, he was amazed to find that it had grown much larger and that the hole halfway to the fork would require a hundred or more Carpet Snakes in length to reach. So the Snake looked about, and saw the Crow looking up and laughing: 'Caw, caw, koo kaw, well done, I have had revenge, what a blow to the mothers, won't they weep, what a great sorrow will be theirs, unable to rescue their babies.'

'Hello,' said the Carpet Snake, addressing the Crow, 'you seem happy over the growth of this tree. This is the tree where we got our meal. There was always one in the new moon, somebody left his baby child here whilst they went gathering mussels in the lagoon or picking wild herbs for food. This new moon the tree is changed, there is food upon it, babies belonging to the pelicans; I can smell them, my spirit tells me there is food there.'

'Oh yes,' said the Crow, 'there are six little Pelican babies up there. The tree was a small one, about an ordinary tree. I sang the Forest Song, causing it to grow, so that their parents or mothers would be unable to rescue them.'

'Oh, you interfering and wicked old Crow, you are always making trouble of some kind. First you are doing an injury to the parent, which does not concern me; secondly you take my food or remove it, so that I am unable to procure it. Oh, you nasty thing.'

'Oh, wait a moment, let me think awhile, perhaps I shall be able to cause the tree to come back to its former size.'

So the Crow thought and thought, but he could not think of a way, song or witchcraft, that would cause a tree to come back.

'No, I am unable to call upon the little magic worker who caused the tree to grow. They are such tiny little men, and have wonderful power in causing trees to grow, I cannot understand why they will not respond to my wish.'

The Crow did not know that the Tuckoonie were little Spirits that came to do Good and not Evil. They came at the song of the Crow to cause the Wirri to grow because the little fairy good Spirit knew that the Carpet Snake would be on his way to this particular tree. So they sent the Tuckoonie along, and at the singing of the Crow danced around and made the tree grow, to place the children beyond the reach of the Carpet Snake, which was their salvation.

Now the little Tuckoonie had their instructions, they knew that something would take place. Their mission so far was ended. But they were allowed from the unseen world to witness the wonderful deliverance of the babies of the Pelicans. So the Crow hurriedly bade the Carpet Snake good-bye, and hastened on his journey down the Murray River.

Now the Pelican mothers began to feel anxious about their babies, so the two sisters hastened back from the fishing-ground to where they had placed their offspring. When they arrived, they saw that the tree had grown far beyond the other trees, and what was more, they were unable to see and speak to their babies. But they could hear them crying, and it made them so sad that they beat their own heads with the yamsticks and cut their bodies with flint knives, causing deep flesh wounds, to show their grief. And in desperation they sent up a long shrieking wail that sounded all around the lagoon, which had the effect of calling all the Pelican tribe to their side. They saw that they were helpless to do anything for the children and their mothers, so they all sat around the huge tree and wept and wept, until all the other tribes heard them wailing—the Goanna, the Emu, the Kangaroo, the Possum, and the Muldarie—and joined in the wail.

After they had wailed for an hour, the Kangaroo called for volunteers. The Goanna and Possum responded, and said they would attempt to climb the tree. Now when the tree began to grow, it grew in size and thickness. Just at the fork of the trunk was a growth below the trunk, like a bracelet; that became large too and made it impossible, when they had climbed to that point, to go any farther. Now, the Goanna was the first to make the climb. Up and up went the Goanna, then wended his way around and up the tree until he arrived halfway to the fork and the obstacle that had enlarged itself since its growing. He came back to the earth again and told the Pelicans and the others that the difficulty was greater than they imagined.

'Give me an axe to cut my way when I've reached that obstacle you see growing beneath the fork.'

An axe was given to the Goanna, and up and up he went. He reached the obstacle and tried to get beyond by cutting his way, but failed, and with disappointment he descended to the earth the second time.

The Goanna told the Pelicans that he did not think they would be able to rescue the babies. 'But perhaps the Possum may be able to climb the tree and overcome that one difficulty just near the babies.'

So the Possum ran up the trunk until he reached the obstacle. The Possum tried to surmount the difficulty but failed, so in a sad and disappointed spirit he descended to the earth. When he told them of that one difficulty, and that if someone would only be able to surmount it they would deliver the babies safely to their mothers, the Kangaroos, Possums, Goannas and Muldarie began to weep with the Pelican tribe.

The little Blue Wren with his two wives heard this great cry, and they came slyly along from shrub to shrub and from bush to bush, until they were able to hear and see what caused the whole trouble, and without uttering a word to the weeping crowd he spoke to his wives: 'Oh Narpin Nhoenow (oh my two dear little wifies), I cannot bear to hear the great strong Pelicans, Kangaroos, Goannas, and others, cry. Such big people like those to be so helpless to save the babies. Now you both stay away in this bush. Do not allow yourself to be seen. I shall go along and ask my cousin, the Woodpecker, to come and rescue the babies. Now there is not one able to climb the tree like he can. I have never known him to fail. Goodbye darlings, I will not keep you waiting long.'

With that the Blue Wren hurried away through the great gum trees. It was a great undertaking for so small a Bird. But the little Wren was spurred on with a good spirit, a loving spirit, that spirit that makes small men do great and noble deeds. This spirit carried the Wren on wings like those of the mighty Eagle.

He sped on his way through the boughs of the huge gum tree in search of the wonderful climber. Presently the Blue Wren stopped suddenly, because he heard the familiar voice of the Woodpecker and was wondering which tree that sound came from. There away, two trees farther on, he saw the Woodpecker approaching him timidly.

He said: 'Oh Cousin, will you come and rescue the babies of the Pelicans that are upon the tree that has grown since they were placed upon it. The Goanna tried, but failed. The Possum climbed, reached a certain place on the tree, and could go no farther, and he had to give up further attempts and came down a most disappointed person. Oh come, the mothers of the babies are two sisters and they are weeping and will eventually break their hearts.'

So the Woodpecker told the Wren to return and inform the Pelicans that he was coming, and would rescue the babies. So the Blue Wren, with a little heart filled with overflowing gladness, came to the Pelican tribe, and in comforting words told them that the Woodpecker was coming and would restore the babies to their mothers. So everyone—the Pelican, Muldarie, Kangaroo, Possum, and Goanna tribes—anxiously awaited the presence of this wonderful climber.

The Woodpecker came along unobserved by anyone, but there, right before their vision, standing at the foot of the large Wirri, was the Woodpecker.

Then he said to the little Wren: 'Bring the Kangaroo along to me, I would like to say a few words to him.'

So the Wren went to the Kangaroo and whispered into his ears: 'Kangaroo, the Woodpecker would like to have a word with you before he begins to climb the tree. Will you hurry to his side?'

So the Kangaroo made a couple of bounds and was at the side of the Woodpecker in a moment of time. Then the climber told the Kangaroo that everyone must stand away from the base of the tree; no one must speak or whisper and no one must look up, but that everyone should bow their heads and close their eyes—no one was allowed to see him go up and return. So the Kangaroo told those present the wish of the Woodpecker and they promised to do just what he desired. When all those present sat upon the ground and bowed their heads and closed their eyes, the Woodpecker began to ascend, and he climbed over the obstacle and tied one child on his back with a rope made from the fibre of the ti tree, and came to the ground with a baby, and placed him in the charge of the Kangaroo. He ascended the second time and brought another. He climbed the tree six times and rescued the six babies and delivered them to the Kangaroo.

The Pelicans and the mothers of the children still kept their eyes closed and did not know whether he had succeeded in delivering their children or not, until the Kangaroo told the people that they could open their eyes and see for themselves. They were all hesitating to open their eyes, fearing that they would not see the children beside them. But the mothers, so anxious, opened their eyes and, behold, what a sight met their vision, for sitting upon the earth were their babies. They shouted with joy, rushed forward, and embraced the children, and when they looked around to thank the deliverer of their babies, he was far away. He did not wish to be made a hero. He did not like them to sing his praise for the wonderful deliverance of the babies, because he said to the Kangaroo before he departed: 'I feel that I have done my duty and I am proud to be of service to help those in distress. I am glad that I have been able to fulfil the duty that was entrusted to me. Nup ill Ghee in ill (Now I leave you).'

When the Kangaroo saw that all the excitement was over and that the babies were once more in the safe keeping of their mothers, he said to the others present: 'Now, this thing has been done by some enemy. It should be the duty of everybody here to find out who caused the tree by some witchcraft to grow to such height in so short a time. Can any one of you call to mind an incident that has aroused your suspicion leading to the event of such unusual phenomenon? Before leaving for your homes, I would plead with you to give this your serious consideration.'

Up jumped the little Blue Wren.

'Will the audience allow me to make a statement? When I and my two wives were enjoying our customary outing, we were attracted by your crying. So I suggested that we should come and investigate what was the cause. So we cautiously wended our way from bush to bush until we came in full view of the large tree, and you all looking up eagerly. So we looked and saw the Goanna making an effort to reach a spot, and then we saw the Possum, and we also heard the babies crying up on the tree. We came a little nearer. Then we heard the sad news that it would not be possible to rescue the children. Our hearts were greatly moved. "Come my wives, let us go to yonder bush and discuss the matter." So we moved away to yonder shrubs. When we arrived at that spot, there was, to our surprise, a stranger, a person we had not seen or heard. He looked such a wicked person, and he was in conversation with the Carpet Snake. I heard this stranger warning the Snake not to say anything about this incident to anyone, lest it should come to the knowledge of the Pelicans, who gave him such a nice bed to lie on and good and appetizing food, for to break the law of hospitality would mean death. The Snake replied: "Well you had better run for your life, and do not stay until you reach Mookpool thou wong." So the Crow without another word ran away. Now,' said the Blue Wren: 'come let us go to the Carpet Snake and surround his mia mia and demand an explanation which he is able to give about the magic art of the tree growing.'

And they all arose with one accord, and the Kangaroo said: 'Now then, little Wren, you and your wives will please lead the way in search of the Snake.'

The little Blue Wren led them on until he came to where the Carpet Snake and his wife were camping. So they formed a circle around him, and the Kangaroo called to him to come forth as they would like to have a few words with him. So the Snake came out of his mia mia, and, confronting the Kangaroo, said: 'It is not customary for you as a representative of the Animal tribe to approach me, a Reptile tribe. It was your duty according to custom to have asked the Goanna alone to seek me and ask me to attend any conference with other tribes. And not only breaking one law, but you have, by your impudence, broken the law of relationship, you a Ying gawatcherie, have the effrontery to ask a Noo Paa. You, belonging to the hairy tribe, break the law by asking the feathered tribe to accompany you to find me, a non-feathered or haired tribe. This violation of a strict law, you, oh Kangaroo, must answer for. One more, the feathered tribes are nearer related to me than to you. You have no relationship to them whatever.'

The kindly and wise Kangaroo patiently listened to the angry Carpet Snake. After a few moments of silence he addressed the Snake. 'I am well aware of the law of all races that sets a line of distinction, and I am also acquainted with the importance of that law. And there is no one in this company that endeavours to maintain and observe them as I and my tribe. But as you know, and those present know, there is only one thing that all law, custom, and tradition gives way to, and that one thing is when a child or children are in danger or require assistance, and law, creed, and caste vanishes.'

When the Kangaroo finished replying to the Carpet Snake, the audience cheered and cheered again: 'Kay hey (Well done) Whangunhund, we all agree with what you say, oh Kangaroo.'

Then turning to the Carpet Snake again, he said: 'You have heard the voice of the various tribes on this matter, Animal, Bird, and Reptile.

Does it not clearly show that you as a family of the Reptile tribe stand alone? Come now, let us be friends, join us to find the person who did this cowardly act to innocent and helpless babies. Remember, oh Carpet Snake, that you have children of thine own. Some day you and your wife may be in the same position as the Pelicans were. You will require the assistance of the various tribes. Think not so much of thyself, oh Snake, but for the love and helplessness of the weaker. Think.'

So the Carpet Snake, approaching the Kangaroo with head bowed, said: 'Oh Kangaroo, I admit that I have been rather hasty in my reply. I am also sorry of accusing you of breaking the law, custom, and tradition of our race. Will you forgive me?'

The kindly old Kangaroo, with tears rolling down his cheeks, said: 'Oh Snake (Kryunda), it makes me weep with joy to know that you are really sorry for the remarks you have made. I am always seeking to avoid hostility, and am always ready and willing to forgive any who have said nasty and wicked words about me. I can assure you that I have forgiven you with all my heart. Come now, tell us, who this stranger is that did this wicked act?'

So the Carpet Snake told them that the person who worked this magic of causing the tree to grow so rapidly was none other than the mischievous Crow, who was sheltered and fed last night by the Pelican family.

'But,' said one of the Pelicans, stepping forward, 'how can it be? The Crow claimed relationship with our tribe. He addressed us as Rhong-hund (brother-in-law). How is it possible that one who has married our sister stoops so low to a most despicable act? It cannot be. Oh Snake, be careful, lest you may with a sore heart repent the day thou accused an innocent person.'

'Friends,' said the Carpet Snake, in a more sympathetic tone and feeling, 'I am very sorry that I have been beside myself in using such expression. I ask the Kangaroo, will you forgive me? I come of an ancient race and we have, in caves and trees, carvings and drawings, from time immemorial of the family tree of all tribes. The person that was your guest last night is not your brother-in-law. He is a deceiver. He is of the Evil One.'

'Then,' said the Pelican, 'we have been deceived and have fallen victim to his cunning device. Come, let us follow him and destroy him from the face of the earth.'

'Pardon me, Pelican, let us not be too rash in vowing vengeance upon this Evil one. He will soon exhaust the evil that is within him. His own evil designs will come back upon himself, which may cause his own destruction or his repentance. The only way open for us is to send someone along and warn the other tribes to be on the alert for this cunning one. Now, who will volunteer?'

Before the Kangaroo had time to proceed further the little Blue Wren jumped right before the Kangaroo and in his soft sweet little voice, said: 'Send me. I am willing to undertake the task.'

And the little Jinny Wrens came forward and stood on either side of their lord and master, Mr Blue Wren and with such a small, tiny and musical voice, said: 'Narpin nharhgon (our husband protector and companion) volunteers to go on a dangerous mission into strange lands. We go and share with him the difficulties and hardships and the dangers as well as if it should be to meet death.'

When the other Birds, as well as the Animal and Reptile tribes, saw the spirit of sacrifice so evident in the little Blue Wren and his two wives, they sent up a loud cheer: 'Kay hey,' and the kindly Kangaroo said: 'Three more Kay heys for the two Mrs Wrens.'

Again and loud the volume of sound was sent in the air: 'Kay hey, kay hey, kay hey!'

Like a mighty wind came the sound, and with the suddenness of lightning came an object from the sky, rending the still air; right into their midst, bowing politely, came the Falcon, the terror of the Bird tribe.

Turning to the Kangaroo, he said: 'Oh King of Animals, I have been sent by the King of the Birds to bring you his compliments, wishing you every success in your effort to keep goodwill and harmony among the various tribes. The King of the Birds, who is now sailing majestically in yonder sky, saw all that was going on, and he sent one of his attendants, the Kite, with a summons instructing me to come and offer you my services. The King of the Birds was so pleased to see one of his most humble subjects, the Blue Wren and his wives, that in appreciation of his courage and that of his wives, he has entrusted me with the honour of presenting them with the Royal Colour.'

He handed the badge to the little Wren. 'This is from your King, the Eagle Hawk. Accept!' and the Falcon, bowing, stood aside.

Again the crowd cheered: 'Kay hey,' and the Wren, turning to his two wives, said: 'Take my honour, dear wifies.'

The two Jinny Wrens stood on either side of their husband. 'We share the honour and the glory when it is upon thy breast.'

So they pinned the Royal Colour upon the Wren, and that is why he wears it today, because of his willingness to undertake so great a task.

Everyone was pressing forward to take a glimpse of the little Wren who was decorated with this beautiful colour, and the wives of the other Birds were looking with envious eyes at the two tiny little women standing shyly beside their husband. Presently the Falcon, addressing the Kangaroo, said: 'The Eagle desires that the Wren and his wives shall not undertake this mission. But,' and turning to the Wren, 'can I have your consent to go in your stead?'

The Blue Wren answered: 'Go and fulfil the desire and will of the King of the Birds.'

So as suddenly as he came, so he departed.

So after everyone presently had paid their compliments to Mr and Mrs Blue Wren, they departed to their homes. And the Pelicans, when they arrived at their mia mia, consulted one with the other that they would no longer place their offspring upon shrubs or trees. They have kept their vow from that day to this. They rear their babies on the ground, or I may say, that the Pelicans lay their eggs upon the ground. They will never take the risk again of placing their young upon the trees so that the little Pelicans have to content themselves lying in the soft sand, and it is much safer to enjoy themselves playing on the ground, and they are much easier to find.

Now the Falcon went in search of the Crow, as he flew up in the clear sky, his trained and keen eyes taking in every living object beneath. At one time he thought he saw the Crow, and steadied himself in mid-air to catch another glimpse. But the object disappeared as suddenly as it came. He flew around and around, gradually widening in a spiral, feeling sure that the object he saw was the Crow. Then he flew around, getting or coming towards the centre, but seeing no more sign of the Crow. And then he flew to the nearest cliff and sat resting himself for the following morning's scouting, spending the night upon a tree branch on the side of the cliff, it being a clear still night. He fell into a deep sleep. Presently he felt a light touch upon the shoulders, looked up and saw the Owl sitting beside him. The Owl, for it was him that woke the Falcon from a deep slumber, whispered into his ear very softly indeed, still fearing that the clear night air would carry the sound to some other prying folks. He said: 'There is a stranger in these parts. I saw him in the twilight just as I and my neighbour the Bat peeped out of our den in the deep valley yonder. He was acting rather suspiciously, his very walk and actions seemed to us that he was being chased by someone, or it may have been an evil conscience.'

The little Bat put in an appearance, sitting down on a branch a little above the Falcon, grasping it by a hook on its wing, allowing himself to hang head down near the ear of the Falcon. He said: 'I saw a stranger, it seemed by his actions that the had committed something wrong not a long while ago. I was up the valley. I saw an object, first I thought it was my friend the Owl who sits on the other side of you. This something went up into the sky so wonderfully quick, then when it reached a certain height it shot forward like a meteor, leaving a shower of light behind. I became so afraid that I hastened to my den and stayed there awhile. So when I thought that all danger had passed, I came out to seek my friend, the Owl, to warn him of this unknown danger, this dreadful enemy, this wicked monster, making his way down the Murray. I saw you sitting here, and I also saw the Owl sitting beside you, so I availed myself to inform you of this occurrence.'

'Yes,' replied the Falcon, 'I am commanded by the King of the Birds, my King, to capture this stranger who is causing trouble and sorrow among the various tribes.'

When the Crow escaped from that scene of action of the babies of the Pelicans, on his way down he met the Pee wing ie, resting on the limb of a dried gum tree and berating his failure to capture a Kangaroo Rat.

'Oh,' said the Crow, 'now I come to think, are you not my brother-in-law?'

'Well, I don't know what relation exists between us. You are a perfect stranger to me and these parts.'

'So I am. Without a doubt this is the first time that I or any of my family have come to this country. But will you allow me to ask you one question? Is not your totem the Palletis (a grub that is found in honey-suckle trees and roots)?'

'Oh yes,' said the Pee wing ie, 'how came you, a perfect stranger, to know that?'

'That is one of the secret records of our race, the race I belong to, the Marrunhoniyie tribe. So you are my Rhongee.'

'All right,' said the Pee wing ie, 'let us be friends.'

'Now, will you sit here while I go to see whether I shall be able to catch a Rat?'

So the Crow hastened away into the scrub, and made a place similar to the hiding-place of a Rat, and took the spikes from the back of a Porcupine and stuck them into the ground where what appeared to be the home of the Kangaroo Rat. He came back and from a distance he beckoned to the Pee wing ie to come quietly and to follow him. The Crow leading the way, they came to the trap that he had laid for the Pee wing ie, and pointing before him, he said, whispering: 'There in those grasses rests the Rat. Go steadily.'

The Pee wing ie sneaked up until he came near enough, then the Crow, making signs, said: 'Jump onto the hiding-place and you will capture the Rat.'

So the Pee wing ie made a jump right on top of what appeared to be the resting-place of the Rat, and instead of a Rat, there were the spikes of the Porcupine stuck right into his feet.

'Oh, oh,' said the Pee wing ie, writhing in pain and looking around to see where the deceiver was. There was not a sign of him, he had disappeared suddenly. The Pee wing ie sat down, groaning with pain; he was unable to extract the spikes from his feet; he called loud and long, but no one heard him calling. He called again and again until he became exhausted with intense suffering, and he lay himself down to die.

The Magpie was on his way home and noticed the Pee wing ie lying and struggling to rise, but unable to do so on account of those dreadful spikes in his toes. So the Magpie came and attended to him and supplied him with food until the wound healed with the Porcupine spikes still in his feet and toes. And ever since that time he was able to take hold of his prey more effectively, because the talon entered into the flesh. Before this accident the Pee wing ie would take hold of a prey which would struggle and struggle until it freed itself and escaped. But now his claws were shod with something from which nothing would escape. And now instead of the Pee wing ie looking upon the Crow as an enemy, he looks upon him as a friend.

Again the Crow met another victim—the wife of a Death Adder. She was outside her home one beautiful sunny morning, bathing herself in the sunlight. Now the Death Adders were an inoffensive people, if anyone did them an injury they would rather suffer than retaliate.

'Now,' thought the mischievous Crow, 'what a lot of surprises there will be. I shall place this Wirrie (a stick that is stuck into the body of a dead person and allowed to remain until the body is decomposed, and the stick absorbs the poison and becomes a fatal weapon should you allow it to puncture the flesh, which sets into blood poisoning).'

So he stealthily crept up to her, looking about him to see whether there was anyone about to see him doing the deed. Now he came right up to her, and looking at her to see whether she was really asleep, touched her gently on her brow. She did not move. He thrust the Wirrie in her tail and jumped up and ran away and got behind a bush to see what would be the effect. But she lay quite still without moving. The point of the stick entering her tail had caused terrible pain and she had fainted. The Crow once more came to the victim, shaking her to arouse her, but without any good result. She was entirely unconscious.

Suddenly, from above, the Falcon pounced upon him. The Crow struggled to free himself, but the Falcon held him fast, and said to him: 'I have been ordered by my King, the Eagle Hawk, to take you prisoner. You have been causing great anxiety among the tribes with your mischievous deeds, and now you shall give an account of the wickedness.'

During the struggling of the Falcon and the Crow, the other members of the Death Adder family arrived from their hunting and saw the poor woman lying dead, and they began to wail. Their cry went up, and carried by the wind into the valley and upon the hill-top, the Bird, Animal, and Reptile tribes heard. They recognised the voice of the Adder, so they hastened to see what had happened. They gathered around the body and they too wept with grief for the harmless Adder. And they all were anxious to know the cause of her death, for she appeared to be dead.

The Falcon said, 'The Crow has Wachan (stabbed) her with a Wirrie.'

They shouted: 'Away with him, bury him alive, he must be buried in the same grave as his victim.'

So they raised the body of the Adder, placed her on a striped three-stick, V-shaped at the wide end, and with the sticks tied together, and conveyed the body to a gully nearby, all marching in a procession, with the Crow led by the Emus and Kangaroos. The Wombats dug the grave, and when it was sufficiently deep, they prepared the body, carefully wrapped in ti-tree bark for burial, and told the Crow to get into the grave. So he hesitatingly leapt into the grave. When he touched the bottom he suddenly and mysteriously disappeared. A Wombat jumped into the grave to see whether there was an opening in the side of the grave. To his great astonishment there was one, leading south. The Wombat was a great tunnel-maker, and he knew by sight which way it was leading, and the distance to its next opening up to the surface of the earth. So he shouted to those above: 'Away to Pumbala (this is low-lying country in the south-east of South Australia).'

The Falcon was up on his wing and in a moment was tearing his way through the air toward Tintinarra like a mighty wind. Not seeing any sign of the Crow, he continued his journey right on to Mount Bension beyond Kingston, and upon this Mount he sat and with his telescopic sight viewed the surrounding country. But not a sign could he see of the Crow. Becoming restless, or in suspense, he flew into the sky until he became a mere speck, then he circled around and around, gradually wider and wider, until he had covered many hundreds of miles. Still no vision of the Crow, and no one was able to give him any information as to his whereabouts.

All this while the Crow discovered a great many subterranean tunnels, and he considered that it would be safe if he stayed in the tunnel awhile until the Falcon would think that he was dead. The life underground became tiresome and uninteresting, so he decided that he would come out and enjoy the beautiful fresh air during the night, and he continued to do this for some time.

And he said within himself: 'I shall take advantage of the early morning before the sun rises, and I shall enjoy myself before the Falcon is up on his duty.'

So he continued to do this from one new moon to the following new moon, and again said within himself: 'I shall come out all day and take the risk.'

And once more the Crow enjoyed the bright and beautiful days that came and passed on to begin another day. So he boldly began his usual routine of living, going about to see who would be his next victim.

When the Falcon began his search from Mount Bension, in his flight in a spiral he saw the Adders in great excitement. The dead had come to life, or out of the unconscious state that she was in caused by the Wirrie (poison stick), and the wound was healing rapidly. The Wirrie had grown into the flesh of the Adder, and all the Birds and Animals were so afraid to come near to touch her, or they would not allow the Adder to touch them because she had a dreadful sting. So from that day on, the one-time despised, and the ones who were kicked and cuffed, were equipped with a weapon that caused death to anyone unfortunate enough to receive a blow or a thrust from it. The Falcon alighted among the Adders and inquired what all the excitement was about, so they told him what had happened.

Once more he took to his wings and flew up the Murray, from Tatearra, right away to Mookpool thou wong, beyond Murray Bridge, to where he was to report to the Eagle Hawk about the doings of the Crow. The Eagle Hawk was sitting on a huge dry gum awaiting his arrival.

The Falcon came and took a seat beside the King of Birds, and addressing him, said: 'Oh Eagle Hawk, the harmless Adder has become a victim of the mischievous Crow, and now they are endowed against their will with the sting of Death.'

'On and away,' said the Eagle Hawk, 'prevent him from transferring his wickedness into the other members of the Reptile family.'

Again the Falcon was upon the wing, hastening towards Tatearra and Tintinarra, stopping now and again, giving the Goannas and Lizards warning to avoid the Crow: 'Do not speak to him, whether he feigns hunger or thirst or illness, do not assist. Let there be a large margin between you and him.'

And when the Falcon inquired of the Goanna: 'Where are the other members of your race (the Snakes)?'

The Goanna said: 'Oh, the Crow invited them into the subterranean passages. With tearful eyes and almost a broken heart, I have pleaded with my tribe not to be so thoughtless as to listen to the flattery of the cunning and mischief-making Crow. The Lizard family, with the exception of the two Snake families, the Carpet and Python, gave heed to my warning and have refused the invitation. The rest of the Snakes are already guests of the Crow in the caves.'

Now the Crow took the Snakes into the beautiful caves and prepared a great feast. And the Snakes sat in the interior of the cave.

Then the Crow, addressing the Snakes, said: 'Will you kindly allow me to retire for a while, as I have an important matter to attend to.'

The Snakes replied that they would endeavour to make themselves comfortable and await his return. So the Crow hastened out of the caves into the sunlight, and flew straight into the air, and circled round as he ascended, until he thought that he was out of the danger zone of the Hawk family. Then, looking down from his high position to locate the home of the Adder, he saw an excited assembly below. Like a bolt from the skies, he descended into their midst and beheld a sight that gave him great pleasure, for there upon the tail of the Adder was evidence of something that should fulfil a mission for which it was intended—the sting.

Then, turning to the Adders congregated, he said: 'Yhun na mind dauthum; Lukice kainall kuldri auld wirrund (Have I not spoken the desire of my heart? Grow, oh Wirrie, poisoned pointing bone, into the flesh of the Adder). Oh Wirrie, you must become part of the Adder. All the hatred of your soul shall enter the Wirrie and it shall become the sting of Death. Have I not desired too that it shall not only remain in your individual self, but that thou shalt transfer it to thy children and thy children shall pass it on to their children through all generations for ever.'

Suddenly, before the eye could blink, the Crow seized the Adder and carried her to the cave.

Now, on his return with the Adder, the assembly of Snakes [was] fast asleep. They had ate and ate until they had gorged themselves, and then lay down in a stupor, and they were dreaming of feasting and seeing sights that were beautiful. The Crow tried to arouse them but there was no response. He looked into their faces and noticed that they seemed to be smiling and looking happy and contented. He tried again to arouse them, but failed. The Snakes were in this state for months; the Crow became baffled and did not understand the position. He did not know what to do. He had brought the Adder to show them what an effective weapon she possessed.

And a thought struck him: 'Now, if they are in a happy sleeping state, I shall make this cave ring with laughter. I must go and ask the Koo ka ka burras; they are such happy-go-lucky chaps, they should fill this cave with laughter.'

So he hastened out to find them and invite them. So once more the Crow went out and discovered the Koo ka ka burras down by what is known as the Reedy Creek, in the south-east of South Australia. So he told them that the Snakes had been feasting and eaten too much, which had caused them to go into a stupor, and that, although in that state, they seemed to be happy, with smiling faces in their subconscious state.

'Now here is an opportunity for you to bring that wonderful laugh of yours to some good use for the benefit of waking the Snakes.'

'Well,' said the elder of the Koo ka ka burras, 'I know the laugh we possess is infectious. When we laugh we bring life and light to weary broken-hearted ones. Our laugh makes it a delightful voyage for those passing to the land beyond. We shall come, lead the way.'

So the Crow flew before and they followed until they arrived at the beautiful cave. When the Koo ka ka burras looked around them they saw this wonderful sight. They were amazed, they had no idea that such wonderful sights existed below the surface of the earth. There came before their vision the deplorable sight of the unconscious Snakes. They began to be sad. And when the Crow asked them to laugh they were unable to do so. They replied that the condition in which they were in caused the laughter to leave, and that they were feeling down in the dumps.

'It's a feeling that we are not accustomed to. No doubt if we were to take the Snakes into the sunlight, it would give back to us and to them, life.'

But the Crow thought, 'If I take them into the sunlight, I shall lose control.'

So he asked the Koo ka kee if there were any other means besides the sunlight that would strike a chord within them to cause a feeling of delight. So the Koo ka kee replied: 'There is only one person or tribe who at all times and all places will touch the chords of happiness within the bosom or soul of our Being, and that is the Frog. His voice penetrates everywhere, near or far. He may be seen or unseen, his voice, oh, if we could only hear that voice, we are sure that it would awaken us to our full faculties of laughter. And then we should be able to laugh the Snakes out of their slumber.'

So the Crow hastened out of the caves into the sunlight in search of the Frogs. All Nature seemed to be simply basking in the sunshine, there was no sound of life anywhere. So the Crow flew into a large gum tree and sat there with ear alert, waiting to catch the sound of the Frog. This was about midday. Just in the late afternoon, the sound of the Frog was carried by the soft wind to the Crow. Away he shot through the air towards a creek that was hidden by high trees and shrubs and reeds.

And there in a clear space was a little clear pool, and in it were Ploongee and small scaleless fish that frequent fresh water streams, and many, many happy and merry-making Froggies all out to enjoy themselves. Whilst the Mother Frogs sat under the shade of the trees just by the bank of the pool, away among the water-weeds were the Father Frogs, hunting food and procuring water-grubs for their wives and children. There were some of the little Froggies playing upon the bank, running and jumping leapfrog, others running out on the roots of the trees and leaping into the air in a graceful curve and coming head first so neatly into the clear water. Other little Froggies would be testing one another with the power of endurance, swimming from one side of the bank to the other, for speed and the most trips. Other Froggies would be testing their lung capacity against another Froggy for distance diving, and also staying longest beneath the surface. Other Froggies, with mischief gleaming in their eyes, would sit upon the overhanging twigs and watch the Ploongee swimming by and would leap upon their backs and steal a ride, whilst their sister Froggies would be laughing. This was a great day for Froggies, skipping and romping and making all kinds of antics. The Crow stood awhile admiring the lithe and muscular form of the Froggies.

Then the Crow, approaching the mothers, said: 'What wonderful and happy children. Where are their fathers? I would like to speak to them.'

The Mother Frogs gave a call that was answered by the Father Frogs who, replying, said: 'We are coming in a moment.'

So the Crow sat awhile admiring the little Froggies. Now the Father Frogs came to their wives, and, placing their afternoon's catch upon the ground, sat resting awhile. Then the Crow told them his mission, that there was no one of any tribe that could make the Koo ka ka burras laugh but the Frog, and they were at this moment in a very melancholy mood, sitting in yonder cave.

'Now will you come and bring your children with you? There is a great and noble mission for your race which shall not be forgotten. Come!'

The Father Frogs all agreed that they would be pleased to render their service for the benefit of others, so they all hopped off towards the cave, leaving the Mother Frogs with the babies to look after the home and cook the food and await their return. Of course all the boy Froggies were delighted to visit the cave. They were led right into the midst of the cave, and what beauties they beheld. Then the Crow showed them the Snakes in their stupor, and told them that these silly idiots ate and ate until they nearly burst.

'Ho Ho Ho,' laughed the older Frogs, and the sound of their voices was heard all around up to and beneath the cave, 'Ho Ho Ho.'

And the Koo ka ka burras turned their heads from side to side.

'Hello,' said one of the elders, 'I fancy I hear a familiar voice.'

The Crow noticed the change in the Koo ka ka burras, and he was so pleased with himself that he took the little Froggies to a little pool that was in a line of vision of the Snakes and burras, and instructed them that they could enjoy themselves in this beautiful bath, and the elder Frogs were seated above the pool, tier above tier like an amphitheatre. Then the Crow addressed the Frogs and pleading, asked that they should do their best to make the Koo ka ka burras laugh and that the laughing would have an effect upon the Snakes, bringing them out of their stupor.

So the Frogs began singing: 'Oh Koo ka ka burrund, Young a mutch ham carkar roomie Ghee ill itch Yarrow allie nhun cknow; Nem ill ind aitch? (Oh Koo ka ka burras, where is that infectious laugh, that laugh that gladdens the hearts of wearied and broken-hearted souls? Did it leave you, escape from thy throat? Which way did it fly from you so that I may go to capture it. Or did you leave it at home in the hollow of the gum tree?)'

'No,' shouted the Koo ka ka burras, 'we have it with us. Come now, hear us laugh.'

'Look there,' said the Crow. They turned their eyes and saw the Froggies leaping and skipping, doing all kinds of acrobatic feats, some of the little Froggies imitating the Kangaroo's leap, others the Emu dance, picking berries from shrubs. Another party of Froggies imitated the clumsy Goanna stalking its prey; the Pelican was another that was imitated by the Froggies. The sight of the scenes that were played in a humorous fashion caused the Koo ka ka burras to laugh.

'Oh,' said the Crow, 'it worked like magic. Just hear them laughing. I wonder when will they stop.'

No, they kept on laughing, until the Snakes in their dreams heard the infectious laughter and they all threw their heads up, opened their mouths, and laughed so heartily that they woke themselves.

Hastily the Crow asked the Frogs and Koo ka ka burras to retire, so they left the cave and went back to their respective homes. Then the

Snakes, who were now wide awake, asked the Crow for what purpose they were invited to the cave and secret passages.

'Oh,' said the Crow, 'I have something to show, something that it would be well to have in your possession. Look!'

And he presented the Adder to them. 'See whether any of you notice a change in this person.'

The Snakes looked and looked at her and remarked to the Crow: 'Only do we see a Wirrie grown to her body. What advantage is that?'

'Wait a moment,' said the Crow, 'you shall witness this day one of the greatest surgery feats of the age.'

He had hid away in a crevice of the rock a Wombat. He called him forth and he came out. He ordered the sleeping Wombat to tread upon the Adder. As soon as he made the attempt, the Adder swung her tail and struck the Wombat on the front leg, causing a wound.

'Watch and see the effect.'

Presently they saw the poor Wombat's body quivering and then fall to the ground a corpse.

'There, would you all like to have a weapon like that, only you shall have it in your mouth? Will you permit me to present you with these Wirrie? Stick them in your top jaw, and rest yourselves in this cave until the Wirrie grows to you, so it becomes part of you and you part of it.'

So the Crow performed his operation upon the Snakes. And this is how the Snakes became in possession of the deadly fangs, the Gift of the Evil Crow.

Then, when the time arrived when the Snakes should leave their hiding-place, the Crow thought it would be safe for himself to seek other climes, so he took his journey to Mount Gambier and lived there awhile.

Now, the Snakes with such new gifts, began to seek victims on which to try its effect. There were Kangaroos, Wombats, Emus, and other smaller Animals being killed by the deadly bite and sting of the Adder. So the Animals called a meeting to discuss the great danger that would wipe out the whole race unless something was done to prevent or stop it.

In this meeting of the Animal race, the Wombat said to the Kangaroo: 'I think from what I have gathered that the Reptile family are divided among themselves. The Lizards have decided to fight against the Snakes at any time. They are not favourable to them now since they visited the Crow and were guests at the cave and secret passages. So

I think it would be wise if we could invite the Goannas and Sleepy or Blue-tongue Lizards, and hear what they should suggest.'

'Good,' said the Kangaroo. 'Bandicoot, will you oblige me by running a message for me to the Goannas and Lizards?'

'With much pleasure,' said the Bandicoot. 'When would you require my service?'

'This very moment. Here, take this message stick and wait for a reply.'

The Bandicoot hastened on his errand until he came to the home of the Goanna tribe's hunting-ground, and he asked of one who was lying in the shade of the tree:

'Where can I see your Chief?'

He was told to go to a large gum tree that fell some years ago and was quite dry and had a hollow in the trunk on the south side. So the Bandicoot went along until he arrived at his destination and knocked at the open door.

Presently, a little Goanna peeped out, and asked: 'What do you want?'

'Oh,' said the Bandicoot, 'I have brought this from the Kangaroo (holding out the stick) to deliver to the Chief of the Goannas.'

So the little Goanna took the message stick into his father, who was sitting pondering over the grave danger that was confronting them, the deadly bite of the Snakes. He was analysing some of the herbs that were recommended by their Mooncumbulli, who said that it would counteract the poison of the Snakes. When the stick was brought in, he laid aside his work and read thereon the message from the Kangaroo, his dear old friend. So he hastily scribbled on a stick beside him the message: 'I and my family will accept your invitation to a conference, in which we shall discuss the awful danger that is confronting us. Let us meet at Cool lim what.'

The message-stick was delivered to the Bandicoot, who ran and ran until he safely arrived at the home of his Lord and Chief, the Kangaroo. After reading the message, he gave instructions that they must at dawn tomorrow leave and journey to the appointed meeting-ground.

Oh, it was a great gathering—Animals, Birds, Reptiles, and Insects. The Goanna told the Animals, Birds, Reptiles, and Lizards that the only remedy was to join forces and wage war against the Snakes.

'I have made a discovery of a herb that will counteract the poison, and it does work. I was out the other day and met my cousin, the Why yee (brown snake). I asked him where I would be able to procure food for my children. In reply he spoke an angry word. Well, that was more than I could stand, so I grappled with him. And we fought a great battle. He bit me just by the shoulders. I felt the sting smarting me very much. I ran away and plucked some of the herbs that I now hold in my hand, and began chewing and chewing and swallowed them. And it had an instantaneous effect. The pain disappeared like magic; and seemed to give me greater strength. I returned, and there was the Snake lying quietly beside a shrub. Oh, he was surprised to see me alive. First he thought he saw my ghost returning to haunt him. But I spoke and said: "Oh mine enemy, and the enemy of the whole tribes, I am no spirit. I am myself, the one who fought you half an hour ago. Come, let us do battle." With that said, we grappled with each other. I took him by the throat and I gripped him firmly. You see, as I said, the herbs gave me double strength so that I strangled him to death. But there is this about these herbs, what is my cure will not cure you. So I think if we all join forces and declare war against them I am sure they will become friendly or be exterminated. So it will be for them to choose.'

So they agreed that they would send for one of the Snakes. Away went the Frilled Lizard and asked the Tiger Snake to attend, representing his family. So he came and listened to the Goanna.

'Oh Tiger Snake, tell your family that the Animals, Birds, and lastly your cousins, the Reptile family, have vowed to join forces to exterminate you. Go think it over.'

The Tiger Snake returned to his family and told them the message. But they were not themselves agreed upon it, so that is the position today. The old Goanna and Hawk are always at war with the Snakes. The Goanna especially is a most hated foe of the Snake, so is the short, stumpy little Blue-tongue Lizard. Many a time this little Lizard will tackle a Snake five or six times its length or size.

The reason why the Lizards, such as the Goanna and Blue-tongue Lizard, have such hatred against the Snake is because before, when the Snakes were void of their poisonous fangs and when they were harmless and unable to defend themselves against their enemies, it was the Goannas and the Frilled and Blue-tongue Lizards that stood up for them, fought their aggressors, and provided food and sheltered them during the cold wintery weather.

Sometimes the Koo ka ka burras and some of the Hawk family would delight themselves in sporting and hunting, delighting in capturing and destroying the harmless inoffensive Snakes. The little Lizard was the sentinel of the Snake family, and often when there was danger threatening the Snakes he would give the alarm to the Frilled Lizards and they would go forth to fight. Now it happened that these Birds were slaying the Snakes, and the Koo ka ka burras were laughing as they watched their writhing bodies upon the ground. And it attracted the Jew Lizard, who, without a moment's notice, hastened to the Frilled Lizard, and he gave the war cry and rushed forward, followed by his friend, fully armed. They charged the Koo ka ka burras and the Kites, and they fought and fought until the blood flowed.

Now it seemed strange that this battle was fought only by the Frilled Lizard family against the Koo ka ka burras and Kites; no others interfered, because, fearing that all their tribes would participate, the Emu, the Commander-in-Chief of the Bird tribe, gave instructions to all others of his race not to take part in it; whilst the kindly and venerable Kangaroo gave orders to his race to show sympathy to either side; the Goanna, Chief of the Reptiles, acted the same role as the Emu, giving instructions to the others not to join forces with the Frilled Lizards.

They fought from midday until the sun set in the western sky, and they both fell to the ground with exhaustion.

'No one, not one of either side, shall give assistance to both tribes and their wounds or in any way minister to their needs. They must do for themselves,' said the Kangaroo and Emu.

They gave this proclamation not because they were heartless, not because they had no sympathy or love for their race, but because of two reasons: one was to teach them the dreadful result of hatred and war, and the other was to find out whether there were any among the whole races—Animal, Bird, Reptile, and Insect Beings—who would be moved with a spirit of self-sacrifice and give way to higher and nobler ideals than obedience to their Chiefs.

All the Animal tribes were represented at witnessing the battle. All the Bird tribes were there to witness the battle. So were the Reptile families there to witness this battle. They stood in silence with heads bowed in sorrow. This great gathering gradually melted away as each respective tribe went to its home, some weeping and others sobbing. Now all the

Animal and Reptile tribes were gone. The Cockatoo, Parrot, Lyre Bird, Pelican, and Magpie went home sobbing, and just one more family, the Swan, remained a little longer than the rest. Then they followed, bowing their heads in grief.

Just one more of the Bird family remained. They were just common little Beings with no great record of battles fought. All others, as they left with feelings of sorrow lying heavy upon their hearts, would very much indeed have liked to minister to the bleeding, suffering, and dying Lizards, Koo ka ka burras, and Kites. But it seemed up to this time no one came forward but the little Robin Redbreast, for it was they who had remained to the last of the great assembly. They would not turn their backs upon bleeding, suffering, and dying. They would not heed the command of their leader and Chief, or the leaders and Chiefs of other races.

'What do we care?' they said amongst themselves. 'We live for higher and nobler ideals. Come, let us stay the bleeding of the wounds. Come, our duty is to the distressed and dying, not to the well and perfect.'

But the little men Robins turned to their wives, bidding them go home and prepare the evening meals for their babies and to keep the home comfortable for their return in the morning. So the wives of the Robins hurried home, filled with joy that their husbands had responded to a higher calling, submitting to the voice within.

Now, each little Robin attended to the wounded and stopped the flow of blood, staying beside them until they were able to rise and go to their home and bury the dead. And just before the morning star arose in the eastern sky, heralding the coming dawn, the Robins completed the noble work and returned to their anxious and loving little wives and babies. They told their wives of the awful misery of the wounded, and heartrending messages that the dying told them to deliver to their aged mothers and wives and orphan children. The little wives of the Robins listened with mingled feelings of sorrow for the suffering and dead, and joy for the service rendered by their bold little husbands, who sat talking and telling them of the difficulty which they had had in lifting the heavy bleeding bodies of the Frilled Lizards, Koo ka ka burras, and Kites, and showed the blood upon their breast which came or flowed from the wounds.

They forgot that the time was passing swiftly and that the sun shone brightly. The little Jew Lizard raised the cry: 'Oh, come and see where the wounded and dying were when we left, behold there is no one. Who has broken the command of the Chiefs of the Animals, Birds and Reptiles?'

Everyone rushed to the battlefield of the previous day. There was no one to be seen. The Chiefs sent orders that everyone should come to the assembly and give an explanation of their disobedience, which must end in death.

So all the Animals came, feeling proud that they had not broken the order of their Chief. They were proud soldiers who obeyed their superiors. The Reptile tribe came, feeling proud too that they had no occasion to be afraid of the challenge. The Bird tribe came hurrying, thinking surely there is not one of our race who would be so foolish as to disobey the command of the Emu. The Cockatoos, Parrots, Lyre Birds, Swans, Pelicans, and others of the family presented themselves, assured that none of them would bring disgrace and dishonour upon the Bird tribe.

The Kangaroo gave orders that all the Animals should stand in order, the Koalas in one rank, the Wombats in another rank of their own, the Dingo family alone, and so forth. The Reptile Chief, the Goanna, gave orders to his tribe that they should stand in order, each family a rank to themselves: the Frilled Lizards a rank to themselves, the Blue Tongued Lizards a rank to themselves, the Carpet Snakes a rank to themselves, and so forth, until each of the Reptile families were in a rank to themselves. The Bird Chief, the Emu, gave a similar order as the Animals and Reptiles, that each of the Bird families should occupy a rank to themselves: the Cockatoos a rank to themselves, the Swans to themselves, the Pelicans to themselves, and so forth all in order until they came to the smaller families. The little Blue Wrens and other small birds were in their own rank and order. Lastly came the Robins; they fell into a rank, each of the Robins wearing a cloak made of the fibre of rush that grows on the river banks. The Animals occupied the northern side of the ground, the Reptiles the southern side of the ground, the Birds stood on the eastern side of the ground. On the western side of the ground, like an ordinary football oval, stood the Chief of each tribe, the Kangaroo, Eagle Hawk, and Goanna.

The Goanna was the first to address the assembly, expressing how grieved he was that someone had disobeyed the command. The Eagle Hawk, following on the remark of the Goanna, said that a command broken was a capital punishment, resulting in death.

Lastly the kindly old Kangaroo rose to his feet, and all eyes were fixed upon him. He stood silently awhile with bowed head, with mingled feelings which went out to the person or persons who broke the law, and who no doubt did it moved by some good impulse. Raising his head and looking round at each tribe represented, he said in a loud and firm voice that everyone could hear distinctly: 'Someone has broken a command. Who will find him and bring him before this assemblage?'

Not one moved. Again the Kangaroo said: 'Will some of you, I do not mind of which race, step forward and deliver up to us, those who have dared to break our command.'

Suddenly, from the third rank of the first nearest and facing the Chiefs of the Animals, Birds, and Reptiles, the rank of the little Robins, wearing the cloaks fastened firmly about the breast and neck, marched in order from their position round the oval, passing the Chiefs and coming to their starting-point again, stood in front of their friends and family, the Bird tribe. Sharply turning and facing the Chiefs, marching abreast, facing the Eagle Hawk they stood awhile and did not say a word. They stood thus until the Kangaroo, Eagle Hawk, and Goanna looked a bit puzzled.

Then the Kangaroo, addressing the Robins, said: 'Well, my little people, are you the volunteers? Will you arrest the offenders and bring them to us?'

Then each little Robin nodded his head.

'Right about face, quick march, forward!'

Instead of responding to the marching orders, they tore from their breasts the cloaks they were wearing and revealed to the astonished Kangaroo, Eagle Hawk, and Goanna, the bloodstained breasts. Instantly, the old Kangaroo bowed his head, with streams of tears trickling down his cheeks. The penetrating eyes of the Eagle Hawk were gradually filled with tears, and he, too, bowed his head. The Goanna turned his head first this side and that side, looking with one eye focused upon the Robins' breasts, then turned the other eye to focus upon the Robins to make sure that his sight was not deceiving him.

'Yes,' he said to himself, 'it is the stain of blood upon their breasts.'

He caught the same explanation as did the Kangaroo and Eagle Hawk, that these little Beings, moved by nobler ideals in spite of the command, attended the needs of the wounded and dying. So he bowed his head and wept.

The Animals, Birds, and Reptiles were amazed at the action of their Chiefs.

'What makes them weep?'

After the Kangaroo, Eagle Hawk, and Goanna had overcome their emotion, the Kangaroo gave orders to the Robins to face the audience. The little Robins, without a fear, turned smartly and stood facing the Animal, Bird, and Reptile tribes. They, too, bowed their heads, because never before in the history of the Animal, Bird and Reptile tribes had such a spirit of self-sacrifice been displayed.

And the Kangaroo called with broken voice: 'Volunteers, volunteers, slay the offenders.'

Not a Being stirred. They were all willing to die rather than take the lives of such noble little Robins.

'Well done, ye Animals, Birds, and Reptiles. You have witnessed this day a spirit that I hope will be immortalised throughout the ages to come, until time shall be no more.'

And so today, as a reminder to the Animals, Birds, and Reptiles of this spirit of sacrifice, [the Robin] still carries the bloodstain upon his breast where the head of the bleeding Lizard rested before going west, to the Mystery Land.

At this time when all these events were taking place, the Crow was sitting upon what is known today as Mount Gambier. Weeping, he reviewed his past life, and was deeply sorry for the wrong he did, weeping for forgiveness. And he looked upon his past life, everything was a failure, no good came out of it.

But presently, as if from nowhere, came the form or the Being of the little Blue Wren, and he spoke and said to the Crow: 'Oh Evil One, good always comes of wrong doing. When the little Pelicans were the victims of your cunning and witchcraft, it awoke in me the spirit to think of others. I hastened again and brought along the Woodpecker and begged his service to deliver the little Pelicans. See my colour of honour conferred upon me by the Chief of the Birds, brought from the sunlight.'

And the Blue Wren disappeared as suddenly as he came.

When the Crow looked around he saw before him another form, the little Robin Redbreast. 'Cheer up, oh Crow. Thy mission has been of some good. What if thou gave to the Adder and Snakes the sting of Death? It has caused much sorrow through the death of many. We have all been selfish, thought too much of our own self. See, I bear upon my breast the bloodstain of the Frilled Lizard. All pain, suffering, agony, and death awakens within for all Beings a spirit of sympathy and love and sacrifice.'

In a twinkling of an eye the Robin disappeared.

A dark cloud overshadowed the Mount on which the Crow sat. From out of the dark cloud lightning flashed, the thunder rending the still mountain top. Rain and hail poured in torrents, and the wind blew with fury, tearing limbs from the trees.

'This is dreadful,' said the Crow.

Suddenly, as if by magic, the storm passed over, the sun shone brightly, plants grew on, with flowers to decorate the mountain, and in the valley below flowers were everywhere like a sea of colour.

'Thus,' said the Crow, 'I have done some good.'

A light touch upon his shoulder caused him to turn, and he beheld a figure rising heavenwards, who beckoned: 'Come up, a place awaits you in Wyerriewarr.'

Now tonight you will see the Crow, no longer a symbol of Darkness and Evil, but a shining Star, ever onward fulfilling his mission for which he was intended.

Narroondarie's Wives

Narroondarie is the name of one of the many good men that were sent among the various tribes of the Australian Aborigines. Now, the name Narroondarie is better known among the Ngarrindjeri tribes of the Lower Murray, Lakes Alexandrina and Albert, and Encounter Bay, South Australia. Before he came into South Australia he was known or called Boonah, hence the initiation ceremonies. Narroondarie and Boonah are names by which he is known as a good man, as a Sacred Man who is endowed or guided by the will of the Great Spirit, the Nhyanhund or Byamee, Our Father of All.

This messenger and teacher, after coming from the northern part of Australia down into various parts of New South Wales and Victoria, found his way into South Australia, dwelling mostly in and around the shores of Lakes Alexandrina and Albert, and would visit various camping-grounds where the people lived permanently. Some of them would run into the water and hide among the reeds and water plants, and when he saw that the people fled from him he would call: 'Young Hund an,' and they would remain silent and he became annoyed at the people's attitude.

And he would say to them: 'Well, children, if you will not answer me, "Pool jarra wallul." This is a command and a curse. Now you shall all become birds and shall remain thus for ever.'

And they suddenly became birds at the command of Narroondarie. And whilst there were others who summoned sufficient courage and came at his call, these were or are the tribes that remain this day around Lake Alexandrina.

Now this should have been the completion of his mission, so he chose two bald hills, which were free from trees, with only low shrubs and grass trees growing, as his last home on earth, the surrounding country being dense growth of Mallee and Pine, Honeysuckle and She-Oak, and a few species of Gum tree and other shrubs. He made the choice of these two hills because he was able to have a view of both lakes. And it was his intention to rest here until the Great Spirit should call him to take his place in heaven among the other Great Company that had gone before him.

On one of his fishing expeditions, he was passing on his way to Lake Albert when he saw in his path two grass trees, young and tender, swaying so gracefully in the Kolkamia (south wind), and his attention was so arrested that he stood for a moment looking upon these two stems of grass trees, and then from the She-Oak's bough came the weird note of song—not of pleasure or joy or happiness, but of sadness. The song was that of the two bound up in the stem of the Grass Tree. The Selfish Spirit of the Grass Tree kept these young maidens bound thus because they were so sweet, and he delighted to invite Nature—the Bees, Ants, and Honey-birds to come and dine with him. And his heart was moved by their pitiful cry.

Now, these two maidens have captivated many, many good men who, on their way to the Spirit Land, have fallen victims to their wonderful charms. These two maidens had been passed on from stage to stage, sometimes into the form of a butterfly with beautiful colours, sometimes found or imprisoned in the Karldookie (flower-tops of reeds). Various trees, shrubs, and plants have gone forth with the endeavour to keep these two maidens prisoner because their chief delight was to captivate all the great men. So it was at this time an effort of the Grass Tree to keep them bound up; it was the last of the Vegetable Kingdom and all were wondering whether it would succeed.

So that is why when the Great Man Narroondarie stood looking at the Grass Tree's stem, that the boughs of the She-Oak began to wail as the wind was passing through the wiry leaves. Now the sounds seemed to come from the She-Oak, but were coming from the Grass Tree. These cunning maidens knew that if they were at this moment to try to use their charm to win this Sacred Man they would fail. But to touch the chords of pity—surely this good man would pity them and release them. On this move they were sure he would set them free. They were conscious the Grass Tree was not a good medium through which they could send their message on to Narroondarie. So when the Kolkamia (south wind), breathing upon all Nature, caused their sorrowful cry of distress, as if some loved one had died and they were mourning, then Narroondarie stood, and being a Great Man, heard the cry of the two maidens and said: 'Yaka yakatumburra (Oh, I pity! Oh, I pity you both)! Mackaunda ngool purpe (Why do you both so weep, or what makes you weep?)'

'Menpeel nullum. They have placed us into this Grass Tree and our flesh with its sense of taste, smell, hearing, and touch is dead, and only this subconscious state which is still alive makes us accept this prison home. Our bodily form and human flesh have become the form of vegetable flesh. Oh Great One, take pity upon us and release us and we shall become your servants.'

And Narroondarie thought and thought. And these two maidens, with the cunning of many, many years' experience, began to use it upon this Sacred Man. And he listened and then he began to think within himself how nice it would be to see what would be the form of these two Spirits enclosed in this Grass Tree.

'It will not be any harm for me to look upon them although I am forbidden to associate myself with women. I will assist them and cause them to come forth and then after look upon them for a while.'

So he bade the Grass Tree body to give the fair maidens their liberty. In the twinkling of an eye the maidens stepped out of the Grass Tree a Punerrie (picture) of beauty. Their perfect form and their wonderful Peel langga (eyes) so captivated the Great Man that he fell, a victim to their charm. And he decided that he would make them both his wives. So he told the maidens that now he had given them their freedom, he would ask them to be his wives. Instead of going a-fishing as he intended he returned to his home and asked them to be seated, and then he gave them something to eat.

After they had enjoyed their meal, he began to tell them of the various laws and customs that he gave to the people, and that some of the laws were very drastic, that is to say when broken would result in the death of the offender. For instance, in the making of the youth into men, no woman is allowed to look upon them or to give or offer them food, or their portion of the flesh of a Kangaroo and Emu, or fish such as the Pondi (cod), Tcherie (freshwater bream), and especially the Thookerri (silver-scaled fish and extremely bony). No woman is allowed to eat this fish under penalty of death. Now, this fish is much sought after by the Aborigines.

So as time went on they were passing through new experiences and the whole woman's tendencies began to exert themselves, and there began to arouse in the mind of Narroondarie some coming trouble. He would not allow them to remain at home by themselves, but would ask them to accompany him on his fishing expeditions. One day they were out fishing on Lake Albert; he was in his canoe whilst the maidens were wading in the shallow water along the shore, with a net made from the rushes that grow on the bank of the lakes, made in a cone shape constructed after the fashion of the old-style candle extinguishers, only a great deal larger. They would place this at the opening of a dense growth of reeds; one would go along the bank and enter the water and reeds at the other end and splash the water, causing the fish that were between her and the one with the net to escape, so that the fishes would swim toward the entrance and enter the net and be trapped. And they would take the net to the bank and empty the contents, and there would be fishes of different kinds—Tcherie, Pillulkie, or Pummerrie.

Unfortunately on this occasion there were three beautiful white-silver Thookerri, and they looked around, trembling with excitement. They covered the fishes with weeds and rushes and went on their way with the net, feigning to fish, but they were so overjoyed with their catch that they paid no attention to what they were doing. They could not stand the strain much longer and so decided to go home, and looking out into the lake their attention was attracted by a column of smoke that rose against the clear sky looking north-west.

So they called their Chief and husband, Narroondarie, and he came to them, and the elder of the maidens pointing towards the smoke said: 'Look! A message to be sent.'

So he sat down waiting for an impression. Suddenly he arose and told them that Nebalee had sent a message asking that he would like him to come to his Now wondie (his home) Rowhokkun (Point McLeay Mission Station) now, so he would leave at once and they should make themselves comfortable at home; so they parted.

The young maidens said: 'We will stay here and watch you cross over to the other side of the lake and then we shall go to our home.'

So Narroondarie got into the canoe and paddled across the lake.

When the maidens saw that he had landed safely and was on his way to Rowhokkun, they turned around and went towards a heap of weed and rushes and removed from beneath the coveted prize and food and they sat looking and looking, turning the fishes over and over, and after they had finished admiring them, they rose and walked toward home; in fact they ran all the way until they reached the camp, and then began hurriedly to make a fire of She-Oak tree bark. When the wood had burned, leaving a nice red coal, they placed the fishes beside the fire. First they placed a layer of soft grass—a grass that retains the fat of animal bird or fish (no flesh food is cooked without it)—and then they took two thin, dry, or sometimes green, sticks, about a foot or sixteen inches long and about half an inch in diameter or less, and placed or took these two sticks between the thumb, and the first and second finger, lying between the thumb and index finger on top, and by a trained manipulation of the thumb and two fingers, took a coal of fire, as you would with tongs and placed it upon the fish, then covered the fish with live coals and allowed it to remain for a while, and then they removed the coals from the fish over the cooked side which they lay upon the grass, then they placed coal upon the side that was lying upon the grass in the first instance, and the fishes were repeatedly turned over several times; and when cooked thus the fat comes out and explodes like fat in a frying pan.

And Narroondarie heard the fat on the Thookerri frizzling and he said to Nebalee: 'Do you hear that sound as if someone, a woman or women, is cooking the forbidden fish? I shall not sleep here tonight but I shall leave you just before sunset.'

So after the fishes were cooked, the maidens sat down on top of the hill so that they would have a vision of the surrounding country and should anyone be passing or come to their camp, they would have plenty of time to hide the remaining portion of the fishes so that they would not accuse them of having eaten a forbidden fish. They sat in the sunshine eating and chatting, expressing their delight of enjoying such sweet food: 'Ah, the men are clever! They know what are the nicest foods, and so they make laws to prevent and deprive us. But we have been too clever.'

So they ate and laughed and made merry. Now they had completed their meal and were reclining on the grass enjoying a rest, listening to the song of the birds in the valley not very far distant, but just as the sun was halfway down the western sky they came to themselves, and rose to a sitting position, looking into each other's eyes enquiringly, then spoke:

'Oh, what have we done? We must not stay here any longer. It is very strange, do you not smell the oil of the Thookerri? The grass shrub and tree have retained the smell. Come! We cannot stay here and be asked questions when our lord and master returns.'

They awoke to their sense of guilt, so the elder said: 'Come, let us flee.'

'But,' said the younger, 'whither shall we fly? Let us stay and face the wrath of Narroondarie. Stay and be placed back and embodied in a tree-shrub plant lest when we are caught fleeing he may cause us to be into something more dreadful than these.'

'Come!' said the elder, 'there is no time to discuss the matter; we may go into some strange land and win the affection of a Mooncumbulli, become his wife, and no one shall dare to interfere with our liberty.'

So without another word they both gathered a great bundle of grass tree sticks and carried them to the waterside and bound them together, forming a raft, and they shoved the raft into deep water and sat upon it and paddled across the western side of Lake Albert, and slept at the point near the estate of the late T. R. Bowman.

Now this happened during the night, the crossing of Lake Albert, and it was late in the evening that Narroondarie arrived home. When he was about a hundred yards or more from his mia mia, he was struck with the smell of the Thookerri fat.

'Ah!' said he, 'those silly and frivolous maidens have eaten the forbidden fish and now they must be punished.'

When he entered his mia mia there was no one about. Then he called: 'Young who Nhod (Where are you both)?'

No answer, only the screeching of the night Owl, which was a sign that there was something wrong. The culprits had fled. So he lit a fire and sat down for a while pondering over the misdeed in his two young wives. He was thinking deeply what excuse he should make to the Great Spirit for releasing those maidens from the prison of the Grass Tree into which they had been placed by the last victim—the Proolgie (the Spirit Native Companion). He must have had an excuse.

'Now, to what form of punishment or prison shall I put them? Well, before I can decide I must capture them.'

So he lay down to sleep and before the sun rose he took his Plongee (a weapon about eighteen inches long with a knob at one end the size and shape of the smallest child's football with a handle at the other end about a foot long and about an inch in thickness). Now, this is a weapon for the bruising of the body of a person who transgresses a law, and it means a slow, painful death which will give them time to think and repent of the misdeed. He also took a boomerang and his Possum skin bound around his shoulders, and set off walking slowly down to the shore of the lake, and then the sun rose and he began to walk faster, still casting his eyes upon the ground, looking for footprints. When he got to the lake side he made for the place where they left their net, and saw that there were the scales of the Thookerri upon it; and now he was satisfied of the reason for their absence from camp.

He got into his canoe and paddled across the lake and landed at the same point, and saw the kindie or raft made with a bundle of grass trees, and he walked around among the bushes that grew on the bank of the river and saw a fire and a place where they had slept. Then he began to follow their tracks leading toward the Coorong—that is a strip of water between a strip of land hummock lying north-west and south-east in Encounter Bay, South Australia—and he saw again where they had constructed another kindie and had just gone across a few hours before his arrival. So he thought he would rest and make the attempt of fording the Coorong in the morning.

When the sun arose, he crossed over the Coorong and began his search for further tracks of his wives. But in this he failed and he was wondering in which direction he would go; never before was he baffled. And so he had to decide which way he should go, and he chose to go south-east, following the Coorong. He walked with great speed, and he covered about seventy miles, and rested awhile, thinking that he must come before the maidens if they had come in this direction. But no one passed; so he built a small camp made of the boughs of shrubs and grass, and at midnight he went to sleep. He was so tired with the previous day's journey that he slept soundly long after the sun rose.

And he would have slept on but he felt a touch and heard a voice calling: 'Awake, sleeper! Beware! Thine enemy is near.'

So he rose and looked around, but saw no one. But the visitor was Puck nowie, the Grandmother Spirit, the Guardian Angel of good people that is ever beside them and warns them of danger. So he broke his fast and made preparations to meet the unseen enemy. Then he began his search for his two wives.

Now, away among the Punbbaalee tribe there lived a very cruel man who had become a disciple of the Crow, and like his Chief caused a great deal of mischief; and he too was transformed from a human being into a Wombat. And this Wombat wandered among the sand hummocks all alone and, as Narroondarie was walking along, he saw it and threw his spear and struck it in a vital spot, right into the heart. He withdrew the spear and allowed the blood to flow from the wound upon the white sand, and then he picked up the Wombat and carried it to his Mia mia and tied it upon a pole. And just as he was about to sit down he missed his spear, and remembered that he had left it where he had speared the Wombat. So he returned, and behold, he saw that the blood of the Wombat was developing into a man, so he sat and watched it.

Presently there was a man lying upon the ground, breathing as if in a deep sleep; so Narroondarie, instead of taking his spear, left it, thinking perhaps it would become of use to this man. So he went away among the Ti trees and made several Yundi (spears) and returned a second time to his Mia mia. And this time he pondered over the man that had developed from the blood of the Wombat. As a servant of the Great Spirit, he was aware that there were Spirits of good and bad men embodied in tree shrubs and plants. But this discovery was something new. A Spirit to be within the lifeblood of an animal! So he began to experience an uneasy feeling, as if something unpleasant was about to take place; so he returned to see what the person was like—whether he was a friend and would assist him in the discovery of his two wives; and he began to cautiously wend his way until he came to the spot and saw that the person had disappeared, so he looked around, hoping to see footprints which would lead to him. But there were no footprints and now he was convinced that this strange person was an enemy. A friend will always leave a footprint—this is the teaching of the Aborigines. So he thought to himself, like all wise men do, that he would be always upon the alert; and during that day he was not seen.

On the second day of this event Narroondarie sat upon the peak of a high sand-hummock looking first Wolkundmia (north), then Tolkamia (west), Kolkamia (south), and Karramia (east). There was no one to be seen. Then he sat down and debated within himself as to which direction to take. Presently he heard the voice of someone laughing. It was not the laugh of joy or amusement, but a laugh of scorn, so he leapt to his feet and immediately his eyes caught a vision that almost froze the blood in his body, and a cold chill ran down his back; for there before him stood the Arch Enemy of the Good Parrimparrie: the Evil One. So Narroondarie grasped his Rarrabarr, standing erect with the weapon held firmly in his hand ready to hurl it at the approaching figure.

Parrimparrie stood about two hundred yards away from the base of the hill on which Narroondarie stood and, calling, addressed him thus: 'Yar Raa Rhonghund Ta Now ind Glan im un (Oh brother-in-law of mine, do you not recognise me?)'

So when Narroondarie heard this friendly salutation he came down to where the Deceiver sat. When Narroondarie was about twenty spaces away, he stood and said: 'Oh Rhonghund un, was it yourself that I released from the body of the Wombat?'

'Yes,' said the Deceiver.

'Now, brother-in-law of mine,' spoke Narroondarie, 'do you claim to be my Rhongee (brother-in-law)?'

'Yes,' replied the Deceiver.

'Then perhaps you may be able to tell me the whereabouts of your two sisters. I am in search of them.'

'Nou, hie um rum un (No I shall not tell you, oh mine enemy). I have waited long and patiently, but during your sojourn among the people in various parts of the country, I was prevented by your followers, those who have gone above, the Peewingie, and Proolgie (Hawk and Native Companion). They have placed me into the body of the Wombat and you have released me, and now you shall die before you reach Wyerriewarr (heaven).'

Now all Great Men have been given the privilege to go to heaven without death.

'Mack kundun yun krook, Rhonghund (Then why did you call me: 'oh brother-in-law of mine')? Kunthun itch mewee (Why have you deceived me now)? Are you not pleased that I have been the means of your release? Were you not at my mercy? Do you realise that I could have slain you? I allowed you to take your present form. Come, let us not quarrel. Nup ghie ell lung (I leave you now).'

And Narroondarie turned and was making in the direction from whence he came, nor-west. Then the Deceiver began to laugh and sing a song. And Narroondarie kept walking and, thinking that he had gone a certain distance, he stood and looked about, and still hearing his enemy singing, thought that he was following, but he saw that he was in the same place and had not moved an inch. He looked around and saw that Parrimparrie was dancing and brandishing his spear in a threatening attitude, with spear raised and poised, ready to send it on its mission of death.

Narroondarie stood awaiting results. Suddenly the spear was hurled with lightning speed and would have entered a vital spot had not Narroondarie seen it delivered in time. With a downstrike of his Rarrabarr, he quickly smote the spear and its point tore a flesh wound on his thigh. Then Parrimparrie began dancing and singing because he had drawn the first blood. So Narroondarie took his spear and placed it into the Thy rall gie (the throwing stick) and poised it well above his shoulder and, like all warriors, uttered a prayer and speaking to the spear, he said: 'Thow, tack (Oh my trusted spear, art thou not my handiwork; have I not made thee for a purpose? Come, now, behave thyself favourably to thy master and do his bidding).'

And with muscle and mind he hurled the spear with lightning speed, and it entered the body of Parrimparrie and pierced his heart. He fell lifeless to the ground with the life-blood trickling into the ground.

So Narroondarie began, as he thought, his journey. He walked and walked, taking no notice of things around him until the presence of a Rich er rook itty (Willy Wagtail) that seemed to be continually in his path drew his attention. So he looked about and saw that he was still in the same place, so he said within himself: 'I have met a great and powerful enemy; although his life has left the body, he is influencing the conditions around that are preventing my escape.'

So he sat down and rested himself awhile before making another attempt to depart and as he sat he noticed that birds or animals that came near the body were unable to go from it, so he came to a decision that the only way out of it was to burn the body. So he rose and gathered a great heap of grass and twigs and piled log upon log until he had a heap twice his height, and then he took the body of Parrimparrie and placed it upon the huge wood heap. Next he took two grass trees; in one he punctured a small hole and then into this hole he put the point of the other, which he held between the palm of both hands and began rubbing and rubbing until a spark was produced. And then he set fire to the wood and so burned the body of Parrimparrie.

And he began his journey. He walked and walked, then looked to see how far he had come, but he was still in the same place. And he said to himself, 'I must see whether I have burned everything that belongs to him,' and looking round he found the congealed blood of Parrimparrie upon the ground, so he made another fire upon the blood and stirred the hot ashes until there was no sight of blood.

And then he began his journey and this time he was able to pass on without any hindrance. He walked so fast that he covered about seventy to eighty miles in an hour. Now he found that he was confronted by the Murray flowing into the Southern Ocean. So he spoke to the Great Spirit, asking Him to make it possible that he could be able to walk across. His prayer was answered; the ground came up and formed a bridge across the river. Now when he had crossed to the other side of the river, he saw the footprints of his two wives that had been made three days ago. And following their footprints, he came to where they had camped for the night and he noticed that the cold ashes had the stained appearance of a Tarrarrie (a lump of fat inside a Mullowie or some call it King[fish]). Now this fat of the fish Mullowie a woman is strictly forbidden to eat, and when Narroondarie saw this evidence he was so greatly grieved and sorrowful in heart that he sat down beside the camp and wept bitterly for the sins of his two young wives. He spent the night there weeping, because he loved these maidens very much. To think it was he who delivered unto the people the word of the Great Spirit, that those who broke these laws would receive the full penalty—Death! And that he who had brought them out of bondage and given them the full living of a human life would now bring about their destruction. And this punishment must be greater than the first. This thought weighed heavy upon his mind, that he must punish them and set them up as an example that the way of the transgressor is hard, and that the coming generations would look upon these two as the well-beloved wives of the Greatest of Prophets among the Aborigines. He prayed for their forgiveness but the answer came: as a person chooses to live, so shall he die.

And now he set out to overtake them and mete out the punishment. He followed their tracks, which led him to what is known as Port Elliot, South Australia and he came to where they had camped two days before him. He saw and examined the ashes and saw that they had cooked Cockles and Periwinkles and Mullet (fish). Again he wept, this time beside a huge rock, and his tears trickled into the sea.

He wept so much that today some of the old folk will point out the place and say: 'This is the spot where Narroondarie wept bitterly for his two wayward wives.' It resembles a soakage of fresh water by the side of the sea, and that which was liquid of salt bitter tears and a sorrowing heart comes as a sweet, cool, and refreshing water to journeying souls to the Land of the Spirits. And when the Aborigines visit this spot you will see tears trickling down their cheeks, the result of their thoughts of their Great Leader, the Messenger and Teacher of the Will of the Great Father of All.

Now Narroondarie, after spending a restless night, rose early and walked rapidly until he arrived at the Bluff, Victor Harbour. He sat there with his face turned toward the west and he saw them in spirit and again he wept, because he saw in a vision what was to happen and that it would be he who should bring them to their timely end before they reached the Spirit Land, Kangaroo Island. So he hurried on once more, while in his bosom waged a great conflict. His lovable nature was willing that they should reach this island and be free for ever of all punishment for their wrong-doing.

Now the maidens arrived in the afternoon opposite to Kangaroo Island. And at the time of the story the island was connected with the mainland but during a severe southerly storm the sea would cover the connecting strip of land. And the maidens, instead of going across that afternoon, spent the time in collecting honey, with the intention of crossing on the morrow. And another reason: there was a keeper on this strip of land on the mainland side who was in charge, and he was known as the Krowallie (Blue crane) and no one would attempt to cross without his permission. He was a very austere person and a very dangerous one to dispute with, because he always had beside him on his person a very sharp-bladed spear that would cause a very nasty and severe wound.

Now, Narroondarie was just four or five miles behind or away from the maidens; he could see them standing on the cliff looking across to the Spirit Land. So he made a little mia mia and went into the bush and procured a Possum and roasted it, and allowed it to cool before eating it. And the maidens did the same, they made a comfortable little mia mia and also a large fire whose blaze Narroondarie was able to see. Now Narroondarie was awaiting a message which would instruct him how to punish the disobedient girls. At midnight the Kroolthumie (Owl) came with the instructions that these maidens should be allowed to walk the strip of land that acts as a bridge to all pilgrims to the Spirit Land, and when they should arrive halfway across then should Narroondarie chant the Wind Song. First he must chant to the Tolkamia (west wind) and sing its Song of Fury to bring up the waters of the mystery land and let them roll with vengeance; then he must sing the song of Kolkamia (south wind) to blow and bring the water that comes from the unknown land; then they may wish to return to land; then he must sing the song of Wolkundmia (north wind) and the water shall all come together and toss and toss them until they become exhausted; then he must command that they shall become rocks.

So Narroondarie rose early in the morning and came near unto the maidens and sat upon the cliff to see them begin their journey of death. They came to the Krowallie and asked his permission to cross, which he willingly gave, and the maidens began laughing and chatting, anticipating the joy and pleasure and happiness that awaited them when they arrived upon the Spirit Land, but most of all they would be free from the Law from which they were trying to escape. Yet little did they realise that within a few moments they would meet the full penalty of their disobedience. Now Narroondarie came a little nearer to the strip of land that led to Kangaroo Island and sat upon a vantage spot, watching and waiting until they were half way over the distance.

When they reached that point Narroondarie began singing the Wind Song: 'Pinkell lowar mia yound, Tee wee warr, La rund, Tolkamia a tren who cun, Tinkalla! (Fall down from above, oh thou mighty Wind; swiftly run and display thy fleetness! Come thou down from the Northern sky, oh water of the deep! Come up in a mighty swell!)'

And the westerly wind burst forth in all its fury and came screeching overhead, while the maidens were pressing forward, struggling against the storm. Then presently the waters were churned and welled and rose just over the way. Then Narroondarie sang a Song of the Wind and the south wind blew and the waters from unknown land came tantalisingly on, raising themselves like miniature mountain peaks, and the waters closed upon them, lashing them and tossing them about like corks. They struggled first toward their goal, Kangaroo Island, then it seemed as if the Spirits were against them and they turned themselves and began swimming toward the mainland. But the Wolkundmia, answering the call of Narroondarie, was willing to do its duty in bringing these two maidens to pay the penalty of their sins.

As they sped on they called: 'We come, we come!'

And the maidens sank with exhaustion and were drowned and sank to the bottom. And the winds suddenly ceased and there was a calm and Narroondarie wept bitterly; although he hated everything that was displeasing to the Great Spirit, he felt within his inmost consciousness that he loved those youthful maidens with all their faults and errors.

And again a voice whispered to him: 'Command that the maidens' bodies be turned into stone to stand out as a warning to all women not to eat of the forbidden food.'

He spoke, and it came to pass as he was told. These two rocks can be seen from the mainland, as well as by passing vessels, and are known today as: the 'Two Sisters'. Before the coming of the White Man, these stones were called and still are to the few remaining Aborigines: 'Rhunjullang'—the 'Two Sisters'. Many were the pilgrimages taken by the Aborigines in days gone by to see these stones and view and contemplate the way of the Great Teacher, Narroondarie.

After this had happened, with tears still welling in his eyes and a broken heart, Narroondarie commanded that the waters should go back, and allow him to walk upon dry land to Kangaroo Island. And on the eastern side of the island was a huge Gum Tree and under its shade he rested until the sun sank into the western sky, the Land of the Spirits. He walked to the west of the island and plunged into the sea and sank into the deep, and was there a long while, seeking in the depths of the sea the Spirits of his two wives, and he rescued them from the watery cold grave and arose with them clinging on both sides of the Great Teacher, and he flew upwards and upwards until he came to the Land of Wyerriewarr, to join that bright and happy group Naboolea, Wy young gurrie, Jeirellang, and Mungungie, and to look down to cheer and comfort and encourage the Korn mar culdar (mankind) to press on to fight all the evil desires that are within, remembering always to obey the will of the Great Spirit.

NHUNG E UMPIE

Human nature is the same in the Australian Aboriginal as it is in the white, brown, or yellow man, irrespective of nationality, language, and religion. We may presume that it makes no difference if we go back to those distant ages; to those earlier periods in which evidences of our ancestors have been placed on record, we find in the remains of ancient civilisations of the great Nenevek, Greece, Rome, or Egypt, great walls and fortunes as a defence against the enemy who attempted to invade their cities. Writing and carving clearly demonstrate this spirit: an eye for an eye and a tooth for a tooth.

Now, amidst the rising and falling of King and Emperor, there arose mighty men who caught a higher inspiration and were filled with knowledge and wisdom. They endeavoured to raise their people to lofty ideals and to instil into the hearts and minds of their respective races a spirit of brotherhood and goodwill. Now it is not necessary for me to mention those noble and inspired characters of every age. The Budha, Mahomet and Christ; these men have established religion and teachings to knit the bond of the race in love and sympathy. The question arises: do these religions and teachings fulfil all conditions for the benefit of the human race? Now, each nation may accept and follow the teachings of a Budha, a Mahomet, and Christ, each were great men in their time and their influence is felt and they are with us today.

Now, there arose among my people a man who claimed (as others had) that he, too, was sent by God with a message and teaching and we speak of him as Narroondarie. He was a sacred man and, like all Prophets and teachers and Philosophers, found that he was confronted by a great social problems of his race: how was he to overcome the vile nature of the human race? Spears, Nulla nulla, boomerangs, pointing sticks and bone witchcraft could not allay this cankerous disease. Now Narroondarie, as if inspired, instituted the custom of Nhung e umpie.

Now, Nhung e umpie is a portion of the navel cord at birth from mother and child. Now, the gut or intestine is treated in a way that preserves it, for it is kept for a considerable time. It is then placed within a roll of Emu feathers and then wound round with fibre from the bark of the tree or mallee. This makes it safe and transferable from one hunting ground to another, and when it is sent on its long mission as a bond of friendship. Now, it is only the privilege of a certain female member of the tribe who is selected to give the gut; she must be the daughter of a mother who also was selected for a navel gut. These mothers must come from a direct line of noble womanhood, of good pure moral character. She submits the gut to a Mooncumbulli; that is, the Philosopher of the tribe, and it remains in his possession until he sees fit or thinks it proper to present it to a tribe. But supposing that there should be a break in the line of these women, then the woman who is the next of kin on the mother's side takes up this great and important position. This custom among the women is a coveted one, each girl when they are educated to become good women strive for this position. No one knows that from some one of themselves a selection will be made.

At this stage, I would like to call your attention to the Christian faith: in one of the Gospels [Luke, Chapter 1, Verse 42] you will find these words: 'Blessed art thou among women and blessed is the fruit of thy womb'. Also in Verse 46, Mary said: 'My soul doth magnify the Lord,' and in Verse 47: 'And my spirit hath rejoiced in God my Saviour,' and in Verse 48: 'For he hath regarded the low estate of his hand maiden: for, behold from henceforth all generations shall call me blessed.'

Now, this gut or part of the intestine of mother and child has a great significance to us. We look upon it as coming from within a part of a woman where dwells all good wishes of pity and sympathy. There are two parts embodied in this one gut. First, that of the well-trained moral of perfect womanhood which is recognised with a great deal of reverence. Secondly, there is that portion of the childish innocence and purity which offers itself for a great development of life: to prove in itself as a challenge its capability to develop itself and to prove the inheritance of a mother's quality. Thirdly, the navel cord is symbolic of a string that binds the peculiarities of mother to child. As a mother and child are linked to each other before birth, so the Nhung e umpie must be linked as mother and child. The navel cord is a physical reality, so Nhung e umpie should be so: true love, true fellowship, true pity. Let this symbol so bind you. Now we look upon the navel cord with reverence, just as there is Christian reverence towards the house of God, its fount and Altar and Sacrament. It is an all-powerful custom that can bind any two tribes to a bond of good fellowship and brotherhood. Distance makes no difference; wherever it is conveyed and is submitted to a tribe, it is accepted with honour. It is a law in itself.

The Pondi (Murray cod) totem tribe and the Pummerrie (cat fish) totem tribe are continually at war, one with the other. Then another tribe—the Thookerri—steps in, not to take any part in battle or to decide with either. But being of a peaceful nature, they are desirous of settling the dispute in a satisfactory manner that will be advantageous to both.

The Thookerri totem tribe perhaps will approach the Pondi Tribe and say: 'Why do you continue fighting the Pummerrie tribe? Don't you think it better to become friends?'

The Pondi will reply: 'I will not cease until my tribe shall conquer and wipe out the Pummerrie.'

Then the Thookerri goes to the Pummerrie and pleads with him, but he is adamant. So the Thookerri goes home and summons the elders of two or more tribes who are of a peaceful nature and they will hold a conference so that someone shall go to either tribe, the Pondi or Pummerrie. Perhaps he has decided to go and make his home with the Pondi, and perhaps within a month or two months they are expecting one of the wives of the Pondi totem tribe to give birth. And through some means, when the child is born, then he procures the navel gut and gives it to the Mooncumbulli and advises him to send it hastily through the Preeg ghee to the Pummerrie tribe.

Panp Parl Lowa: Spirit of Help among the Aborigines

There are traditional customs of my race that have come down the ages from generation to generation for thousands of years until they have become hereditary. Several stand out more prominently than others. The first is: 'Panp parl lowa', which may be literally translated as 'Do unto others as you would that they should do unto you.' I feel safe in stating that this golden rule is taught by all people, irrespective of colour, creed, or religion, primitive or civilised.

So in my race that rule exists. It is the foundation of our social and religious life. It is upon the foundation of this law that our educational system is built. It consists of various degrees. First, the mind is trained to control pain through concentration, and to master appetite, human desires, and fear. When the boys and girls have passed through these initiations, they are declared to be men and women, and they are then expected to take upon themselves responsibilities of manhood and womanhood. They must think of their duty to their tribe and to the whole of the race belonging to other tribes. They fulfil this rule not by work in teaching, not in writing on rock or tree, but by deed.

The Chase

At Pursechoul (this is a call of daylight), each young man goes forth, some with a Yundi (a plain spear without a barb, nine feet long and two and a half in diameter) and a Yarnabarr (a small weapon for killing animals), others with a Pint (a fishing spear twelve feet long and two inches in diameter at one end and with two prongs made of hardened stick) and a reed Kykie (a spear made from the reed that grows on the banks of the rivers, lakes, and lagoons, with a wooden point made from the oak, fixed on a reed of wood in diameter not more than half an inch and five to six feet in length).

The one with the Yundi wends his way into the bush stealthily in a crouching position, passing from shrub, keenly watching for any passing object. A swish, then like a bolt from the sky, the Yundi is sent on its errand like a flash and completes its mission; a Wallaby lies dying with the warm blood trickling from a vital spot. The man goes on until he has captured three or four. Those in their canoes return with their spoils of Murray Cod, Murray Bream, Cat Fish, and Turtles. All the Kangaroos, Wallabies, Fish, and Duck [are] passed [by] their mundi. The elder of the tribe comes and the food is distributed to the members of the tribe. After everyone is supplied, the hunter receives his portion, which may consist of the head of a Kangaroo, the head of a Cod, or the head and neck of a Swan, and so forth. The hunter receives these trifles without a murmur, satisfied that he is fulfilling the will of the Great Spirit, the Source of Good Deeds.

Duty to the Old

In like manner, the wives of the young men take upon themselves the responsibility of making the lives of the old and infirm, the widows and orphans of their tribes, happy and comfortable. They supply the vegetables and food. All animal foods are taken as food in the early hour of the morning and late in the evening. Vegetables are taken at intervals from eleven midday to four o'clock in the afternoon.

The young men and their wives continue in this good work until they become old and infirm, then those who in the meantime are being educated take [up] the responsibility. This goes on for generation after generation, each living for the other, the strong caring for the weak.

No person or tribe will ever attempt to have more worldly possessions than the other. Perhaps the hunting-ground of one tribe might be a lagoon, and the food consisting chiefly of fish and wild fowl, and a neighbouring tribe's may be the bush, the food consisting of the flesh of animals, in which case they would barter or exchange fish and wild birds for animal and herb food, gum and wild honey.

No Trespassing

No one of either tribe would trespass upon the hunting-ground of the other. To do so would mean death, it being a capital offence to take food from another tribe's hunting-ground. There are occasions when one tribe will ask another, or be invited by another to spend two or three months to enjoy their hospitality, and the visiting tribe when it returns home will invite the other. Thus there always exists a spirit of friendship.

There are, however, many instances where the Chief of a tribe becomes dissatisfied with his hunting-ground and becomes a menace to surrounding tribes, which will combine forces and drive the offender right out of the country, and the defeated tribe gradually becomes absorbed into other tribes and ceases to exist.

Sport

The spirit of sport is universal you will witness it among all nationalities and colour and language, and in all climes. There are many different forms of sport. The English-speaking race have their schoolboys and girls, youths and maidens, with their cricket outfits, their tennis balls and racquets, lacrosse, golf, football, rowing, and yachting. Each one in company contesting one with the other, each displaying their strength and skills to win prizes and gain the approval of the onlooker.

Wrestling and running, I suppose, are among the most ancient of sports. These two forms of sport can be traced right back to the Romans. Now, it may be interesting to know that wrestling or running, a race between two or more persons, was a common everyday scene witnessed among my people, especially among the boys and young men. There was another form of sport, and that was the throwing of either a spear, Nulla nulla or boomerang, to a certain distance to demonstrate their proficiency.

Now, let me endeavour to explain the form of wrestling among the Aborigines. The idea was not to link or grip their opponents in a way to overpower him or to make him helpless to move. Not so much of the strength was displayed, but skill and agility in grappling with the opponent, to throw him to the ground clear without him holding you. First, there are three persons selected from the Emu totem tribe, another three from the Pelican totem tribe.

A clear ground, free from shrubs or rocks, must be a soft sandy spot. Before the contestants arrive, the members of the respective tribes congregate to witness and to barrack for either side. Now the boys or young men arrive, their bodies may or may not be smeared with oil and red ochre. Presently a person steps forward, he holds in his hand a boomerang and Rarrabarr.

He turns to the contestants, addressing them: 'Now then, boys, you are called upon this day to uphold the honour of your tribe. One of you may win or take the coveted prize.'

And he holds before them a new[ly] made boomerang and a Rarrabarr (a weapon made from a certain kind of mallee, partly from the stem and root). This is a kind of weapon much sought after by the boys and young men, it is principally used in the hunting of the Kangaroo, Wallaby, Emu and Wombat when these animals are fleeing from the hunter. These weapons, the boomerang and Rarrabarr, are placed into the ground like you would the cricket stumps. The referee then calls to the boy who will defend these weapons. Perhaps the Pelican tribe steps forward. Those who come to witness this scene shout: 'Kay hey!'

Now the Pelican boys stand in front of the boomerang and Rarrabarr, facing the Emu boys, who stand ten to twenty yards away. Then after a while, the referee calls to the Emu boy: 'Moor ruck all (Take the weapon from the Pelican boy).'

And one of the Emu boys walks forward to take the weapon and at half the distance he is met by a Pelican totem boy, who grapples with him to prevent him coming any further. Supposing the Emu boy throws the Pelican boy to the ground, he rushes forward and he is met by number two Pelican boy, and he serves the second boy the same by throwing him upon his back and he almost reaches the coveted prize but he is met by number three Pelican boy. And now the tug of war begins. The Pelican boy strains every muscle of the body to defend the prize as well as the honour of his tribe and both fall to the ground and up they rise. The Emu boy getting is nearer and nearer; he reaches out one hand to take hold of the Rarrabarr but fails and he gives up further attempts to capture the prize and he returns to his fellows with a feeling of defeat. Number two Emu boy makes the attempt, but he may not have the strength or skill because he is the younger of the three.

Now comes the third Emu boy; instead of walking he runs and perhaps knocks the first Pelican boy down, and meets the second boy and throws him to the ground. And now he grapples with the third

Pelican boy and throws him to the ground and he takes the Rarrabarr and returns to his two other companions amidst the cheering, feeling a proud boy.

Now they are given a rest, perhaps an hour or more. The referee takes the boomerang and places it on the side of the Emu Totem boys. And, facing the Pelican totem boys, says in a loud tone so all those present may hear: 'Moor ruck all (Take the weapon from the Emu totem boys).'

A Pelican boy goes forward and is met halfway by an Emu boy, they begin wrestling, and perhaps the Emu boy in some way throws him upon his shoulder and carries him to his companions. The Pelican boy is defeated easily and it comes to the third Pelican boy to arrest the prizes but he fails. Then the barrackers of the Emu tribe become excited just as the winner in a football match begins shouting with joy, because the Emu totem boys have won the prizes—the boomerang and Rarrabarr. The Pelican boys in their defeat take it in good spirit and will wave their hands to the Emu totem boys as a sign of friendship, expressing a desire to meet them in future in a similar challenge.

Their foot racing is something similar to the European running. There is no method of training competition. Then there is the throwing of spears. First, there is the selection of boys or young men. This time the Dingo totem boy and the Wombat totem boy meet in a challenge to test their strength and skill to throw their spears for distance; the spears are made of reed that grows on banks of the Murray or Lake Alexandrina and Albert. The reed is three feet long, little more than three-eighth inch in diameter, with a pointed stick fixed into one end about another three feet, which makes the spear six feet long, and a woomera stick. The Dingo totem boy outclasses the Wombat totem boy in distance. Now the Wombat totem boy challenges him at target throwing, in which the Wombat boy excels, and wins the prize, which may be a newly constructed shield.

Now there is one game that is played by my race and it is a game any one not acquainted with would think there existed a spirit of hatred. But it is only a friendly game in which they enter without signs of any friendship. Let us imagine a large Wail lar roo mundi (a large camping ground) where half a dozen tribes represented have assembled. They are just sitting around in groups enjoying their breakfast.

Presently, without warning, a person appears on a hilltop not more than three hundred yards away. He shouts so loud that the whole tribe hears every word uttered and all attention and eyes are turned towards him. Then he says: 'Whong kun peen jull Kropung (Climbed an Emu to the top of the hill belonging to the Kropinyeri tribe).' (Kropung is the name of the locality of a tribe which are called after the place. Just as the tribe's name rendering Jesus of Bethlehem is the Bethlemite so Kropung is the Kropinyeri.)

Again the challenge is shouted: 'Whong kun peen jull!' and he has in his hand a bunch of Emu feathers. Waving them about his head, he dances around and, imitating the Emu in flight, dodges the spear, and shouts once more:

'Whong kun peen jull!' and suddenly leaps into the air. The Kropinyeri cannot bear this challenge much longer, they rise to their feet and give chase. The man who gave the challenge runs towards his tribe. Just as the Kropinyeri are about to grab him, everyone of the whole six tribes stand to their feet to witness the struggle that shall take place. The Kropinyeri are determined to take from him the bunch of Emu feathers. The tribe that sent the challenger forms a ring around him, joining hands, and the man with the Emu feathers is in the centre. Now, there may be a hundred or two hundred men the Kropinyeri must pass before they arrive to him. The Kropinyeri are pressing their way in until they come to the man with the Emu feathers, and they wrestle with him and take the feathers from him; this may take a whole day to accomplish. The Kropinyeri are looked upon as the heroes of the whole camp.

In another game, Koone, thirty or more boys will stand in a row extending seventy or eighty yards and two boys at the end stand in a parallel line forty yards away. They have in their hands a weapon made like a cross, or two sticks nine inches long, three in width and half an inch thick. And the first boy that has it throws it to his companion who stands seventy to eighty yards away and it spins along the ground; the boys who stand in a row have spears or boomerangs or Rarrabarr, just weapons that each boy fancies. With their weapons each tries to stop its motion. Or, in other words, that cross weapon thrown like a hoop is supposed to be wallaby or Kangaroo; this sport is to teach the boys to become hunters when the game is running away.

Another game that is popular among my race is Pul jung kgee (ball). They are picked men, young men or old men fifty years of age, about six men representing perhaps the Water Rat totem tribe and the other six representing the Eagle Hawk tribe. An Eagle Hawk tribe will stand beside the Water Rat tribe just like they do in football. Presently, the Water Rat tribe throws the ball to his companion, then the Eagle Hawk will try to catch it. Perhaps he does and he throws it to his companion and perhaps his companion catches it, and they try to keep the ball between themselves, catching and throwing and dodging the Water Rat. And this is kept up indefinitely until one party, the Eagle Hawk, tires, or perhaps they will keep going until the sunset and both agree to abandon the game until the following morning. And they begin the game, and continue until some one of another tribe, perhaps the Ibis totem tribe, steps in as referee and declares it a draw.

Just as the modern hunter with his gun finds more exciting sport with his gun in shooting the bird when on the wing, or when the rabbit or other animals are running, then there is another great sport, the boomerang throwing. This is the game that men of fifty years as well as young men and boys will take part in.

First, the Turtle totem tribe will send a challenge to all the surrounding tribes for three or four hundred miles. On a calm clear day a smoke signal is sent up and a telepathic message is sent that the Turtle totem tribe has made a number of boomerangs that have no equal. And it is anxious to meet all tribes that are willing to accept its challenge. Will they come to Moor ang eng on the bank of Lake Albert? This is plain country, away from trees or shrubs. Now each tribe begins to make and test their boomerangs—it is a busy fortnight. Each tribe comes out onto the ground equipped, painted in all kinds of fashion, their boomerangs carved in various designs to represent each tribe.

The Turtle is first to demonstrate their boomerang, perhaps they are made to circle around the performer or thrower three times before hovering about his head and descending to the earth at his feet, or within a circle of twelve feet. Then the Goanna totem tribe will next enter the ring to accept the challenge. He throws his boomerang and it goes straight from the thrower about seventy yards, and will gradually work itself around and pass across the line about forty yards, travelling in a spiral towards the performer. Next time it passes the line, it comes within twenty yards and comes nearer until it hovers about the Goanna totem Man and spins until its momentum is exhausted. It touches the earth perhaps inside the circle about two feet.

The Story of the Mungingee

Mungingee is the Australian Aboriginal name for the cluster of stars known to most people as the Pleiades. It is the belief of the Australian native, as it was of the Ancient Greek, that certain legendary women are responsible for the lustre of these stars. The usual native name for a girl between the ages of eight and fourteen years is pummi (plural, pummar). Yartooka are the girls who have reached the age of adolescence. It is to certain of the Yartooka of olden times that the Australian Aboriginal owes the beauty of the Mungingee. These names originate from the Ngarrindjeri tribe which inhabits the lower Murray and the Coorong, and the Ruminyeri tribes of Cape Jarvis, South Australia.

According to legend it was the Yartooka who, in the early days of my race, perceived the necessity for the submission of the body to the mind—a submission that would mean the restraint of physical appetite and of the effects of pain and fear. They saw that without this there could be no racial advance. Accordingly they presented themselves to the Elders of the tribe for trial by ordeal. The Elders explained to the Yartooka that the test was a difficult one, but the girls were firm in their resolve.

So every morning for three years, in a place apart from their brothers and sisters, the Elders, to teach them moderation, gave them a small portion of the usual food, consisting perhaps of a piece of fish, or flesh of the emu, kangaroo, or wombat. This they received twice a day at the hour of sunrise and at the hour of sunset. At the end of the third year they were taken for a long journey through the dense bush and across the plains and rivers, travelling through the heat of the day, ever onward, the thorns scratching their flesh, and often almost fainting from fatigue. After a week had passed thus, the Elders called the Yartooka before them and enquired whether they thought they were better able to control the appetite.

To this the Yartooka replied, 'Our minds are made up. We will control the appetite.'

The Elders then said: 'You are asked to fast for three days, and during this fasting we will travel for three days.'

So the Yartooka set out with the Elders on the journey, and the way was long and difficult and they were weak from the lack of food. The blazing sun seemed to them more ruthless and the way more rough and thorny; but in their determination to conquer they kept on their way undaunted.

On the evening of the third day they arrived at the appointed camping-ground. The Elders prepared the food for the following day. On the fourth morning they were given a yonguljee (flint knife), and instructed to cut from the kangaroo or emu the amount of food they required. How tempting was the smell of the roasted flesh to the Yartooka, who had travelled unceasingly for three days without breaking their fast. The craving was strong to cut a generous portion and satisfy the craving for food. Each cut herself the ordinary portion, and the Elders cheered the girls and praised them.

'Kay hey,' they said, 'you have proved yourselves so far, but there are other appetites and it is for you to control them as you have controlled that of hunger.'

And they replied: 'We are ready to undergo any tests you please. Our minds are made up to conquer.'

They then submitted themselves to various tests in order for further control of the appetites, each test more difficult than the last, and in every case they were triumphant.

Then the Elders told them that it was necessary to overcome pain, and again they submitted themselves to the guidance of the wise men, who decided the form of operation they should undergo. In the presence of the other girls and boys they took the Yartooka away to a selected spot, where all sacred ceremonies are performed, and they ordered them to lie upon the ground, while they took a Mardpung (stone axe) and a pointed stick about eight or nine inches long. They told the Yartooka one by one to open their mouths, and the point of the stick was placed upon a tooth of each, and the Elders raised the axe and brought it down upon the tooth, breaking it off and leaving the nerves quivering and exposed. The girls then rose from the ground and sat awaiting the further commands of the Elders.

They were asked whether they felt the pain, to which they replied: 'Yes we felt the pain.'

Then the Elders said: 'Are you willing to have another tooth knocked out?'

And the girls replied: 'Yes, our minds are made up. We are going to control pain.'

And again the Elders asked at the conclusion of this test: 'Are you willing to undergo more severe testing?'

And the Yartooka replied as before: 'Yes, our minds are made up. We will control pain.'

They were then led to another camping-ground and commanded to stand in a row and an Elder of the tribe approached each with a flint knife. He stood before the Yartooka for a while, and then drew the knife silently across the breast of each of the girls and the blood flowed. Another Elder then took the ashes of a particular wood and rubbed it into the wound. The effect of this was twofold; it intensified the pain and helped to heal the wound.

After a day or so, to allow the wounds to heal, the Elders again called the Yartooka before them and enquired whether they were still willing to submit themselves to further testing.

They replied: 'Yes, we are willing to go through any tests. Our minds are made up.'

The Elders then went along through the bush and selected another camping-ground for the girls. At bed-time they were led to the spot and told: 'It is time to retire to rest. This is your camping-ground.'

The girls then threw their Possum rugs on the ground, weary and eager for rest. The night was dark and moonless and very warm. They lay there for a little while, and presently they felt things crawling over their bodies. And they were afraid, but refused to give way to fear. Maybe each girl was afraid of what the others would think of her if she failed, and so each helped the others to be brave. Then they felt and discovered they were lying on a bed of ants. All through the night they lay there and the time seemed very long. These girls had journeyed far, fasting, and their poor bodies were still tender with half-healed wounds. In the morning they presented themselves to the Elders, smiling and showing no signs of the terrible night they had passed.

Still their journey continued, and they had to undergo further tests, such as the piercing of the nose and the wearing of a stick through it to keep the wound open. And they were bidden to lie on a bed of hot cinders. Before each fresh trial, they were asked if they were willing to undergo the test. Their reply never varied: 'Yes, we have made up our minds to conquer pain.'

Now the Elders were very pleased with the Yartooka, and very proud of their powers of endurance, but they realised that it was necessary for them to overcome fear as well as the appetites and pain, so they called them together and said: 'Yartooka, you have done very well and proved yourselves of a wonderful hardihood and endurance. The next stage is the control of fear. Do you wish to continue on the way?'

The Yartooka stood there in all their youth, with glowing eyes, and repeated the old formula: 'Yes, our minds are made up. We will conquer fear.'

On the fresh camping-grounds in the dark night, with the campfire gleaming on the trees and casting dark, gloomy shadows, the Elders told them tales about the Bunyip and the Muldarpie. The latter is a Spirit which assumes many shapes. It may come as a kangaroo or a wombat or a lizard or reptile. They were fearful stories of dreadful Beings and of ghosts, to which the Yartooka listened tremblingly. The more highly strung could scarcely refrain from crying out, and found themselves looking back over their shoulders and imagining that the dark shadows were the Bunyip or the Muldarpie, and other Spirits. For hours they listened until it was time for bed. After the Elders had made the sign of good-night, they told them that the place where they were camping was the burial place of their great-grandfathers. They lay down to sleep, resolved not to be afraid of any ghosts or spirits.

But the Elders crept round the camp making weird noises, so that the hair of the Yartooka rose and the blood ran cold. Besides these sounds, there were the usual bush noises, such as the howl of the dingo, the shriek of the owl, and the falling of decayed branches. But the little Yartooka were not to be turned from their purpose and lay there until the break of day. Then they rose and presented themselves to the Elders, showing no sign of their disturbed night, their faces placid and their eyes clear and shining. The Elders knew that they had conquered fear and their hearts were glad with pride. They sent out invitations to the adjoining tribes and there was great rejoicing, and many corroborees were held in honour of the girls.

But the Yartooka were not content that they had conquered the appetites and pain and fear. They desired that their sisters should do the same, so the leader of the girls stepped out from the group and said: 'Yartooka, we have passed through the testings our Elders have prescribed, and suffered much pain. Now it is the desire of the Great Spirit that you should go through the same testing. You must know that the selfish person is not happy, because he thinks only of himself. Happiness comes through thinking of others and forgetting self. Greed and pain and fear are caused by thinking too much of self, and so it is necessary to vanquish them. Will you not go and do as we have done?'

The Yartooka of the other tribes eagerly assented, so proud were they of the victory of their sisters.

Then the Great Spirit was so pleased with them that he sent a great Star Spirit, and the Yartooka were transferred to the heavens without death or further suffering, that they might shine there as a guide and symbol of their race.

On clear nights ever since, the Aborigines look into the skies and revere this wonderful constellation, the Mungingee, remembering what the Yartooka have done, always thinking of the story of how they were given their seats in the heavens.

The Voice of the Great Spirit

It is interesting to learn how all races of men have wrestled with the problem of good and evil. The Australian Aborigines have a greater and deeper sense of morality and religion than is generally known. From a very early age the mothers and the old men of the tribe instruct the children by means of tales and stories. This is one of the many stories that is handed down from generation to generation by my people.

In the beginning, the Great Spirit spoke directly everyday to his people. The tribes could not see the Great Spirit but they could hear his voice, and they assembled early every morning to hear him. Gradually, however, the tribes grew weary of listening to the Great Spirit and they said one to the other: 'Oh, I am tired of this listening to a voice I cannot see; so let us go and enjoy ourselves by making our own corroborees.'

The Great Spirit was grieved when he heard this, and as the tribes did not assemble to hear him but went and enjoyed themselves at the corroborees, the Great Spirit said: 'I must give the people a sign that they will understand.'

He sent his servant Narroondarie to call all the tribes together again once more. Narroondarie did so, saying: 'The Great Spirit will not speak again to you but he wishes to give you a sign.'

All the tribes came to the meeting. When every one was seated on the ground, Narroondarie asked them all to be very silent. Suddenly a terrific rending noise was heard. Now, Narroondarie had so placed all the tribes that the meeting was being held around a large gum tree. The tribes looked and saw this huge tree being slowly split open by some invisible force. Also, down out of the sky came an enormous Thalung (tongue), which disappeared into the middle of the gum tree, and the tree closed up again.

After this wonderful performance Narroondarie said to the tribes: 'You may go away now to your hunting and corroborees.'

Away went the tribes to enjoy themselves. After a long time some of them began to grow weary of pleasure and longed to hear again the Great Spirit. They asked Narroondarie if he would call upon the Great Spirit to speak to them again.

Narroondarie answered: 'No, the Great Spirit will never speak to you again.'

The tribes went to the sacred burial grounds to ask the dead to help them but the dead did not answer. Then they asked the great Naboolea (the same as the English Nebulae), who lives in the Milky Way, if he would help them but still there was no answer and the tribes at last cried aloud with sorrow and regret. They cut their bodies with sharp stones and painted themselves white. They began to fear that they would never get in touch again with the Great Spirit.

The tribes finally appealed to Wy young gurrie, the wise old black-fellow who lives in the South Cross. He told them to gather about the big gum tree again. When all were there, Wy young gurrie asked: 'Did you not see the Thalung go into this tree?'

'Yes,' answered the tribes.

'Well,' said Wy young gurrie, 'take that as a sign that the Thalung of the Great Spirit is in all things.'

Thus it is today that the Aborigines know that the Great Spirit is in all things and speaks through every form of Nature. Thalung speaks through the voice of the wind; he rides on the storm; he speaks out from the thunder. Thalung is everywhere, and manifests through the colour of the bush, the birds, the flowers, the fish, the streams; in fact, everything that the Aboriginal sees, hears, tastes, and feels—there is Thalung.

The Water Rat who Discovered the Secret of Fire and How it was Taken from Him by the Eagle Hawk

Among the Animals, Birds, and Reptiles that have made a name for themselves and their tribe are such names as those of the little Bat, with that wonderful boomerang which was invented by the Lizard; the Koala (Teddy Bear), the great astronomer, philosopher, discoverer, and navigator; the Pelican, the great manufacturer; and the Water Rat, the discoverer of fire for cooking and heating purposes. Now, before this wonderful discovery, all flesh and vegetable food was eaten raw and in cold climates during the winter season they suffered great misery. The little Dingos, Wombats, Kangaroos, and Bandicoots would always be crying and shivering, as their clothing was not sufficient to keep them warm.

One day a young Rat went seeking for a comfortable home spot for his wife, and his wife said to him: 'Nun kar wat pag ar rallin (Oh dear me, I had a most beautiful dream). You will remember the billabong where you used to come and visit me where those lovely water-lilies were blooming. I was sitting there on a log by the water thinking of our courting days, when presently out of the clear water came a dragon-fly, and, hurrying to a water-lily, sat upon it for a while, then hurried back to the spot from whence it came, hovering about the surface of the water. Presently a big clear bubble rose and floated towards the water-lily, and the dragon-fly followed. Presently a great many dragon-flies came and gently raised the big bubble from the water, carrying it carefully and placing it upon the water-lily. I sat gazing in wonderment at this strange sight, thinking, when like a flash a clear beam passed before my vision. It was the spirit of the water-lily dancing around it and leaping skyward. At that moment the bubble burst. Oh dear, what a wonderful sight! A beautiful baby Retculdie (Water Rat) was lying peacefully in the bosom of the water-lily.'

The young Retculdie sat seriously thinking for a while, but presently he rose and, kissing his wife, hurried away to that little spot and walked round the bank several times in search of a suitable place to build a home for his wife. He selected a place over the pond and began digging under the roots of a large gum tree until he came to an obstruction. It was the root of the tree. He was annoyed and, not wishing to abandon a place that meant so much to him and his wife, he began to use his teeth as an implement to cut a way through. Biting and gnawing his way into the root, suddenly he kindled a spark. Again and again this occurred. After completing his work, the home furnished with soft grass, he hastened to his wife and invited her to follow him.

They wended their way silently to their new home. She walked inside and, sitting down by her bedside, a feeling of rest and comfort crept over her. She quietly went to bed and fell asleep. When she awoke, her husband told her of his wonderful discovery and performed before her the ceremony of producing fire, the much-needed blessing. Then he hastened away and told his father, mother, brother, and sister and they spread the news to other members of the Retculdie tribe. They all came and saw and felt the energising heat that came from the fire, and the Retculdie tribe vowed that they would endeavour to keep the secret to themselves and not reveal it to the Tortoise, Water-fowl, Kangaroos, Dingos, or any other tribe.

So the Retculdie tribe lived in comfort in all weathers and in all climates. Now the Kangaroos, Wombats, Goannas, and Tortoises could see the light through the weed, but the Retculdie were too wise for the Turtles, who would crawl through the grass, sneaking towards the home of the Retculdie to find out what it was. But the Retculdie would see them coming and hide the fire. Then they asked the Hawk tribe to approach the Eagle Hawk to wrest the secret from the Retculdie.

The Eagle Hawk consented, and on a sunny morning, when there was not a cloud to be seen, he began his mission. Up and up into the blue sky he soared until he appeared a mere speck, and still on and on beyond their vision. With telescopic eyes piercing the distance, scanning the river and every object, he saw the Retculdie rubbing the sticks and producing fire. Like a bolt from the sky, he sped on earthward, faster than an express train, with greater speed than an aeroplane, rending the air as he came with the noise of a mighty wind. All life was spellbound and even the Retculdie was paralysed. The Eagle Hawk swooped and, taking the Retculdie up in his mighty claw again, mounted in the sky, where he hovered for a while.

'Ask the Retculdie to give me your secret,' he said, 'or I will drop you to earth.'

The Retculdie preferred telling the secret to losing his life, and thus it was taken from his selfish tribe by the Eagle Hawk.

Whowie

The Whowie was the most dreadful animal in existence. It was a Being or Reptile like the Goanna, only much more or a great deal larger. Its length would be something about twenty feet. The funniest thing about this strange creature was that it possessed six legs, three on either side, something like the Goanna's legs, and it had a tail. It had such an enormous head like a frog's head. Now this animal was very treacherous and would attack anything that came in its way, and devour it. The people in those far-gone days would flee in terror from it, and it would take about thirty or sixty people to make a meal for it. It was not swift in its movements, but very slow. Sometimes it would come across a camping-ground when the people were fast asleep and without making a noise to show its presence, would swallow first one and then another, perhaps a mother and child together, and what it could not swallow it would take in his mouth to its den.

Now, the home of the Whowie was in the Riverina district, and it was about this locality that it lived and hunted. Its chief abode was on the bank of a river, a cave leading away from it for miles away. During the hot summer days, it would bask in the sunshine upon the bank of the river or among the sandhills. The sandhills were the result of the footprints of the Whowie; that is how they came to form in the Riverina district. Now, this dreadful animal was taking great toll on the people; the Itty itta (the Kangaroo Rat) were the greatest sufferers, so they held a meeting between themselves as to what step should be taken. And the Chief of the Itty itta said unto his fellow Beings: 'We are a very small race in stature, and we are gradually dwindling. There will be none of us left unless we clear out and take a journey into some distant country; to stay here means that we shall be all eaten up and none will be left to represent our race. So now I leave it to you all to decide what to do.'

So the Chief Itty itta sat down beside a log, waiting for his subjects to suggest a step to be taken. Then from among the assembly there arose an elder with long flowing beard, and he began to address the others of his race: 'Oh my children, I am far gone into years, and for me to think of taking a long journey would be out of the question. And it is not only that, but I have spent many, many happy days wandering up and down the Murray and in the surrounding country. Those were delightful days, plenty to eat, many mussels we gathered from the river, fishes were plentiful and so they are today. But we dare not go to the river side for fear of the Whowie, our great enemy. So I do not feel inclined to leave; let us think of some other means by which we shall overcome this great danger without a great loss to ourselves. We must endeavour to gain the assistance of three or more of the other tribes.'

So their Chief ordered that they should build many bonfires first thing after the rising of the sun. So they all retired that night, and whilst some were sleeping, others were on guard to give the warning cry should the Whowie appear in their camp. During the watching hours, one number of Itty itta would keep up for a time and that number would be released and go to sleep; this is how they kept guard whilst the family slept.

Now, after the sun rose, every Itty itta busied himself collecting wood and boughs and made many fires here, there, and everywhere. When the other surrounding tribes saw that there were many smoke signals, that was a sign that it was a message of distress and that it was also a call for help. There were smoking signals sent up all round—messages that all were willing and anxious to give whatever help was required. The messages also said that they would be there on the following morning, about the same time. So all the Itty itta set to work, hunted and captured as many fish as possible, and some gathered bags and bags of mussels; some were roasted upon the live coals, others baked in the oven holes dug into the earth. Oh, it was a very busy day among the Itty itta, making great preparations for the many tribes that would arrive in the morning, whilst some were away spying out the country to see the whereabouts of the Whowie, whether he was at large hunting food or basking in the sunshine. But that day he was nowhere to be seen, so some of the bolder Itty itta went away to the cave of the Whowie by the bank of the river and went quite close to the entrance of the cave for sign of footprints. And after a careful study they saw—or were convinced—that the footprints led into the cave. Now, it would take the Whowie a whole week before he came to the end of the cave, because it was such a long one and there were no other holes but this one.

Now, on the following morning, just at the time appointed, people came from all directions, marching with their spears, Nulla nulla, and some had their stone axes. Now the Animals, Birds, Reptiles, Kangaroos, Possums, Platypuses, Eagle Hawks, Crows, Magpies, Cockatoos, and every member of the feathered tribes, the Lizard and Reptile tribes, were represented in full force. When the spies returned to camp and told the others of the result of their scouting, that they felt sure that the Whowie had entered his home in the cave and would take a week to reach the terminus, they spent the day and night in entertaining themselves with dancing and corroborees, feeling safe.

This rejoicing lasted for a day and a night, and after that they set about to attack their great enemy, the Whowie. Now everybody set about gathering sticks and making them in small bundles, just large enough to carry into the cave, because they would have to carry them up into the cave a long way. And the people of various tribes began in earnest, beginning from the early hours of the morning till late in the evening. This was kept up until they thought that the Whowie would have reached the end of the cave, then they had stacked half of the length of the hole of the cave, and they stacked a great heap at the entrance and set fire to it, and the wood began to burn away into the cave and caused a great trail of smoke that filled the cave, which by now had made it rather uncomfortable for the Whowie, who began to force his way out, battling with the heat and smoke. And he began to roar like an angry beast, as if in deadly combat with some mighty foe.

This struggling lasted for six days and on the seventh the Whowie came out of the entrance, blinded and dazed in a stupor. And when he got free or right out of the hole, the Animals, Birds, and Reptiles began to attack him in earnest with spears, Nulla nulla, and stone axes, beating him all over the body, causing great wounds, with blood flowing freely; and with much beating and bleeding he fell to the ground, dying.

And now when the gentle night winds are blowing to the cave you will hear as it were the sighing of the Whowie. And when the little Aboriginal girls and boys are naughty and disobedient, mother will say: 'Look out, the Whowie is listening,' and the children will crouch up against their mother's bosom for safety, looking round with staring eyes expecting to see that Dread Dragon, the Whowie of the Riverina.

Why All the Animals Peck at the Selfish Owl: The Coming of the Light

My race, the Aborigines of Australia, has a vast tradition of legends, myths, and folklore stories. We delight in telling stories to the younger members of the tribe. These stories and traditions have been handed down orally for thousands of years. In fact, all tribal laws and customs are, first of all, told to the children of the tribe in the form of stories. Just as the white Australian mother first instructs her children by nursery stories, etc.

A legend I call 'The Coming of the Light' is a very old and popular one among my people. Of course, it must be understood that the mothers or the old men of the tribe, in telling these stories, drag them out to a great length, putting in every detail, with much gesture and acting. The story goes thus.

Long, long ago, before there was human life, there was only Animal life. There was the Bird tribe, the Animal tribe, and the Reptile tribe. Once a year, in the springtime, all these different tribes met and held a great festival called a 'Munmundi'.

The Bird tribe were great talkers. The Cockatoos cried: 'Come and let us prepare ourselves for this great Munmundi.'

So they retired into the bush and decorated themselves with leaves and bushes. When they came out again, they began to dance in their decorations before the Kangaroos, the Carpet Snake, the Goanna, and all the others of the Reptile and Animal tribes.

The Animal and Reptile tribes cheered and praised the feathered tribe's dancing. This admiration and praise made the feathered tribe very conceited. The Cockatoo, who was always a very cheeky fellow, went to the Eagle Hawk, Chief of the feathered tribe, and said: 'Oh Father Eagle Hawk, are not we feathered tribe, greater than the Kangaroo and Carpet Snake, the Goanna, and all the tribes?'

The Eagle Hawk answered: 'Oh my son Cockatoo, of course you are superior to all the other tribes.'

Now, the other tribes overheard all this, and it made them very angry. So after much wrangling, the feathered tribe challenged the other tribes to fight, and to prove who was the superior.

But there was one family, the Bat tribe, that stood alone and would not take any part in the dispute, nor would it consent to join forces with either party in battle. Now, the Chief of the Bat tribe called his family and told them that they were to stand by prepared for battle, and when they saw that one of the combatants was winning they must join in to decide the battle.

And how the battle raged. The Animals and Birds were throwing their spears and waddies, others were hand-to-hand fighting with Nulla nulla. Just when the battle was raging fiercely, it seemed as if the Bird tribe would win. They were pressing the Animal tribe so much that the Kangaroo and his army were driven back. At this moment the Bat shouted to his family: 'Come join the Eagle Hawk and his tribe. Onward, slay the Kangaroo and his army!'

So the Bat family stood side-by-side with the Cockatoo, Koo ka ka burra, Crow and Magpie. The Bats were experts in the use of the boomerangs, they threw their weapons so fast that the boomerangs about the armies resembled a huge cloud. But presently the Kangaroo called to his army and, speaking words of encouragement, stood waiting for the approach of the enemy. Now, when the Animals saw their Chief and General facing the foe, they fought with greater courage and drove the Bird tribe back.

Now the Bat saw that he had made a blunder, and called to his family: 'Retire from the ranks of the Bird tribe and quickly join the Animal tribe,' so the Bat joined the Animal tribe fighting against the Birds. Now the armies of the Animal and Bird tribes were swinging like a pendulum and the Kangaroo and Emu were in mortal combat.

'Oh Emu, why should we fight, it causes so much bloodshed, pain, misery and death.' The Kangaroo, extending his hands, said: 'Come let us shake hands.'

So the Emu clasped the hands of the Kangaroo in friendship and said: 'Let us be friends.'

When the Animal and Bird tribes saw them shaking hands, the Cockatoos were shaking hands with the Dingos and the Koo ka ka burras were shaking hands with the Wombats, and there was a general shaking of hands among the Animal, Bird, and Reptile tribes which resulted in friendship. But the little Bat tribe did not know what to do, as they had been false to both parties. So the Bat tribe had to go and live with the wicked Owls, who always lived away by themselves and who delighted in the dark.

Now the Sun, the great ruler of all, saw this fighting and killing among the Animals. So the Sun became very angry and hid his face; and all the earth became dark. Now the Animals, Birds, and Reptiles were grouping in the darkness and life became a burden.

The Emu came to the Kangaroo and said: 'Oh Kangaroo, what shall we do? The children are unable to enjoy themselves and we find it difficult to provide food and clothing.'

The Kangaroo thought awhile; presently an idea came to him. He said to the Emu: 'Build bonfires, here, there and everywhere.'

So the Emu went and asked the Crows, Pheasants, Magpies, and Cockatoos to assist in bringing in a supply of wood to keep the fire burning. Now they were burning and burning the wood until there was a shortage of fuel. Once the Emu approached the Kangaroo with the seriousness of the position, again the Kangaroo thought and thought.

He quietly said to the Emu: 'Summon the whole tribe and let them meet me in conference and we shall discuss the problem of light.'

So the Emu went around to each camp and invited them to this meeting, so all the Animal, Bird, and Reptile tribes came and sat in conference to find some means of discovering a way of providing light or bringing back the sunlight. There was no one able to solve the problem. Now there was a little Lizard sitting beside the Kangaroo, and he was thinking hard.

Presently he addressed the Kangaroo: 'Oh Kangaroo, the Owl and Bat know how to give us light. I have heard a whisper that they are able to bring back the sunlight.'

So the Kangaroo said to the little Lizard: 'Will you go along and ask the Chief of the Owls and Bats to attend this meeting? I would like them to.'

The little Lizard went on his errand in search of the Owl and Bat and he found them, and he said: 'Oh Owl and Bat, the Kangaroo wishes that you should come along and attend a meeting; will you come?'

'Oh yes,' said the Owl and Bat, 'we are coming, we are coming.'

The little Lizard hastened back filled with joy that he was able to return to the Kangaroo with the great news; that he was able to procure the consent of the Owl and Bat.

When they arrived, the Kangaroo said: 'Owl and Bat, will you give us the light or bring to us the sunlight?'

'Oh,' said the Owl, 'I cannot do that because I love the darkness and my children delight in it.'

Then the Curlew called: 'Oh Uncle, you would not refuse me, thy nephew. Oh, for the sake of my children and the children of other tribes, give us the light.'

Once more the Owl refused: 'I will not.'

Then there arose a great cry among the Animals, Birds, and Reptiles: 'Oh, give us the light. Oh, give us light.'

The cry was so pitiful that it smote the hardened conscience of the Bat and all the past wrongs that he did came before his vision, so he said within himself: 'Now I can atone for what I have done.'

So he shouted: 'I will give you the light, I will give you the light!'

So the Animals, Birds, and Reptiles ceased crying. Then the Bat asked: 'Has anyone a boomerang?' and the same Lizard that brought the Owl and Bat to the meeting answered: 'I have a boomerang, I will give it to you.'

So the Lizard gave the boomerang to the Bat. Once more the Bat spoke to the assembled crowd: 'I feel the great cost that I am making, I loved the darkness and my children delight to romp and skip and play in one continual darkness. But I know that when I make this sacrifice I shall have their approval.'

Then he took the boomerang and with a mighty force hurled it towards the north, and it travelled away north and came back from the south. Again the boomerang was sent on a mission towards the west; it travelled around the earth and came back from the east, and just as the Bat was about to throw the boomerang the Koo ka kee said: 'Wait a moment Bat, we do not want an exhibition of boomerang throwing, we require the light.'

'Yes, I know that you are all anxious to have the sunlight. But I am dividing that great darkness; I am going to give you light and I shall retain unto myself the darkness.'

And again with greater force he hurled the boomerang towards the east. It travelled around the earth and came back from the east and was hovering about his head. Then the Bat shouted: 'Look towards the east the light is coming, the light is coming!'

The Bird tribe looked and they became so excited they began chattering and twittering and whistling. At the approach of dawn, still the Bat shouted: 'The light is coming, the light coming!'

Presently, the boomerang touched the earth and the Sun arose. Oh, what a joy. The Kangaroo yelped with delight, the Dingos scrambled and turned somersaults and the Koo ka burras laughed with gladness. And the Bat returned to his home in the cave, waiting till the sun sank in the western sky. So now when the Owl ventures out into the daylight, all the feathered tribes will fly around seeking an opportunity to peck at him because he was so selfish in refusing to give them the sunlight. But if the Bat comes out at sunset, or on a dull evening before sunset, no Bird will ever attempt to molest him because he was willing to make amends for the wrongs he did by his act of kindness in bringing once more the glorious sunlight which all creation is so much depending on for life and energy.

As for the little messenger the Lizard, he still loves to sit and gaze at the Sun, and if you look closely at his neck you will see he still has there the Boomerang that the Kangaroo gave him.

Why Manparrie (Frogs) Jump into the Water

The powers of observation in the Australian Aboriginal are very keen. The habits and characteristics of all the animals and birds are watched closely, and then in time that information is woven into the legends of my race.

My people delight to give a reason for everything they observe, as well as to draw a moral lesson from it all. The moral lesson that we try to teach in the legend of the frogs (Lower Murray, Lake Alexandrina and Narrinyeri tribes) is that man is incomplete apart from woman, and that if the males try to live alone, they fail and succumb to every fear. The overcoming of fear is the strongest feature in the training and culture of my race. This is the legend of the frogs.

Once, all the male Manparrie (Frogs) became discontented and left their wives and sisters. Each male Manparrie went and lived by himself.

One night while the male Frogs were cooking their evening meal, each of them had the same experience. Each felt a Presence come up from the south. They could not see this Presence; they could only feel it. Presently a voice asked for some food. The Frogs looked, but could not see anyone.

'Yes,' said the Frogs, 'we will give you something to eat; but who are you? We cannot see you.'

'Oh, never mind,' said the Voice, 'later on you will see me. I am tired; I have been travelling all over the world. Give me something to eat.'

Each Frog gave the Voice some fish to eat. The Frogs could see the fish being moved about and disappearing, but could not see who was eating it. After the meal was over the Voice said: 'I am tired; may I sleep here tonight?'

'Oh yes,' said the Frogs.

In a very few minutes the Frogs could hear the Voice snoring. The Frogs, however, could not sleep. They jumped up and ran about, crying: 'Who are you? Let us see you, and let us feel you.'

The Voice answered: 'You will see me coming across the plain tomorrow.'

In the morning, the Voice was up before the Frogs and before the Frogs could ask any questions, they could hear the Voice just moving away from the camp very gently and quietly.

Next evening each Frog stood on a high place near his camp, watching for the Voice to return, and all he could see was a small whirlwind (a willy-willy) coming across the plain. It came over the plain and circled around the Frogs' camp.

A Voice said to the Frogs: 'Here I am again.'

'But,' said the frogs, 'we cannot see you; we want to see you with our eyes.'

'Well, then,' answered the Voice, 'You will see me again tomorrow night.'

Now, all the frogs lived by the river-side close to the water. When the next evening came, each Frog jumped up to the top of a big log to wait for the coming of the Voice. They looked across the plain and saw a huge willy-willy coming. It began to blow fiercely and a hurricane struck the camp. The storm blew around the camp, big gum trees swaying under its mighty force. Presently there was a terrific blast of wind and a Voice began: 'I am . . .'

But the Frogs had become so afraid that they did not wait for any more and dived into the river, and kept under the water until the storm had passed.

Aboriginal elders tell this to their children and they point out to them that the frogs jump into the water at the slightest sound of wind.

'Look, look,' they say, 'how afraid they became from living by themselves. And that is how you will become if you ever desert your tribe.'

Witchcraft

As a convenience, I shall adopt the term 'Medicine Man', who is a person that performs magic. There are men in every tribe who profess to possess supernatural powers and they are looked upon as doctors because they are able to diagnose a disease—the cause and effect—and are able to prescribe a herb or herbs for the complaint.

Now, at this stage I would like to guard against a mistake that may easily occur. That is, a Medicine Man is not always a doctor, Rain-Maker, spiritualist, or magician.

A Rain-Maker, or a man who professes to make rain through some incantation, causes a change in the weather. For instance, it may be a clear morning without a cloud in the sky or a visible sign of rain to the ordinary person. This individual is not a Medicine Man; he is one who may have released the elements. Lightning, thunder, rain, and wind are totems, or they are the totems of a tribe to which he belongs. One or more members of the tribe make a special study of the weather and they make good meteorologists. They are able, by observation, to predict a coming change.

Supposing a person of his tribe caused him an annoyance. He would await the opportunity and when he noted a coming thunderstorm that would arrive within three hours, he would begin his incantation and his wife would advise all present that they should warn their children that a storm was coming. The little children look about but see no sign of it. But after a while, black clouds appear in the distance and a flash of lightning, then a thunder peal. The children hasten to their Mia mia and the storm is all about them. They are terrified.

The Rain-Maker leaps out of his Mia mia, chanting his song, calling to the lightning, thunder, rain, and wind spirits, repeating the words: 'Thou hast heard my call, thy coming to my call convinces the people that thou art my friend and servant and come at my bidding.'

The children and youths and maidens are astounded at what they consider a wonderful performance, and an event like this is instilled into the minds of the young people, and they become easy victims and grow with such convictions. So members of the tribe are very careful indeed not to offend him but endeavour to please him by ministering to his wants, such as food and furs of animals for clothing. This profession belongs to this particular family and not to the tribe. Whilst these persons may be weather prophets, they may know nothing of the pointing bone, not in the using of it, only that they believe in its deadly effect, so that a Rain-Maker is neither a magician, nor a doctor, or not necessarily a magician, or a doctor.

A Medicine Man is one who is able to use the Pointing Stick, or bone, or pebble and the wirrie, the crystal, the Thumie, or the Nugoongie, which is fragments of human hair and fragments of flesh or pieces of bone, which are generally the remains of someone's meal, or may belong to a member of his tribe or that of another tribe or tribes. They take these bits of bone and flesh and bind them to a stick that is about four inches long and about the thickness of an ordinary lead pencil, gradually tapering from one end to a sharp point. At the blunt end the flesh and bone are bound by kangaroo sinews. Then the gum of the pine tree is placed over the flesh and bone and placed away in some cold place. In most cases, these are taken away to some secluded spot and buried in the earth twelve to eighteen inches below the surface, though some choose to place them in the hollow of a rock or tree, until the service of the Nugoongie is required.

The Wirrie is another charm stick, similar to the Neil yeri; it differs only in that it is placed into the body of a dead person and allowed to remain until the body decomposes, after which it is taken from the body and wrapped in Emu feathers and Kangaroo or Wallaby skin. This is looked upon as the most dangerous weapon or instrument of death. It requires very careful handling, as a prick from the point of the Wirrie would cause blood poisoning.

Now, the person who makes a special study of the pointing stick or bone and the crystal, the Nugoongie (fragments of flesh and bone and human hair), and Wirrie has his knowledge confined to this subject alone and not to rain-making. He professes to point the bone or stick and cause it to enter a body and it is he who takes it, or extracts it, from the body, sometimes with the help of Puck nowie—a Spirit who lives in the sky and comes to his aid and operates on the patient when required. Sometimes he confines a period to the composition of a song to the Spirits of the departed ones and to hold communion with them as to some coming event. When the Medicine Man comes in touch with a Spirit, the performer tells us that the Spirit does not speak to him, but when granting a request they give the answer indirectly through some medium—perhaps a sound, a rap on a tree, the rustling of a bough, the breaking of a bough on a tree, and sometimes, if beside a river, the message comes by a splash of water, and these sounds the Medicine Man is able to interpret.

Now, a Mooncumbulli is looked upon as superior to a Rain-Maker and a doctor. His profession is supposed to be unlimited. Because he is well versed in all tricks of the Medicine Man, and his knowledge of weather and conditions of climate, he knows by his keen study of animal, bird, reptile and insect life the effect of a coming temporary change, and the change of seasons. He is an astronomer, geographer, zoologist, ornithologist, and ichthyologist. He understands the animal life, gives the names to the various bones and muscles, ligaments, the organs of the animals, birds, reptiles, fish and insects and classifies them in their order. He is looked upon as a greater person than the Medicine Man or Rain-Maker.

The use of the Pointing Stick and crystal is a common means of revenge of one tribe or tribes against each other to do an injury. Now supposing the Frilled Lizard totem tribe is desirous of doing an injury to the Carpet Snake totem tribe. A member of the former tribe would seek the aid of another person, say a member of the Possum totem tribe. The Frilled Lizard man would instruct the Possum man to make the acquaintance of the Carpet Snake man. This would be done by asking the Tortoise totem man. After some palaver, the Tortoise man would introduce the Possum man to the Carpet Snake man and they would both sit by the fireside in the evening and exchange their thoughts and ideas on hunting and fishing and on the general topics of the day.

This would go on night after night for a week. One night the Possum man would whisper into the ear of the Carpet Snake man a word of warning, saying that the Frilled Lizard man was in possession of a great number of Neil yeri, and was in the act of preparing them, by dipping the points into the fat of a dead person and continually heating the Neil yeri in hot ashes and laying them beside the fire [and], to a primitive mind, that heat and fire symbolise intense pain or destruction, and he, the Possum man, furthermore heard that one of the Neil yeri was to be used on the Carpet Snake totem family, so that he should be on his guard.

As the Possum and Carpet Snake men are sitting around the fireside exchanging thoughts and ideas about hunting and fishing and the chief topics of the day, the trained eye of the Carpet Snake man catches a vision of something which strikes terror to his heart. There yonder, about fifty yards away, sits the Frilled Lizard man with eyes fixed upon him (the Carpet Snake Man), and in his left hand is held a something which is only too well known—a pointing bone.

The Carpet Snake man turns to his companion and asks: 'What is the Frilled Lizard man doing yonder?'

The Possum man says: 'Do you see what is in his hand? It is only too plain that it is a Neil yeri. And there is only one object, and that is you, that he sees at the moment.'

The Frilled Lizard man is holding the pointing stick in his left hand straight toward the victim, and the right hand is drawn along the left hand and extended forward suddenly with the palm of the hand open, and whilst in motion he gradually closes the finger as if grasping something, and quickly thrusts the arm forward and at the same moment extends the fingers in a direct position toward the victim.

The Carpet Snake man speaks in a whisper to the Possum man, saying: 'Come let us rise and retire to our Now wondie (a small hut or shelter made of boughs, a temporary home of the Aborigines better known as a Mia mia).'

And so they both quickly rise and enter their abode. During the night, the Carpet Snake man is brooding over the deadly pointing stick and spends a restless night. He is the first to rise and he sends for his companion of the previous night and tells him that he had a most dreadful night. He relates the vision or dream that he had been waylaid by some dreadful enemies. They were men with the appearance of a Keli (Dog) head, the body of a Wombat, and feet like the Emu; whilst others had the head and neck of an Emu, legs of the Kangaroo, and the body of a Thooyoungie (goanna), and still others with the head and body of the Eagle Hawk and legs of the Proolgie (Native Companion). These were all anxious to devour him, but he was favoured by the Great puck nowie (Grandmother Spirit) who dwells in the Dark Spot in the Nebula. She saw the danger that threatened him and she came like a streak of smoke or white cloud and enveloped him so that the enemy were unable to find him or see him. Thus, by the timely protection of Puck nowie, he was saved and now was able to relate the incident of the night.

'That dream or vision,' says the Possum man, 'is an enemy who possesses great and varied qualities so that you will be unable to escape him. And there is only one such tribe that you are to fear, and that is the Frilled Lizard. Since we saw what he did last night, I am convinced that he pointed the stick at you, and as you are looking unwell, I think you had better see the Medicine Man.'

So the Carpet Snake man decides to consult the Doctor. But the cunning Lizard man has seen the Doctor and with bribes he retains his services. The poor, worried, and despairing Snake man pleads with the Doctor, saying: 'Oh Doctor, is there no hope for me? Can you, or will you stay the influence of the stick, or take it from my body?'

The Medicine Man, in most cases, when summoned by a patient, carries with him a bunch of feathers from the wing of the black swan or pelican. The totem and feathers are divided and these are used in the incantation for beating away the evil spirits and also to beckon the aid of the Puck nowie—the life-giving spirit. And he has also smaller feathers plucked from the breast of the swan or the black duck near their wings. Two or three of these are tied to a stick about twelve or eighteen inches in length. After the display of the number one feathers he sits quietly at the door of the Mia mia gazing into the sick man's body. Presently he closes his eyes as if to shut out a bad vision. Then he will profess that he is speaking with the departed spirits and relations of the patient. After the supposed consultation, he will offer two feathers and instruct the sick one to place the feathers before his eyes and to look through the feathers at his body. The patient becomes startled because he fancies that the body of the Medicine Man appears to become transparent.

The Medicine Man inquires: 'What do you see?'

The patient answers: 'It seems that I am able to see your Pam erie (the spirit shadow), and your Nul thee (flesh) has disappeared.'

Then the doctor orders the patient to remove the feathers from his eyes and whilst doing so to close his eyes, which he does until told to open them.

The Medicine Man then tells the patient that he has been endowed with the power of the Grandmother Spirit which gives life or takes away life from the body, but there is a great deal of opposition coming from other spirits which are greater in number: 'There are the great-great-grandfathers with their families and their grandfather with their families, and lastly your father and mother and brother and sister's spirits are awaiting you. They are here, just beside your bed. I can see them. They are pleading to me in the spirit language to allow you to pass over to them, and it is for me to consent to their request.'

Then he will place the feathers (number two) before his eyes and look into the body of the sick one, and with a few passings of the hand across his body, pull and tug and produce a broken stick which was concealed upon his person, saying: 'I take a part of it; your departed loved spirits have prevented me taking the whole from your body, so nothing more can be done for you, they are determined that I shall not heal you.'

The Medicine Man silently sits watching the man, then he begins crying softly with tears flowing down his cheeks and bids the patient goodbye.

After the Medicine Man departs, the relations and friends congregate at the sick man's Mia mia, and he tells them of the Medicine Man's verdict of no hope, and that he must submit to the wish of his loved ones who are standing beside him ready to welcome him to the spirit world. So he turns his face toward the west, that mysterious land, and allows his spirit to take flight to join in that one continual hunting and singing, after which they sit around and have a great feast. Thus passes the soul through the power of suggestion.

The Nugoongie is another form of witchcraft; we believe that whatever we touch in the way of foods, the fragments that are left retain our thoughts and feelings. Or anything that belongs to us, that are parts of our body, such as the hair of the head and body, finger and toe nails, wax from the ear, mucus from the nose and throat, have in them the image of the individual. Such is the strong belief of my race. Hence, after meals, all fragments of bone, flesh, feathers, hair of animals, birds and reptiles, and those belonging to the human body, are burnt. The fire is the only thing that destroys the image.

When any person has failed with the use of the pointing stick, bone, or crystal, he resorts to the Nugoongie. It is a custom that all members of tribes take, and are educated to collect, from one another fragments of food and human hair, finger and toe nails, and wax from the ear, and they barter one with the other.

For instance, the Dingo totem man has in his possession the brain of the Black Duck collected from a meal enjoyed by himself and the Kangaroo Rat totem man. It happened that the Kangaroo Rat man was enjoying the back and neck and head of the Black Duck, and through forgetfulness, hastened away to his camp for a stone knife or axe, leaving the head behind, and when he returned the head had disappeared. He inquired of the Dingo totem man what had become of the Black Duck's head. The Dingo man says: 'I don't know as I left the camp a moment after you to see whether my camp was all right, and perhaps a Wild Cat (native) or a Crow took the head [in] our absence.'

Then they begin raking up the refuse of their meal and commit it to the fire. The Kangaroo Rat man watches his opportunity and procures a portion of a Murray cod head or eye from the Dingo man through a little strategy. The Dingo man is aware that the Kangaroo Rat man has it in his possession. Each family of a tribe has someone's Nugoongie and this somebody has someone else's.

The Nouthongie noughoungie is another form of witchcraft adopted to take away the life of a person or to cause his death. To my race, this is more dreaded than the Neil yeri. With the Neil yeri, it is possible for a victim to avoid it but not so with the Noughoungie. Now the person who operates with this must be an expert—one who has the power of concentration or clairvoyance, or telepathy. It is not any person but, as I have already stated, he must be a person with a good many years' training.

Now in performing the Nouthongie, a person will take one of the many from a great collection kept in store. Let us suppose that he has one of the Coongnurrie Black totem men. Perhaps some years ago the Coongnurrie man caused the death of a Rhingarriparrie and now after failing to use the Neil yeri effectively upon the Coongnurrie man, he adopts the Nouthongie. He selects one of the Swan tribe and every night when all have retired to their camps to sleep, the Rhingarriparrie, instead of going to sleep, takes a bag made of Kangaroo skin and empties its contents and also that of the one belonging to an individual (Yhong keeng by name), places it by the fire to keep it warm, and then he will place the other very carefully into the bag again. After he goes out of his Mia mia, he looks about to see that everyone is in bed and returns to his fireside and takes the Noughoungie into his left hand, utters a word or so, softly, so that those in their Mia mia are unable to hear him:

'Shoo ho now werrund (Let the breath leave thy body).'

Then he begins to chant a song of hate, and after singing thus for an hour or more, he warms the gummed part of the stick in which a portion [of] the brain of a black swan is enclosed.

With closed eyes, he will concentrate his mind upon Yhong keeng until he is able to see a mental picture of him and with all the hatred at his command, whisper: 'Porn al low! (Die)'

Then he lays upon his bed as if intending to sleep and will be in this position for an hour. He rises and sits and takes up the Noughoungie, concentrates his mind upon his victim until he catches another mental vision, then whispers the death words: 'Shoo ho, Porn al low (Let the life breath leave thy body, and die).'

He goes through this performance about five times, and the sixth time he takes the Noughoungie and places it at the chimney or an opening left in the centre of the Mia mia that answers the purpose of a chimney, then he will again lay upon his back as if asleep but his mind is concentrated upon Yhong keeng. He sees him plainly before his mental vision and says: 'Shoo ho.'

He does this all through the night until the early hours of the morning, then he silently steals away from his camp, making his way toward his victim's mia mia. And seating himself within a shrub about ten to twenty yards away, he begins to concentrate his thoughts upon Yhong keeng. He carries a bag; in it is his Rarrabarr, Karnark, and a bunch of Emu feathers that have been placed under the arms of a human dead body in a decomposed state. He takes them in his right hand and extending the arm to form a square he waves his hand forward and backward, whispering: 'Tun tall how (Go to sleep soundly into a state, to be unable to feel).'

He does, or goes through this performance for about two hours, and then he stealthily creeps towards the mia mia of the victim until he arrives at the door. He peeps in to see whether there is any firelight, but there is no light. He is on his hands and knees in a position for flight if Yhong keeng is not soundly asleep, and he listens intently. Perhaps the victim is feigning sleep and waiting with a Karnark to strike the offender should he come near. But in this case the victim is very much asleep, as he can judge by the snoring or deep breathing. When he is satisfied, he creeps forward and places the Emu feathers near the head and gently rubs the feathers about the face so that the smell may be left on the face, so that when Yhong keeng awakes in the morning he will complain of a nasty and stinking smell which he puts down to a Noughoungie. He summons his relations and tells them about it and that he is unable to get rid of the smell in spite of the washing with mud or pipe clay and water.

Something should be done. Their relations make inquiries as to the person or persons in possession of a Noughoungie belonging to Yhong keeng. They go from camp to camp until they come to the Rhingarriparrie, who does not directly admit it, but who says that it would be a wise thing if a general enquiry be made where he would be willing to discuss the matter, and would be willing to send out an invitation to all the surrounding tribes to attend and bring their collection of Noughoungie. And that the Yun who noom me (Court) should be held at Wing garrawarn, a locality on the southern shore of Lake Alexandrina, at the time of the next full moon.

At the first appearing of the new moon, tribes from a distance make their journey to Wing garrawarn about two or three days before the appointed time. Every tribe within a radius of a hundred miles has arrived and pitched their Mia mia. On the day before the night of the full moon, every Chief of the tribes represented comes together and then they discuss the matter in a formal way. And they will give an undertaking that they will do their utmost to get the respective members of the tribes to bring and show their Noughoungie, so that they may barter one with the other to gain the possession of a relative's Noughoungie.

The night of the full moon is looked upon as a very important one. It is a night on which all the Mooncumbulli meet. There are men who are specially gifted as well as trained in spiritualism, clairvoyance, and telepathy. And they also claim that they are able to send their intelligence over a distance and make observations as to what is taking place. And they also possess the power of intelligence to go backward and review the past events. For instance, they are able to look back and see the Rhingarriparrie performance with the Noughoungie on that fateful night, working an evil spell upon Yhong keeng. They will describe every detail of the performance.

It seems remarkable and difficult to understand. It seems as if they are gifted with some supernatural power far beyond human intelligence.

These men, as I have said previously, are looked upon with reverence. They excel the Rain-Maker and the Medicine Man in the art of witchcraft, but they do not make use of their knowledge to do a person or persons an injury. Their one aim and object in life is to do good to their fellow men, either in giving advice or in relieving suffering or pain in body or the troubled mind. They take no part in tribal warfare. They keep neutral, even when their own tribe is at war. The only thing they do is to warn their tribe of an invading army, its strength in number and the time of attack, and will advise the Chief to be on guard against it. They are also the men selected to throw the fatal spear and their lives depend on their knowledge as warriors and their agility.

Sometimes a Mooncumbulli meets with the Chief the night before the attack to give him his Wak kuldi (a small shield which a warrior uses as a defence from spears, Rarrabarr, or boomerangs). He takes this shield and places it so that it becomes a pillow, and rests his head upon it and goes to sleep and during the night, he sees the battle raging, all in a vision.

First, he sees that his tribe is being driven back, and then his tribe makes a stand and holds the oncoming enemy awhile, and then his tribe drives enemy back, and then he awakes. And sitting by the fireside he offers up a Pak irrie (song sung to the spirit of battle), pleading that his Chief may be protected against the spear, Rarrabarrr, and boomerangs of the enemy.

Just before sunrise, he wakes a man who is looked upon as a herald whose duty it is to give the call to rise and have their meal, and he gives the second call to prepare their weapons of war, to see that each warrior has his allotted number of spears ready to hand, and that his attendants who carry the Rarrabarr and boomerangs have a good supply of them. Everything is now in readiness. All the warriors sit with three or four spears, each made out of reed with a wooden point about five feet long and a quarter of an inch thick. The herald then gives another instruction that each warrior shall leave the camp and go and sit away from the rest of the community, so that the women and children will be away from the danger zone. The herald gives instructions in the presence of the Mooncumbulli, who retires and takes no part in the fray.

This is because he has something higher to live for, and that is to try to make each tribe live in harmony. Hence his presence at the New Moon assembly. This is a preliminary meeting. It consists of advice given by the representative Mooncumbulli of two or more tribes. Now, on the morning following the night of the New Moon, the elders of the different tribes will meet, bringing their collections of Noughoungie. The audience sits in a large circle and all the Noughoungie are placed in an open space within the circle. Then a Mooncumbulli will come forward and stick each of these charmed sticks standing in the ground, so that all have a view of them and discern any that contain anything belonging to their person, or anything they may [have] touched or handled.

Supposing a Water Rat totem man has a suspicion, or he has a feeling that a Noughoungie belonging to his elder or younger son is among that number, he asks the Mooncumbulli to find out, and if such is the case, to procure it by barter and he will give up one which belongs to a brother of the person who has shown his collection. The first lot of charm sticks belong, we shall say, to the Crow totem tribe. The Mooncumbulli comes forward and sits within the circle beside the Noughoungie, taking each separately into his right hand and speaks to it as if addressing a human being, saying:

'Do you belong to the Retculdie (Water Rat) tribe?' and if there comes no mysterious answer, which is only known to him, he replaces it beside the others and takes up another and asks if it belongs to the Retculdie. He goes through the whole number and perhaps he receives no any answer, and then the inquiring one is satisfied and retires from the meeting. Now the Coongnurrie totem man from the outside of the circle calls to the Mooncumbulli that there is among that collection one belonging to his tribe:

'We are suspicious that that collection there belongs to the Rhingarriparrie totem tribe, find out whether it is so.'

The Mooncumbulli takes up a charm stick and enquires.

This time we receive an answer from the unknown and with the stick in his hand he turns to the Pelican man, and asks for an answer, and whether the spirits have given a correct answer, to which the Pelican replies: 'Yes! That is so.' Then the Mooncumbulli asks:

'Why did you do such an act?'

He will reply: 'I did that because one of the members of the tribe to which I belong is very ill and we think that the Swan totem man has his Noughoungie. Now if they are willing to give it to me, I will give them theirs,' and then they exchange Noughoungie, and both go to the river and dip the stick into the water and allow it to remain soaking awhile, say about half an hour.

And a messenger is despatched to the Coongnurrie totem tribe to inform Yhong keeng that they have procured from the Rhingarriparrie man his Noughoungie, which has already been dipped in water, which has taken away the spell that was imposed by the enemy. This encouraging message is also sent by the Mooncumbulli, that is he need no longer fear the death dealing effect of the Noughoungie because Puck nowie —the spirit who has the power to return the spirit of a departed one back into the body—will ever be present to prevent the death, until it is the will of the departed spirits of the loved ones and relations that he shall join them.

This message has a magnetic effect upon the sick one. He will rise from his bed and sit beside the fire and ask to be served with food. Now the Mooncumbulli will spend a week selecting the Noughoungie of individuals and will advise the parties to barter or exchange one with the other. Each of the tribes is satisfied with the decision of the Mooncumbulli and will roll up their various belongings and silently steal away, each to their respective countries or hunting grounds.

The other death-dealing practice is the Thymie. This is a rope or string made of human hair which may be taken from a living person or a dead body. The hair is taken from the head and placed lengthwise into strands about the thickness of an ordinary lead pencil, and with the thumb and forefinger, the strands are twisted separately and rubbed with red ochre mixed with the fat of the wombat or possum etc., which retain the twist until the performer places the twisted strands upon his right leg. He sits upon the ground doubled at the knees, with the result that he is sitting almost, or upon the heels. He rubs the two strands with the right hand, while with the left hand he holds the ends of the two cords, and in this manner he twists the two strands until they form a two-stranded rope about half an inch thick or less, and then he makes a rope ten or twelve yards long. Then the rope is placed in a box made of Emu skin turned inside-out, so that the human hair rope will be laying on the feathers.

And when one of the elders of a tribe is sick unto death, the maker of the rope asks the brother or son of the sick one if he would take the Thymie into his bed and place it under his body and lay upon it until he passes from this life, into that of the spirit land. The brother or son expresses the wish to the dying man who gives his consent and takes the rope to bed with him. They watch the sick man closely and when he feels himself going, he bids his relations and friends a last farewell, and they wind the rope round his body, beginning at the hips, around the stomach several times, under and around the arm pits, loosely around the neck, and over the back of the neck and head. Placing one end in the dying man's hand, they take the remaining end to a person standing outside the Mia mia, and they patiently wait until the spirit leaves the body. They leave the rope entwined about the body for several weeks, by which time the body is putrefied or decomposed, and the human hair rope has the strength of the spirit of the departed. This rope is considered to be alive to a wish or a desire of the person or persons who make use of it, providing that he cares for it and keeps it in an emu bag to keep it warm and dry.

The Medicine Man of that tribe will take the human hair rope and concentrate his mind upon it and 'Yun na min din' it (speak to it as if addressing a human being), and give it instructions what to do. For instance, when he has a victim selected from some tribe away down upon the Lower Murray, before taking the journey in search of the victim, he will take the hair rope to a sacred Bora ground, and stretch it to its full length—about twelve yards. Twelve men stand away from it chanting a song of hate and revenge, holding their spears and Rarrabarr. Then they will dance around the hair rope using words requesting the Thymie not to fail them in their mission. After singing and dancing for half a day to the Thymie, they return to their Mia mia and rest for the night without a thought of the enemy.

On the following morning about sunrise, the Medicine Man goes to the Bora ground and makes a clear space upon the ground, free from grass, stick, and stone and makes a mound the length of a man and will mark, or draw, as near as possible the figure of the selected victim. He will then return to the camp and inform the other eleven men that preparations are made for another sacred dance to give the hair rope a greater spell. Then the twelve men go to the Bora ground, and before performing, they paint their bodies with pipe clay and red ochre.

All the women, young men, girls, and boys are not allowed to come near the Bora ground, nor within sound of the chanting or singing of the elders of the tribe who are assisting the twelve performers. The elders of the tribe sit in a circle which is about thirty feet in diameter with the figure of the victim in the centre, lying with the feet toward the east and the head due west. There is a pole placed at or between the feet of the figure, onto which the hair rope is tied, lying along the body of the figure up to the head, and then tied to another stick that has been driven firmly into the earth, and then passed on to another stick placed another thirty feet away from the head. The three sticks are placed in a line east to west. The first tie of the hair rope is upon the earth, and so is the second tie upon the head on the earth, and the third tie on the third stick is about five feet up, more or less. When all is ready, the elders all in unison and at a signal given by the Medicine Man do the death or dying note:

'Shoo ho Punteel itch hum mungee (Let thy breath leave thy body. Thy day has already come to pass on to the western sky).'

They address the figure of their victim drawn on the ground and all the while they concentrate their minds upon the real victim. (The real victim is Kartinyeri of the Korrawaldie, a Lawarrie [Cape Barren Goose, which is the same size as the Black Swan, only with a shorter neck and of a slate grey colour] totem man.)

'Porn al low Kartinyeri (Die thou must, Kartinyeri),' and they beat the ground with the palms of their right hands.

The twelve men who are the chief performers stamp their right feet three times. The man who is standing at the head of the figure stoops and takes hold of the hair rope with his left hand and walks in a crouching position toward the third western stick, gradually raising the position of the hair rope until he stands upright. When he reaches the stick, he then takes his left hand from the rope and, closing his fingers as if gripping something, he throws out his hand westward and at the same time opens his fingers as if releasing something. He stands awhile, facing the west.

'Loll thou wald turl kand (Thou are going, and with the sun dip into the western sky).' He repeats these words three times.

Just as he turns to come back and take his place at the end, the eleventh man stands, about two or three yards from the foot of the figure. The second elder goes through the same performance. He stoops and takes the hair rope in his left hand and goes along the hair rope in a crouching position, gradually rising, and as he reaches the third western stick he is in an upright position.

Taking his hand quickly from the hair rope and suddenly passing his hand westward, he opens his hand as if releasing something, repeating the words: 'Loll thou wald turl kand (Thou art going, and with the sun dip into the western sky).'

The other ten men repeat the procedure, and whilst they are performing, the elders who sit around in a circle are continually beating the ground with the palm of their right hand and chanting: 'Punteel itch hum nuggee.'

They will repeat this over and over again for two or more hours, have a half-an-hour rest, and continue again until sunset. Just as the sun is disappearing over the horizon, the elders who have been sitting will arise and some will stand on the right side of the figure lined toward the south, and the others on the left side, in a line northward facing the west, and of the twelve men who have been performing on the hair rope, six stand at the head of the figure in a line west toward the sinking sun, and the other six at the feet of the figure stand in a line eastward with their faces toward the western sky.

They stand in this position with their minds concentrated upon the victim, Kartinyeri, the Lawarrie totem man. Then the twelve men leave the lines and each takes a spear and stands with the spear in his hand with the point directed toward the figure, awaiting an order from the Medicine Man.

After an incantation the Medicine Man shouts: 'Wakul ('Pierce the body)!' and the twelve thrust their spears into the figure.

Then they all say: 'Shoo ho Kartinyeri, Porn al low,' and they blow their breath toward the west. They show sorrow and cry, with heads bowed for a few minutes, and then they walk in a single file toward the west chanting: 'Yune nut itck pornan (Soon will the victim die).'

They repeat this all the way to the camp and they gradually turn in a curve to their respective mia mia. The Medicine Man enters his mia mia with the human hair rope and before sitting, he coils the rope upon his bed and then sits upon it. They are all satisfied with the afternoon's performance.

It is a strange belief that hair has the power to imbibe into itself the spirit of the departed who took it and slept upon it during his dying hours, and that this spirit has a compelling influence upon person or persons to whom it is directed. For instance, these men wished the death of Kartinyeri, an individual of the Korrawaldi tribe, totem Lawarrie

(Cape Barren goose). The victim lives a hundred miles down on the lower Murray on the banks of Lake Alexandrina. When seven days have elapsed, which they consider the allotted time for the performance to be effective, on the evening of the seventh day they prepare for the journey to the hunting-ground of the Korrawaldi tribe in search of Kartinyeri. They will travel every night and rest during the day. They have a firm belief that the spirit in the human hair rope will guide them safely through thickly timbered country, and will give them, or increase their walking capacity with greater or with supernatural speed. They describe it as if the foot simply glides along, or as if they are carried along by some impelling force which they say comes from the human hair. This rope is made from the hair collected from hundreds of people, living and dead, and they believe that the intelligence of these many hairs, with all their wishes, desires, loves, and hatreds are contained in the human hair.

The act of wrapping the rope around the dying person who submits to death is symbolic. When many wish to the hair rope that someone must give himself up to become a victim to some ordered form or performance to cause death, they willingly do so without any effort to resist. So they think that not only does the power of the spirit assist them in capturing a victim, but that in travelling it guides them through the forest or scrub, over mountain tops, into the fern-covered valley, across rivers, and so on. They say they are walking on air, and that the spirits have made or caused the air for a foot above the earth to become solid and soft, and it acts like a [wing]. The air is moving and they are being carried along with it in a direct line toward their victim.

Perhaps in the line of travel they will pass the camping ground of some tribe and they will strike the trunk of a dry gum tree, perhaps standing or fallen, or, failing to find a tree suitable, they strike two sticks, or perhaps two Nulla nulla. In travelling along river banks, when approaching a camp, they throw a stone into the stream just by or near a Mia mia. When the tribe hears these sounds during the evening, midnight, or in the early hours of the morning, they know that a person or party is travelling with a Thymie, and they need not fear because they have sounded an alarm asking that they be allowed to pass on unmolested.

Sometimes a tribe, or a member of a tribe who is a linguist, stands erect before a blazing firelight so that he may be distinguished, then in a loud voice he will first speak a language, inquiring: 'Who are you? From whence have ye journeyed, and to what destination does your mission take you?'

Perhaps he speaks in the Kalmilaroi language, and when he receives no answer, addresses them, using the same words, in the Waradjuri tongue. There are three knocks upon a gum tree, or three stones are thrown into the river, which means to say: 'Yes, we are the Waradjuri tribe.'

This is a sign of acknowledgment as to their identity as a tribe, but not to their mission, because it is the accepted sign given only by those travelling with a human hair rope. No one will ever attempt to imitate the passport of the Thymie.

Sometimes a tribe will offer the travellers hospitality. They will take up various foods, perhaps fish, swan, kangaroo or possum flesh, food already cooked, and walk some distance, about a hundred yards from the camp, and place the food upon the ground, and the travellers will sit down but no one will attempt to disturb them. After they have finished their meal, they will gather up the fragments and commit them to the fire, as it is the custom to avoid the possibility of anybody taking a piece to make a Noughoungie of one or more of their party. So this shows how careful a person must be in regard to this belief, although they are in possession of one of the most effective weapons of destruction, the Thymie. Before leaving, they strike their Nulla nulla several times, or throw a stone into the river twice, giving a sign that all is well and they are leaving on their journey.

When they come within a night's journey of their destination, they camp for two or three days. They send out one, two, or three scouts to spy the country and find out, without being seen, as much information as possible. The spies leave their companions after resting a few days with them. Perhaps on the third or fourth day the spies go out visiting all the camps during the night. Perhaps they arrive at the camp of the Warrawaldie tribe, totem Black Swan. The members of the families are sitting around the open campfire beside some growing shrubs. A spy will creep up to these bushes and come within hearing distance to find out what the conversation is about, whether he may get information as to the whereabouts of the victim. Hearing nothing of importance, he creeps back into the bushes.

Number two and three spies are doing the same. Perhaps it is difficult to approach the camp as the Mia mia are on the bank of a river with an open or clear space at the back, so perhaps a spy will wade into the river, upstream or downstream about two hundred yards away from the fire. Then he will swim along the side of the bank until he comes to within hearing distance and then he will lay among the reeds or rushes that grow along the river bank, listening for some clue as to the whereabouts of Kartinyeri. Perhaps he hears the name of Tilplup, the name of a member of the Lawarrie totem tribe.

The spy is overjoyed with this knowledge—now they will be able to trace Kartinyeri by shadowing Tilplup. So excited with the discovery, he ascends the bank, slips, and causes a splash in the river. All the male folk of the Warrawaldie snatch up a Rarrabarr and a Wak kuldi (shield). Some run upstream and others downstream, with spears fitted into their Thyrallgie (throwing sticks), or a Woomera ready for action, to bring to justice the intruder who dared to approach their home at night. Such are the thoughts of the Warrawaldie, it being a crime to enter a hunting ground without permission, punishable by death, with spear or Nulla nulla.

But the spy takes one deep breath, silently dives into midstream, and cautiously comes to the surface with his nose and head above the water, takes another deep breath and dives to the other side of the stream, and reaching the opposite bank, he swims about half a mile downstream. Then he strikes across to the bank from which he was driven. The men of the Warrawaldie tribe, Black Swan totem, return to their camp, thinking perhaps it was a splash caused by a water rat or Pondi (Murray cod) in pursuit of food. Reaching the bank, the spy is more careful. He hastens to his companions and tells them of his adventures of the evening, and also that he heard a person addressed as Tilplup—and that name only belongs to the Korrawaldi tribe, Lawarrie totem.

Then they all go out to procure evidence. They each stealthily wend their way through scrub and reeds and bush, with their eyes scanning the ground for footprints. One of the spies finds a footprint of Tilplup's and he follows it cautiously until it leads him to a great Wail lar roo mundi. This is during the late afternoon. He hastens back to their hiding place and perhaps he is the first to arrive, and he patiently sits, awaiting the arrival of the others.

The Medicine Man is the first to put in an appearance and the spy tells him of his discovery of the hunting ground of the Korrawaldi tribe by following the footprints of Tilplup along the river bank, then winding across an isthmus to the northern shore of Lake Alexandrina. Now, when all the others have returned from their hunt, they are told by the first spy that he has been able to locate the camping ground of the Korrawaldi. Then they take their evening meal.

The Medicine Man takes one of the party to accompany him to the Mia mia of Kartinyeri. And they take with them the human hair rope and they use the rope to lead them to Kartinyeri's home. When they come to the camping ground, they sit watching every movement of the individual men and women. They do this for several nights and when they are assured of the tribe's movements, they will select a very dark cloudy night. Then the Medicine Man and his companions will walk about the camp, brushing up against the Korrawaldi men who will take no notice, thinking probably it is one of their own.

After much searching, they find the Mia mia—or better still—they find Kartinyeri, sitting in his Mia mia enjoying a meal. The Medicine Man and companions sit inside a shrub and watch his every movement. They continue this spying upon, or shadowing, of their victim for a week, day and night. To keep an eye upon Kartinyeri during the day, the whole party do its bit toward having him under observation. To make this possible, they have to become acquainted with his daily walk to and from the animal, fishing, wild fowl, and hunting grounds. Some of the spies will climb into trees that have thick foliage, or trees with thick clinging creepers. They will spend a whole day and night watching their victim pass beneath them, and whilst they are thus crouching among the thick boughs or creepers, they will utter the death word to Kartinyeri, silently or softly, so that he will not hear: 'Shoo ho.'

At the end of the week, they feel safe and confident that they will be able to work the Thymie (human hair rope), and that it has become acquainted with Kartinyeri and they will be able to go about their work unmolested.

So on the evening before making the attack upon Kartinyeri, they hold a consultation among themselves as well as with the spirits in the human hair, speaking to them as if they are gifted with human intelligence. And the spirit in the hair rope will give them an answer that Kartinyeri is already under the spell of the magic hair rope. Then the Medicine Man leaves for the shrub that is by Kartinyeri's Mia mia, and spends the late evening there. About three or four o'clock in the morning the others arrive individually, first one and then another, until they number twelve; and now the Medicine Man unrolls the hair rope and places it upon a Karnark (a Nulla nulla), and the person holding the Karnark winds the hair several times round it. Then the person creeps along toward the Mia mia of Kartinyeri who is now sound asleep. He winds the hair rope round the arms and neck of his person. The others have placed another Karnark into the ground and they sit upon the ground in a line with the hair and draw their hands backwards as if hauling Kartinyeri towards them. They do this half a dozen times. Presently Kartinyeri rises from his bed and walks toward the performers, and six men—three on each side—face each other, sitting with their legs doubled beneath them, or in other words, they sit on their heels.

The victim walks and lays himself down on the six men's knees. The hypnotic influence of the Medicine Man, combined with that of the six men and the magnetised human hair rope, has a wonderful effect upon the victim. I have heard of men who have practised with the Thymie say if you are not careful in the use of the rope and the victim is aware of its presence, he can hold it in a way to capture the hunter. So that the Medicine Man places the hair rope, or he orders it to be placed upon Kartinyeri, so that they do not expose themselves to the danger of allowing the sleeping victim to take hold of it with his hand.

From the information or description given to me, I would be inclined to say that Kartinyeri would be hypnotised by the suggestion made to his unconscious self from the day they first saw him, so that sound asleep he becomes an easy prey to whatever suggestions are made to him.

They place the rope once around the weapon of one of the companions, and wind the cord once around the body, or arm, or neck, and those holding the cord are unanimous in their thought suggestion. The victim rises from his slumber as if awake and comes toward the men who are sitting upon the ground, with the lower portion of the knee beneath them, having the appearance of sitting on their heels. He voluntarily walks and lays himself upon their knees with face toward the sky, as if about to rest upon his bed. He lies there and the Medicine Man comes forward, holding in his hand a flint knife expressly made for such an occasion and, drawing the skin of the victim from the hips towards the small rib, he cuts a small hole into the body and thrusts the little finger into the body and scoops out a bit of kidney fat. After removing a small portion of this fat, he allows the skin to go back to its position, and presses the cut with smooth pieces of wood made for this purpose.

Then they remove the victim from their knees and place him upon the ground lying with his head toward the west and feet eastward. He is to lay thus until Puck nowie, the grandmother of the human spirit, comes to the rescue and puts life and sense into the apparently dead person. He rises to his feet and faces east, then he turns to the north and yawns; then turns again to the east and right round to the south and yawns. Then finally he turns to the west, and stretching his arms north and south, gives a long yawn. By this time he has become conscious, and he goes into his Mia mia and lays down to sleep. Then Puck nowie comes and heals the wound so that everyone is unable to see the cut, and takes away all consciousness of what happened a few hours earlier, and goes to the place of the operation and takes away all signs and tracks of the enemy, and the blood, and makes the grass or broken twigs appear undisturbed and then she returns to her home in the dark spot in the Milky Way.

The Medicine Man with the other eleven men return to their homes, feeling happy that they have made their revenge and paid back with a life for a life the death of their relation. When they arrive at their destination, they go the Bora ground and invite all the elders of the tribe to come and see the fat taken from the kidney of Kartinyeri, and the performance is just like the first, the only difference is that now they are in possession of the kidney fat of their enemy. When they are all seated one of the elders comes forward and unwrapping a piece of bark of a gum tree taken from a tender bough—which has been treated and dried in hot ashes and soaked in emu fat, which gives it a polish—he gives it to the Medicine Man with a request that it should be the coffin of Kartinyeri.

The poor victim suffers. He knows that there is a pain somewhere in his body but is not able to locate it. He complains to his wife. Like a good and devoted helper she goes out into the bushes and procures herbs which are used for medicinal purposes, and cooks these in the earth by steaming (this is explained in cooking food) and lays it before her husband and says in a pleading voice: 'Thuckallow (Eat, and thou shall be well because I have sought the best food for thee).'

But the patient with his physical suffering is trying to recall something which happened to him at some period. Sometimes it seemed to have taken place a year ago, then it seems a week ago, but the conscious mind is unable to grasp the exact time.

He says to his wife: 'Think for me, Narpund (my wife), helpmate, and child giver, can you call to mind any incident that may cause you to suspect someone pointing a bone at me or a Nhoughoungie someone has belonging to me?'

The wife now becomes somewhat concerned. She hastens away to her elder brother and asks him to come quickly. 'Kartinyeri is talking strangely. Will you please come to my dear husband?'

He goes to visit his brother-in-law. He understands and knows too well that his relation has been hypnotised by some of his enemies with the aid of a Thymie (hair rope) and that a portion of his kidney fat has been extracted. He vows that the offending party, or one or more of that party, shall give their lives in return in the same manner. They summon the Medicine Man of the tribe to come and see and find out who and where are the people to be found that did this injury which is causing the death of their brother. He tries but fails, so they send for a Mooncumbulli who is living with another tribe a day's journey away.

A smoke signal is given and a message transmitted to the Mooncumbulli to come at once: 'Someone is dying, we require your help to procure from his unconscious mind the person who did the deed.'

The Mooncumbulli comes with all haste, travelling all night and all the next afternoon, arriving at night at the mia mia of the sick one. With his telepathic and clairvoyant knowledge he is able to tell them that a Kalmilaroi did the act; there were eleven men with the aid of a Medicine Man. He will tell them every detail of the days spent in making the acquaintance of the tribe and Kartinyeri, and also the night on which the operation took place and also the distance from the Mia mia, and he will point out the bushes in which they hid themselves.

To give them the satisfaction he will say: 'I can see all that which has been taking place before my vision. What comes before me now, I see that your dying brother sees, but is not able to tell you.'

Then he takes away the covering from the body of Kartinyeri, and shows them a scratch on his loin: 'That is what is the cause of his dying, they have taken his kidney fat.'

That night Kartinyeri gives up the ghost and his spirit returns to the west, to the home of all spirits.

The Korrawaldi tribe holds a party to take the life of a Kalmilaroi man. They go through a performance similar to that which the enemy acted. Then they take a journey into the hunting ground of the Kalmilaroi, and treat a member of that tribe in the same manner, by removing the kidney fat. This goes on continually between tribes.

I would like to state here that when these men have returned home to their hunting ground and Mia mia, and especially to the Bora ground (a sacred spot in which ceremonial rites are performed), after placing the fat in the bark which is to become a casket for the fat life of Kartinyeri, they place that casket containing the fat beside the fire and allow the heat of the fire to come in contact with it. The result is that it gradually melts away, and while it is melting, the Medicine Man chants the death song of Kartinyeri. The elders and the eleven men sit and watch the process. They believe very strongly that as the fat is gradually dissolving, so is the life of Kartinyeri slowly ebbing from his body. This form of causing death was mostly practised by the Murray tribes.

All crystals or small shining pebbles were used the same as Neil yeri. The Medicine Man would profess that it was possible to cause the pebbles to enter the body.

The other form of causing death was the bruising of the body on the back, in the region of the kidney, and also the chest. This process is done by using a weapon with a large head—larger than a Rarrabarr—using the thin end as a handle. The point is to strike the body gently, just sufficiently to cause a little gathering of blood. This is done when the victim is struck with a Nulla nulla at the base of the skull into unconsciousness, and before he returns to consciousness, the performer, or enemy, disappears.

These are the various forms that my people practise to carry out their differences—'an eye for an eye, and a tooth for a tooth'. This, I think, was the cause, or one of the causes, which has prevented the increase of my race.

Wondangar Goon Na Ghun (Whale and Star Fish)

Now, some of you have already read of the great philosopher and astronomer, Koala (the Teddy Bear), of his discovery of the Thousand Isles away in the eastern sea, also of his wonderful achievement and skill in the navigation of a large fleet of canoes, bringing many strange Beings, inhabitants of those lands, to the shores of Australia. There were the representatives of the Animal tribe: the Whingammie (Kangaroo), the Barraal (Wallaby), the Wombat, and others; the Bird tribe; the Peewingie (Eagle Hawk) with all members of that family, the Muldarie (Magpie) and members of that family, the Lyre Bird, the Kookaburra, the Peenjullie (Emu), and other members of the feathered tribes; then there were the Lizard and Reptile family represented by the Thooyoungie (Goanna), the Frilled Lizard, and other members of that family; the Snakes; the Rock Python, the Carpet Snake, and other members of that family. And there were among this multitude of strange Beings, two Beings who were more strange than the others—Wondangar (the Whales) and Goon na ghun (the Star Fishes).

Now when they arrived at Shoalhaven they all landed safely, unloaded their canoes and pitched their mia mia and rested for seven sunrises and on the eighth sunrise the Koala sent the Peenjullie to go among the beings to inform them that at midday he would instruct them what they should do. So the Peenjullie hastened in and out among the strange company, with sign and gesture asking that no one was to leave the camp to go a-hunting but to remain until they should receive instruction from the Koala. So these beings just sat and ate their breakfast, whiling the time away chatting to each other in many strange languages.

Now, as soon as the sun was overhead, again the Peenjullie gave a sign: 'Silence—the Great Mooncumbulli comes.'

Then the Koala mounted upon a stump formed like a pulpit and with sign and gesture called each of the heads of the families and asked them to choose where they would like to live. The Peenjullies came forth and, pointing and giving signs, expressed their wish to travel beyond the mountain Tolkamia (sou' west). The Koala, nodding, gave his consent. Then he beckoned to the Whingammie (Kangaroo) and inquired where he would like to make his home. So the 'Roo, pointing and with gesture, expressed his wish to travel and make his home with the Peenjullie, that is, if they had no objection. The Koala called the attention of the Peenjullie and inquired if he had any objection to the Whingammie accompanying him, and he said: 'We would enjoy their presence on our journey.'

So all the marsupial tribe followed their Chief the Kangaroo, with the exception of the Platypus, who expressed a wish that he would probably go west for a time, but would like to return and travel Wolkundmia (north). Then the Koala beckoned to the Peewingie.

The Eagle Hawk said: 'We do not wish to ask for any particular part. Will you allow us to travel just where we can find food?'

The nodding Koala gave his consent.

When all had expressed their wish where they would like to live, the Koala was just about to close the meeting when the Crow called his attention to two strange beings—the Wondangar and the Goon na ghun.

'Oh,' said the Koala, 'come along up here beside me, and tell me where you would like to make your home.'

They both said in sign and gesture: 'Let us stay here awhile and we shall choose later on. Will you grant us this request?'

'Oh, you are all at liberty to do just what you think would suit you best. But before closing this meeting, I would very like you all before taking your journey into these unknown and unexplored regions, to let us all spend six moons with each other to give some of you time. Perhaps you may change your mind and select some other place. And let us understand each other better before we part.'

So the Animals, Birds, Reptiles, and Insects gave their consent to remain at the pleasure of the Koala.

Now the Wondangar, before the departure of the Koala, beckoned the Peenjullie, so the Emu very obligingly came to him and said: 'What can I do for you? I shall be pleased to be at your service.'

'Very well,' said the Wondangar, 'go to the Koala and plead with him to allow me the sole right and use of all the sandhills or hummocks that are along the coastline, and also to give instructions to others that no one shall live or rest upon the white sand unless with my permission. This I ask of him as a temporary favour, until I shall decide as to my permanent abode.'

'I shall do as you wish,' said the Peenjullie.

So he went to the Koala and asked him whether he would be allowed to present a request from one of the party.

'Oh,' said the Koala, 'speak and I shall listen.'

So the Peenjullie began: 'Oh Mooncumbulli (O thou great and clever One), the Wondangar would like your permission of all sand beaches and hills or hummocks that are along the coastline for a short period until he shall decide definitely at a later date what he intends doing.'

'Go,' said the Koala, 'and tell the Wondangar that they have found favour with me and I shall do as is required of him.'

The Peenjullie went and delivered the favourable reply to the Wondangar, who seemed so pleased that they hastened away and took up their abode among the sand-hills and upon the white sand beaches. They would delight to go surfing and lay upon the dry white sand, basking in the sunshine. They repeated this day after day until they developed lazy habits. They would not even hunt for food, but lay in the shallow water and put their tongues out and wagged and wagged them until some of the fish would become curious and swim round and round, thinking what a funny sight. Some would become more bold than the others and would venture right into the open mouths of the Wondangar, and they would suck them right into their stomachs and the silly and inquisitive little fishes would become a meal for the Wondangar. And the other fish that were looking on became more curious than the first, because they could not understand the mystery of this thing. It seemed a cave, and they too would like to explore and find out all about it and their friends, thinking that they had entered some wonderful place, with all kinds of beautiful and pleasant things.

'Come,' said one, 'let us enter,' and they timidly approached, and suddenly, without warning, they were sucked into the mouths and carried farther on, and they helped to supply the hunger of the lazy Wondangar.

When they found that food was so easily obtained, they became more lazy. They would lie in this way for hours until they had gorged themselves with more food than was good for them. Then they would rise from the water, walk up among the hot sands, and sleep and sleep until they became hungry. This was the everyday life of the Wondangar. They were not like the Kangaroo, who would take spear and Nulla nulla and hunt for food. All the other beings hunted for food, but the Wondangar in their laziness procured their food in this unique way.

Now the Wondangar thought themselves very clever folks because they captured their food in this fashion. But it had a very bad result, for lying like they did for hours and hours like some lifeless object, the little periwinkles thought to themselves: 'What a nice thing to cling to.'

And they came and fastened their homes to the bodies of the Wondangar, and other shell-life came and they too clung to them and some of the tiny weeds, wandering along the coast looking for a home, decided that they too would join in clinging to this object. The Wondangar after a while had accumulated upon their bodies other parasites, lives that were seeking shelter and a home.

Now there is another outstanding feature about these Wondangar. They were beings with such a large head and body but small legs and arms, and they did look such queer people. You would expect that being possessed with big heads they would be great thinkers, but not so. This was one of the greatest defects of these queer beings, [they were] unable to reason.

It was fortunate for them that there lived not far away the Goon na ghun, who volunteered to become the friends of the silly lazy Wondangar. These beings came in a large canoe that kept in touch with the canoes of the Wondangar, and during the voyage their canoes would in a calm sea be tied together and travel in this way, and in rough weather be untied and sail separately, so that they would be in no danger of bumping. And it was in this way that they developed a friendship or, let us say, that the Goon na ghun got to pity and sympathise with the thoughtless and lazy Wondangar.

And now when they arrived in another country, the Goon na ghun took upon themselves to be their friends, to help and advise them in anything that they wanted or liked to know. But, sorry to say, the Wondangar were so dense that they did not know what was their want. Now the Goon na ghun were smart beings. They were rotund in shape, with always a smiling face, and always on the alert to do some good act, trusted every other being, thought no evil of anyone. They lived a perfect life, no one was able to accuse them of any wrong. Being perfect themselves, they thought others perfect. Thus they looked upon the Wondangar as good in spite of their laziness.

The Goon na ghun, with the permission of the Koala, occupied all bays and coves along the coast, or bays where the water was calm and clear, with a white sandy bottom free of rock and weed, quite an ideal spot for such good and perfect beings. Now they were very industrious beings, and built their homes in the rock and made beautiful terraces and canals, made in such a way that the fish swimming into them would be trapped, then they would take trips in the adjoining scrubs or forest and procure berries and grubs, and fill their storehouse with supplies prepared for the coming winter months. How different from their neighbours, the Wondangar.

When a straying Possum, turned out from his tribe for breaking some of their laws, became a fugitive, he would often seek the protection and hospitality of the Goon na ghun. Sometimes the Thooyoungie would take advantage of the good beings and would come with a pitiful story of how he had helped to support the Kookaburras in a time of illness, relating a story how every day he would capture food and carry it to their home in the hollow of a large tree; many were the times he would climb the tree with a bundle of food, sometimes the load was so great that he would be overcome with exhaustion and fall to the ground from a distance which would have killed a Possum or a Koala. And it was a wonder that he was able to be there telling the story: 'I have given my last meal to them, and now I feel too weak to hunt.'

'Come, my friend,' said the Goon na ghun, 'stay with us awhile until you have rested and eaten sufficient to gain your former strength.'

But in this case the Thooyoungie would be telling a lie. He would take advantage of the trustfulness and kindness of the Goon na ghun. When their eyes were turned, he would steal from the larder and run away, feeling satisfied with himself that he was smart in tricking the Goon na ghun.

'Ha, ha,' laughed the Goanna on his way, 'how foolish they were to believe such a story. What a clever chap I must be. Now, won't I have a picnic all to myself. What nice berries and what an appetising smell their preserved fish have.'

Now, as the Thooyoungie was flattering himself upon his cleverness in stealing the food from the Goon na ghun, he sat down beneath a large tree that towered above all other trees and which sent out its branches, making a welcome shade for bird, beast, and reptile.

Presently a voice from among the boughs accosted him: 'Hello Thooyoungie, where did you spring from with such nice and tasty food? I am sure that it's not your own gathering. It must belong to some other unfortunate being who will be looking for his food.'

'What do you take me for, a thief?' said the Thooyoungie.

'You have said rightly,' replied the voice, 'you could not be otherwise. You have always been a thief, and will continue so till time shall be no more.'

Then the Thooyoungie became angry.

'Who are you, and what are you, with such impudence? Come down and I will teach you a lesson not to be insulting to honest people.'

'Ha, ha, ho, ho, hee, hee,' mockingly laughed the unseen being, 'I would not like to quarrel with you, Mr Thooyoungand, oh you silly and weak as a child person. It would be a one-sided battle.'

Just then the Koo ka kee came and sat on a limb not far away, and heard the conversation that was taking place, and heard the mocking remark made by someone hidden among the boughs, and he began laughing too: 'Koo, koo, koo, ka, kee.'

The Goanna said: 'And now what are you laughing at?'

'I am just laughing at a thought that struck me, that a thief is sometimes a coward, or a coward a thief.'

'Do you think,' said the Goanna, 'that I am afraid to do battle with one who calls me a thief?'

'Certainly,' said the Koo ka kee, 'I would not allow anyone who insulted me to go free, but would offer him a challenge to fight with spear and Nulla nulla. Go,' said the Koo ka kee, 'and bring your weapon and teach that impudent rascal a lesson.'

'All right,' said the Goanna, 'take charge of my food until I return.'

So the Koo ka kee took charge, and the Goanna went for his weapon.

Now the being who spoke from within the bough was the Crow. He came down from his hiding-place and said to the Koo ka kee: 'The food you are in charge of is stolen. The owner will be here before the Goanna returns and you will be blamed.'

'Well, if that is so, I do not wish to be found with stolen property. Can I entrust it to you?'

'Certainly,' said the Crow.

The Koo ka kee flew away as fast as his wings would carry him. When the Goanna returned he saw that the Crow was in charge of the stolen food. He knew that he was tricked.

'Now,' said the Crow, 'I heard you laugh of your cunning, and heard you say how clever you were. You forget that there are other beings with minds better than yours. It was I who called you a coward, a thief, and challenged you to battle. Have I not won? See, I have your spoil. It shall not be Thooyoungie that shall eat of the berries and fish, but I, your superior.'

The Goanna bowed his head in shame at this simple defeat of the wily old Crow.

Now, the Goanna was so very very hungry that he became weak and unable to hunt for food. The Wild Pigeon, on his way home, saw the poor Goanna looking despondent and inquired what was the matter, and he said: 'I am very hungry, I have had nothing to eat all day and am feeling weak with hunger.'

The Pigeon hastened on and told the Goon na ghun of the plight of the Goanna. So they hastened along, taking with them food and herbs and berries and fish. They wended their way through the scrub until they reached the Goanna. When he saw them he felt greatly ashamed of himself, because here were the beings who gave him hospitality, and what was more, instead of thanking them for their kindness, he had stolen their food. They knew all about the theft and yet when the Thooyoungie was hungry, they came to his assistance and offered him food.

Then he said with sign and gesture: 'Why do you come with food and with kindly smiles upon your faces? Are you not aware that I stole your food?'

'Yes,' replied the Goon na ghun, 'We saw, and pitied you, and said to each other, and let this impress upon your mind—that he that steals, from him also shall be taken that which he stole. Never in future, oh Thooyoungie, think thyself too clever for others. Remember, they too have minds thinking the same. If thou are clever, let others speak of it. But thou must strive to become better every day and with a humble mind and spirit endeavour to improve thyself.'

The Thooyoungie sat with bowed head, listening to the kindly words of advice of the Goon na ghun. Then, placing the food before the conscience-stricken Thooyoungie, [they] instructed him to eat.

'But,' he said, 'have you forgiven me?'

'Certainly, we forgave before we came to you. Goodbye.'

And the Goon na ghun returned to their homes beside the seashore, where they lived happily with their wives and children.

Now, they were noted for their sympathy and kindness, always seeking to do good and to relieve the distressed. Many and many kind deeds were shown to the Koala, Whingammie, Peenjullie, Peewingie, Proolgie, and many others of the various tribes. And for this they were honoured and respected. None dared to molest them, lest they would bring the wrath of the many upon their or his head.

Now, as the Beings were thus living together for a short period before going away to various parts of the country, the younger folk were vying with each other in their own kind. Some of the youths would dress themselves in some of the beautiful colours of the rainbow; some would spend quiet moments away from their relations and companions, developing their voices, and when they thought or were satisfied with themselves, guided by instinct, would sing love songs. Others would choose to be with their better sex during the midday sun in the shade of the large trees. Some would go in the little stream that flowed through the steep mountain-side just by the waterfall. Some felt that they could pour out their souls to the girl they loved, or sought to win, by serenading her at twilight. Some whose hearts were overflowing continued to sing at twilight right on through the still hours of the night under the soft silvery moonbeams, until the deepest night, and the soft moon waned before the sunlight.

Among the Bird tribe the songs were beautiful, each note sounded perfect, conveying to her ladyship the heart-beat of the songster. The young beings of Wondangar and Goon na ghun were each in their own kind singing love songs, each heard by their kind. Thus the young Wondangar day by day on the beach, amidst the noise of the breaking waves, [sang] with voice not heard by the keen ear of Kookaburra or Muldarie, they heard not the sweet note of love that awoke in the bosom of the lady Wondangar a similar note. And yet with the unheard song the Wondangar youth wooed his love, and decided that they would in a few days hence go on their honeymoon.

Now, when all the youths and maidens of the Animal, Bird, and Reptile tribes were love-making, the parents were anxious that the girls should marry someone who would love her and provide a nice home.

Now, the Wondangar had been lying so much in the sea that there were other curious beings, but they were not filled with the curiosity of the silly little fish that made many a good meal for them. But these strange beings were on the look-out for some object that would make a solid foundation on which to build a home. These strange lives, the Periwinkle, Barnacle, and a still stranger being, Weed, all these funny beings made a home on the Wondangar body. And they would roll and roll to try to get rid of them. But they refused to be dislodged, and clung the more.

'Oh, what shall we do?'

Just at that moment the Goon na ghun were approaching their mia mia and heard them making the remark: 'Oh, what shall we do?' and they could see that they were in distress, so they said that they would consider it a pleasure to relieve them of the parasites that clung to their bodies. And the Wondangar lay themselves down upon the white sand whilst the Goon na ghun got busy.

And oh, it was a task. The Barnacles clung so fast that the Goon na ghun had some difficulty in removing them. So the Barnacle and Weed refused to be moved alive. The Goon na ghun would take a firestick and burn them before they would let go their hold; at other times they would take a Nulla nulla and beat them so hard that they would break the shell and destroy the parasite.

Oh, the Wondangar had a very bad time of it. They would often say: 'Oh Goon na ghun, let me rise, I cannot endure the pain much longer.'

'Oh, you must allow us to do just what we think, although it may cause you pain. But it will be only a short time. Better to suffer pain in this way than allow them to eat your body and give you a slow and painful death.'

And in this way the Goon na ghun continued day by day.

Now the Wondangar youths thought that whilst the Wondangar fathers were treated and occupied in that manner, it would be an opportunity to elope with their sweethearts. So they met among the sand-hills and discussed the matter.

'Have we not asked the Wondangar for the hand of their daughters, and they refused? We shall no longer plead to these lazy and silly beings. But let us at sunrise tomorrow prepare our canoes and take our sweethearts to some other country farther south.'

'Yes,' said the other Wondangar youths, 'come, let us prepare and speak to our sweet ones tonight.'

So that afternoon was spent in preparation for the morrow. They patched up the leaky canoes, placed gum into the cracks, made strong as well as light paddles, and went into the bays and creeks to procure fish so that they would not be wanting food. Now all was ready. At evening, when the moon was shining brightly upon the ocean and sandy beach, the Wondangar girls stood upon the beach awaiting their lovers.

Presently they came hurriedly toward them, full of excitement, and they wondered why they were so agitated. And they enquired each of their lovers: 'Oh dear, why you are trembling, your heart seems to beat fast. What is the matter? Has someone annoyed you, or did someone die of your relations? Speak!'

Then the Wondangar youths told them of their intention. 'Your father will not give his consent, and I intend to take you away tomorrow morning while the Goon na ghun are busy cleaning their bodies.'

And the Wondangar maidens said: 'First let me speak to father, and if he consents there will be no need to run away, but if he becomes angry and refuses to give his consent, then I am willing to go with you, even to the uttermost parts of the earth.'

'Well done, girls, you have spoken wisely, so be it as you say,' so pleased were the youths at the intelligence of their lady loves.

Off ran the maidens without hesitation.

'Father, a being has asked me to become his wife and go with him to his people and country to become one belonging to his tribe. Father, I love him, will you kindly give your consent?'

'No, no, my child, I am not going to give my consent, and what is more, as soon as the Goon na ghun finish cleaning my body, I shall not allow them to come around our home seeking your company. Do you hear that? You shall no longer see him. I shall be about to prevent him speaking to you. Now, run away and enjoy yourself, for the day after tomorrow, I shall take away your liberty of speaking to him.'

The Wondangar maidens returned to their lovers, looking very sad, their eyes filled with tears, because they dearly loved their unreasonable fathers. But they felt, too, that they loved their sweethearts more. So they told their lovers of their interview with their fathers, and their refusal.

'But,' said the girls, 'we have decided that we shall become your wives.'

The Wondangar youths were glad at the decision of their sweethearts, but they felt sad that they would have to take the only course open to them, of eloping with them. They sat on the beach a while, watching the moonbeams reflecting upon the sea, and as the rolling waves rose and fell, reflect the moon's ray like a mirror. Then they listened to the love-song of the Swans as they were riding on the smooth still water of the nearby river and freshwater lake. Then from the tree not far on the hill they heard the Muldarie singing his love-song, serenading his lady love. The love-song of the Bird tribe intensified the love within the bosom of the Wondangar beings.

'Now,' said the youths, 'we must part to our homes, for tomorrow will open up to us new prospects with new experiences. Good night.'

So the young Wondangar departed to their respective homes.

Just before sunrise, the Goon na ghun were up and astir, breaking their fast, whilst the Mrs Goon na ghun were placing food into the dilly-bags for their lunch. And they advised their husbands not to be giving too much time to those ungrateful beings, because they were so quarrelsome and treacherous that they would at any moment without warning attack any one.

'Now, this must be your last visit to the Wondangar.'

So the Goon na ghun departed upon their mission of love. Little did they know that their Mewee (soul) would accompany the sun to the mysterious west. They arrived at the Wail lar roo mundi (camping-ground) of the Wondangar, and the sun was shining brightly with a promise of a perfect day. They aroused the Wondangar from their slumber and told them to hurry with their breakfast as they were anxious to complete their work and return home at an earlier hour. And they soon had their breakfast and laid themselves down upon the sands, the maidens clinging to their mothers, fondly caressing them, with the thought that in a few hours they would be far from them, and perhaps would never see them any more—these loving souls who had spent many weary hours during the weeks and months and years in feeding them in babyhood and girlhood, up to the present moment, still loving, still caring.

They bade their mothers goodbye as if in fun. The mothers treated it as a joke.

'Good-bye girls,' and they ran off towards the beach and walked along until they came to a bay.

And there were their lovers waiting patiently. The Wondangar maidens took their seats in the canoes, and away they sped, into the Kol ka nia (sea). Just after midday, the elder Wondangar enquired of their wives: 'Where are the Yartooka (girls)? It seems strange that they have not been home to supply us with water to drink. What is the matter with them? Of all the days since we landed upon these shores, this is the first time they have neglected their duty. Up and be gone, find those silly girls, and I shall flog them severely.'

The mother Wondangar began to think of what the girls said to them. Could it be true? Those words, were they said jokingly: 'Good-bye mother?' The vision of those girls flashed vividly before the mental eye. It must be true, they were gone. So the mother Wondangar began their search for their girls. They followed their footprints all along the beach to the bay, and saw other footprints leading to the water's edge. And it dawned upon them that their daughters had fled with their lovers. And with a heavy heart they returned to their husbands with the unpleasant news that their daughters had gone away with their lovers, perhaps never to return.

As soon as the Wondangar heard that their daughters had eloped with the youths they became very angry indeed, and blamed their wives for not paying more attention to them, and allowing them too much liberty. The mothers made no reply but sat down and wept bitterly. The Wondangar became so angry that they rushed into their mia mia and brought out spears and Nulla nulla and boomerangs and threatened to beat their wives. But the Goon na ghun got in between them and acted as a mediator. The Wondangar turned to the Goon na ghun, and began to accuse them for being a party to the plot. 'No, we came here with one object only, and that was to take the barnacles from your bodies.'

'Yes, that was only a blind,' said the Wondangar, 'that was only to keep us in a state so that we would not see what was going on between our daughters and the youths.'

Then their anger became uncontrollable. They turned upon their wives and began to beat them and the Goon na ghun rushed into the fray to defend the wives. Then the Wondangar attacked the Goon na ghun, furiously striking them with the Nulla nulla, causing great flesh wounds. Oh, the poor Goon na ghun were covered with blood. The Wondangar were twice the size of the Goon na ghun, and the odds were against the smaller beings.

Now, the Pelican has a custom after fishing in the early hours of the morning to seek a place upon the beach or sandpit when the tide goes out, where he can rest awhile. Then, when they have done resting, they take to their wings and fly into the blue sky, circling as they go. Well, it was just then that they looked down upon the lakes, rivers, sea, and land. They saw what appeared to be a battle raging, and from their height they could distinguish the Wondangar mercilessly beating the Goon na ghun, who were fast weakening with the loss of blood. One of their number, a youth, half folding his wings, turned earthwards towards the home of the Koala away on the hill-side, among the tall towering trees, etc. He came with increasing velocity, rending the air as he came, causing a great noise like that of a mighty wind. All beings within that locality looked up and saw the Pelican.

'Hello,' they said, 'it is not often we see the easygoing Pelican travelling with such speed, there must be something very important causing such haste.'

'Prepare yourself, let us arm ourselves,' said the Whingammie, Peenjullie, Thooyoungie, and Muldarie; so they equipped themselves with the Nulla nulla, Kykie, and Bankagee and stood at ease, waiting for further developments.

The Koalas, hearing the noise, came out of the hollow of the trees and from among the thick boughs and out of the rock ledges. The Pelican came right to the door of the home of the Chief of Koalas, and told him what he had seen.

'Oh, the Wondangar are flogging the life out of the poor Goon na ghun. Come quickly, before they are beaten to death.'

When the Koala heard this, he rushed into his home, seized a spear and boomerang and coming out, he leaped from the doorway on to the ground, gave one shrill war note and with the speed of an express train ran towards the home of the Wondangar, with the other Koalas running from all directions following their leader and shouting as they ran. Then the Whingammie, Peenjullie, Peewingie, and Thooyoungie all joined in flourishing their weapons as they went down the hill-side, leapt across the stream, up the hill-top and down, swam the rivers, on to the sand-hill, the Waillarroomundi, the home of the Wondangar, on they ran across the sand-hill. They stirred up the dust as if a hurricane blew, still shouting the war-cry.

When they arrived at the seat of the disturbance all was still, but upon the ground were the wounded and bleeding bodies of the Goon na ghun. The Koala, Whingammie, Peenjullie, Peewingie, and Thooyoungie knelt down beside them, bathing their wounded bodies with the salt water and placing the shell vessel to their lips to slake their thirst.

After ministering to their wants they carried them to their homes and when their wives saw the great company coming, they felt something within themselves that something serious had happened, and when at last they placed their husbands down before them, they began to wail: 'Narpinunda (husband of mine), food winner, protector, and friend. Mee willim manpong (Oh, was it thy kindness, thy bowel of mercy, thy sympathy), ever seeking to do good to friends and enemies alike. And now this reward. Thock kal limdoom ploombie (thou wouldst not listen to the warning given you) of the treacherous Wondangar, but continued to minister to their wants. Tharn und thungara (thou wouldst not even listen to me), thy wife and helpmate. Yan up el lun (Oh, what shall become of me and thy children)?'

They would repeat this over again and again, all through the evening into the midnight hour, and then they retired to rest, with a broken heart.

The Koala with the rest of his tribe, the Animal tribe, the Bird tribe, and the Reptile tribe came very early in the morning before the sun rose to pay their last respects to the dying Goon na ghun. When they arrived all was still, for during the night the burden of sorrow was so great on the wives of the Goon na ghun that they passed on first to the mysterious west, awaiting the coming of their husbands. And the various tribes gathered about and around them, anxious to do some last act to those whose lives were spent in doing kindly acts, by helping to feed the aged and infirmed and the sick.

They felt greatly the passing out of a whole race or tribe so good, and they asked the dying Goon na ghun where they would like to be laid to rest, and they whispered back a reply: 'In the bottom of the clear sea water in the quiet bays and coves where the white sand is free from weed. Place us gently down into the water and let us lie peacefully, do not allow anyone to disturb us, whilst our spirit goes to Wyerriewarr (to the skies).'

So when their spirit took its departure from the torn bodies of the Goon na ghun, the Animals, Birds, and Reptiles wept bitterly, and that night they committed their bodies to the water. And the moon rose and looked upon this great and solemn gathering, and it shone so brightly, lighting up the hill-side, shedding its beam upon the water of the bay. Everything looked so pleasing that the Animals, Birds, and Reptiles expressed the parting wish to gaze one long last look upon the Goon na ghun. They looked and looked with eyes dimmed, with tears of sorrow welling up into their eyes, as if the fountain of grief had broken loose. But they looked more eagerly to impress upon their minds the memory of a good people.

Presently a transformation took place. Was it that their eyes were deceiving them, for behold, beneath the clear water of the bay they saw the stars shining—Naboolea, Nebalee Wy young gurrie, Jeirellang, Mungungee. They looked with wonderment and amazement. They wiped the tears from their eyes to get a clearer vision. And they saw the stars shining upon the white sand bottom, reflecting the moon rays back up through the clear water.

The Crow whispered: 'They are not dead but live, fulfilling the great plan for which they were intended.'

And before parting, the Koala asked that everyone present should come along tomorrow to hold a meeting in the valley:

'To discuss what we shall do with the Wandangar, because they have committed a grave crime, which must not be overlooked, in causing the death of one of the most goodly beings. And also the other matter of considering whether we shall adopt one common language. All previous intercourse we have done by sign and gesture, and now we must come to some understanding so that we can converse one with the other.'

They all shouted: 'Kay hey,' and departed to their various homes, some among the great forest in the valley, others on the hill-side in trees, some among the rock-holes, some down by the lakes and river side, each to their fancied homes. Now, when they arrived at their Mia mia, they sat down, thinking of what they should say and what questions would be asked, some keeping later hours than others. But after a while they were snugly asleep in their warm beds, dreaming of hunting and fishing, etc.

Now when the sun arose with promise of a bright and beautiful day, all life was astir, hastily partaking of the morning meal, all eager to be present at the conference. After everyone had enjoyed his meal, each made their way towards the appointed place in the valley. Every member of the various tribes and families was represented. The Whingammie and Peenjullie took it upon themselves to place everyone in order. They had them arranged, sitting tier above tier on one side of the valley. In the centre of the valley was the stump of what was at one time a large tree. The stump stood about ten to fifteen feet high.

'That,' said the Whingammie, 'will make a splendid pulpit from which the Koala will be able to see every being, and all beings will see him, and from such a position as that he will be able to deliver his address.'

So it was decided that it should be so.

Now they were all seated, and waited patiently for the Koala. Presently, with his bodyguard, he arrived. The Whingammie and Peenjullie went forward to meet him and escorted him to the stump, and with sign and gesture explained that they would consider it an honour for him to mount the stump and address them from it, as he would have a better view and command of the audience. So he expressed himself that it was very considerate of them to provide such an admirable position. So he mounted the stump, followed by his chief bodyguards, who had their spears and Woomera and a Nulla nulla. They stood on either side of him, and the rest of the bodyguards were arranged in order around the base of the stump.

Now, this old Koala was a Mooncumbulli, a philosopher and a linguist. He had during his voyage studied the various languages, customs, and traditions, and during their short sojourn in Australia he became proficient and that is why he was bold enough to summon them all to a conference in which he dared to address each tribe in its own language. Not many of the tribes knew this and they were wondering how he was going to make himself clearly understood. But he first spoke the Bird language and told them of his wish that their language was much better than the others and would they object to the others acquiring it.

'Oh, not at all,' answered the Lyre Bird and Cockatoo, who were the chief speakers selected by the Peewingie and Peenjullie.

The Lyre Bird said that it would be a splendid idea if they would come and be taught by the Cockatoo. Continuing, he said: 'I propose that he shall be selected as a schoolmaster.'

'Yes,' said the Crow, 'I support the proposition made by the Lyre Bird,' and it was carried by all the Birds exclaiming: 'Hick, ka (Yes, be it so as you wish).'

Then the Koala turned and addressed the Reptiles and Lizards in their own tongue, and oh, you should have seen the astonishment upon the face of the Thooyoungie (Goanna). He turned around and addressing the Frilled Lizard, said: 'Am I awake, is this all a dream?'

Turning his head to the right and then to the left, he said: 'I was about to ask you that same question. Something has come over us, or we are affected by yesterday and last night,' referring to the Goon na ghun.

'Perhaps that may be so, but why is it that everything looks so real, nothing fanciful about the visions that are about us? The voice of the Koala is so distinct that there is no doubting the sound of his voice, and I feel sensitive of all my surroundings. And the sun is well, right reaching the home of Naboolea. I cannot be dreaming.'

The Monarrie (Blue-tongue) or Sleepy Lizard was sitting quietly enthralled at the wonderful style and delivery the Koala had of their language, and when the Thooyoungie and Frilled Lizard were whispering to each other and shifting from side to side, they were annoying the Monarrie. He became so angry that he took hold of his Nulla nulla and struck the Thooyoungie and Frilled Lizard such a blow upon their heads, so suddenly, that they leaped to their feet and staggering, they saw stars and it looked as if the earth was rolling over and over and the trees and other objects were being whirled round and round so quickly that it was difficult to distinguish what they were. When the Kookaburras saw what had taken place, and saw the Thooyoungie and Frilled Lizard reeling like drunken men, they burst into a fit of laughter:

'Ka ka ko ko kee.'

The Cockatoo could not remain solemn much longer and joined in the laughter, and all the other Birds, the Muldarie (Magpie) and Tharrangarie (Crow) would have joined in had it not been for the Peenjullie rising to his feet and calling: 'Tou a tou (order, order)!' And they instantly ceased laughing. 'Remember we are not here to entertain Runballarumb, but to consider more matters that are of a serious nature relating to the tragic event of yesterday. Now who is the culprit who has dared to disturb this assembly?'

Then turning to the Koala, the Peenjullie said: 'Will you pardon me, as next in command to the majority of this great gathering, that someone of my race has caused this disturbance? Will you kindly be seated until I shall endeavour to quell their feelings?'

'Thank you,' said the Koala, 'I shall be seated.'

'Now,' said the Peenjullie, 'let the person or persons, the beginners of the interruption, come forward and explain yourself or yourselves.'

The Monarrie rose to his feet and strode forward towards the platform and, facing the audience, said: 'Well friends, I was so fascinated by the flow of language, which was so perfect and delightful, coming from one who is a foreigner to my kind and race, that when the Thooyoungie and the Frilled Lizard, who were as others no doubt filled with wonderment and could not believe their vision nor the sense of hearing, began to express themselves in loud tones which disturbed and annoyed me, I struck them on the head with my Nulla nulla, and now the rest you know.'

Then turning to the Koala: 'You will pardon me, won't you? Your command of my language overwhelmed me, I did not know what I was doing at the moment.'

The Koala rose and said that he forgave him and returned to his seat, and the Thooyoungie and Frilled Lizard came forward and each was given time to make an explanation, which both expressed in the same words.

'First, we were so astounded at your selection of the vocabulary of our language, that we thought all we heard was a dream, and instead of continuing [with] that, we both gave vent to our feelings, and turned first one ear and then the other to be sure that what we heard was real. And what is more, we spoke out so loud that we caused a disorder and annoyed the Monarrie, and he struck us a blow on the head and almost stunned us.'

'Will you forgive the Monarrie?'

'Yes, I forgive him,' and they returned to their seat beside the Monarrie and sat throughout the meeting, satisfied that all they heard and saw was real.

'And now with your permission, shall we be seated?

The Koala replied: 'Will you be seated,' and the Thooyoungie and Frilled Lizard took their seats beside the Monarrie, and they listened more attentively with the full assurance that what was taking place was a reality and not a dream.

And they all agreed to what the Koala advocated—the necessity of one common language.

And at this juncture the Koala announced that they should adjourn for lunch and a few moments' rest, and each respective tribe retired to the shade under the larger trees, others sitting upon the green grass by a little stream nearby wending its way to the mighty ocean, with little fishes sporting in the limpid water. Some of the feathered tribes sat on the bank and caught fishes for lunch and some, who were in such a hurry that they forgot to bring their lunch, hunted among the wattle and honeysuckle trees for grubs to supply themselves with food.

When lunch was over, they sat in the assembly and again the Koala mounted his platform with his bodyguards beside him and upon the ground surrounding the platform.

Then he began his address, calling their attention to another aspect which was of a more serious nature than the former, that is, the cruel assault of the Wondangar upon the good-natured and sympathetic Goon na ghun: 'We shall always remember the untiring labours of these good beings. There is not one family among this great gathering that has not been helped and relieved of their tiresome burden of domestic life and things in general, and not only so when the heart was bowed in sorrow at the loss of loved ones and friends. There was always one who, with kind words, poured the oil of comfort into the wounded heart and pierced soul. What makes it so sad is that there is not one of them left and unlike the others of the great and good beings, they have not ascended into Wyerriewarr but expressed their dying wish to be committed to the water. That wish we have fulfilled. Now what shall be done to the Wondangar? Are we to allow them to go free? They have become a menace to the safety of all tribes. I and my family would have dealt with them more severely some time back, but for the Goon na ghun's sake we did not like to do so. No doubt you have, each respective tribe, had the same thought. And now we must take steps. What shall the punishment be?'

They replied, shouting: 'Chastise them with Nulla nulla or one stroke from the Marpungie' (a weapon like a boomerang, with one end eighteen inches or two feet long, which forms the handle, and this is used to cause a very bad wound, sometimes with fatal results, fracturing the skull).

And the assembly moved that they would suggest that a select number of the Koala family should be entrusted to deal with the Wondangar at sunrise tomorrow, and that all tribes should be present. The Chief of the Koalas accepted on behalf of his family the duty of carrying out the punishment. So the meeting closed, and each one returned, some to their homes, others to hunt food, and the Reptiles went among the rocks and sheltered spots and lay basking in the sunshine.

At sunrise on the following morning all tribes were gathered upon the sandbeach, the home of the Wondangar, waiting the arrival of the Koalas. Out of the shrubs that grew by the sea shore came the Koalas, marching in order four abreast with their leader walking in front. They bore upon their faces the seriousness of the position. The other tribes formed a semi-circle around the Wondangar, with the opening part leading into the sea. Now the forming of this semicircle was for a purpose, as you will see later on. Now the Wondangar were within this enclosure. They were looking half-sleepy and stupid, wondering about this visit.

Then the Chief Koala called the attention of the Wondangar and spoke, addressing them in their own language, saying: 'Oh Wondangar, through your hasty temper with no justification whatever, you have beaten with your clubs unmercifully the Goon na ghun beings, from whom you have derived greater assistance than any of the other beings of the various tribes. And it was whilst in the execution of one of these kindly acts that you attacked with Nulla nulla and spear. And now we, the Animal, Bird, and Reptile tribes, have decided to mete out to you the punishment you so justly deserve. And it will be one severe blow delivered by a select member of my tribe with a Marpungie. Come, rise and receive your punishment.'

But the Wondangar said: 'We are going to fight you.'

'There is no hope of you carrying out your threat. Come Whingammie, Peenjullie, Thooyoungie, take and bind the Wondangar securely with ropes.'

These three beings whose names were called stepped forward and bound the Wondangar, and each select Koala moved forward and raising their Marpungie, delivered such a mighty stroke that it sent the weapon deep into the hard and brainless skull of the victim, burying the point of the Marpungie right up to the handle. And the shock was so severe that it stunned the Wondangar and the Koala withdrew the weapon, covered in blood, and the Wondangar lay so still that the assemblage thought that they were dead.

But presently, each Wondangar took in a supply of fresh air and the breathing caused the blood to squirt up through the fractured skull, and when they awoke out of their stupor and came back to their senses, they were aware of a severe pain in the region of the head. And feeling the warm blood trickling down their cheeks, they rushed into the sea to bathe themselves, diving into the water and rising to breathe, continuing as they went farther and farther out to sea. And this is what they have been doing since that eventful day witnessed by the Animal, Bird, and

Reptile tribes, right up to the present day from time immemorial, in the form of a whale.

And as for the good-hearted Goon na ghun, you will see them lying in the bottom of the sea, victims of the cruel Wondangar. But for their good work in doing for others what they would have others do for them and going further into the work, they did more, by doing for them kindly acts and speaking words of comfort. And although beaten, and with arms and legs severed from their bodies, their good spirit after their death gave them the form and shape of Stars, and their bodies, lying in the deep blue sea, are reflected in the stars above us.

A Wonderful Bun Bar Rang (Lizard)

After a long time the Eagle forced the Retculdie (Water Rat) to give up his secret, telling him that it should become known to all the tribes—Animal, Bird, Reptile, and Insect—for use in their cooking and lighting and to give warmth and comfort in their various homes. And then the Retculdie had demonstrated how to make fire: he rubbed two sticks and the striking of two pieces of flint produced a spark, and when the spark came in contact with fine grass which was rubbed and worked, pulled to pieces then rubbed again and rolled into a ball, it would then burst into flame, and all they needed to do was to place small twigs and sticks and later logs, and they would have a fire large enough to do anything. When he did this, each tribe took away a firestick and made other fires from this stick, which would continually be supplied with fire with sticks and large logs. So that when travelling from one hunting-ground to another they would have or appoint a member of their family and tribe to see that a fire was taken on their journey.

This custom was continued for a long, long while until one day there was a great thunderstorm and rain and wind. Those who lived in the plain country hastened away to the mountain and their fires were all extinguished; in fact all the tribes suffered the loss of fire, even the Water Rat. They became careless and after generations of generations, the children of the various tribes forgot how to produce fire because they had developed a habit of carrying firesticks.

Now all the Chiefs—Animal, Bird, Reptile, and Insect—were allowed to have two wives, who must be sisters. Now the Eagle Hawk made a very peculiar choice in this regard. Every other tribe expected that he would choose from the feather or Animal tribe. But what a surprise, he sent his messenger the Falcon to summon the two beautiful daughters of the Snake with a very red belly. So these two young ladies came along, escorted by their uncles, brothers of their mother. On the way, people were staring in wonderment and astonishment. When they came to the Hawk family camp, the Chief was sitting on his Mia mia and when they came very near, he came down and met them.

Then the uncle said: 'Oh Peewingie, Chief of the Bird tribes, we are proud and honoured that so great a tribe should condescend to choose wives from the camp of your humble servant. We willingly submit them to you. They shall become your servants for now and forever.'

The Eagle Hawk said not a word but held out his hand, taking hold of theirs, and received them unto himself. Now at this point we shall refer to these two sisters as they are known today: Kryang yartooka (Maiden Snakes). The members of their family were distinguished from others as they had a very, very red colour upon their bellies. Red to the Aborigines is symbolic of that fiery temper, warmth of hospitality, and healing effect. Their nature was all this.

At this time of the story all food was eaten raw. One day, whilst the Eagle Hawk was out hunting, these Yartookang kry, or Kryang yartooka, were just before midday basking in the sunshine and at this particular spot there were several Ant-beds, with the appearance of a stump of a tree thoroughly perforated with tiny holes, and they were deserted by the Ants. And on this summer day the sun was shining brilliantly with intense heat. These sisters were resting upon an Ant-bed each, and the heat of the sun and the heat from their red bellies caused a fire to be lit in these Ant-beds, and they both struggled and got off the beds and looked and saw a fire burning without smoke.

'Oh, wonders of wonders!' they both exclaimed, 'what a discovery. Throw sand upon the fire to hide it from the others.'

And from that day on they strictly guarded their secret. Then one day the Eagle Hawk came home with some food, and he equally divided the spoil and he went to sleep before having anything to eat. So the Kryang yartooka hastened to their fire heap, gently scraped the sand from the ant-bed that had already become their fire-place, and began cooking their food. When this was done they covered up their fire again, sat down, and ate their meal. Then they returned to their Lord and Master, the King of Birds, and sat on either side of him.

The Eagle arose, and feeling hungry, asked that his meal should be served, so they both anxiously waited upon him. Whilst he was eating he said to his wives: 'It is strange that I smell cooked food. Have you been favoured with such?'

'Oh no,' they both replied, 'where do you think that we, thy wives, should be honoured above all others with such a long-lost favour?'

'Come now my wives, have I smelt aright, that you both have had cooked fish? Where is your portion? Let me see,' demanded the Eagle.

'We have eaten the allowance you gave us.'

But this is where they stopped speaking—they did not say whether cooked or raw.

The Eagle did not say any more but flew away in search of more food. He returned and divided the food and this time, he did not go to sleep, but sat up and ate his food straightaway. And he asked his wives that they should join him but in this they both declined, asking to be excused.

'Why?' said the Eagle, 'you have been accustomed to eat as soon as I give you your food but of late you eat in secret. Come now my wives, eat.'

But they still refused. Then the Eagle said: 'I go a-hunting. Good-bye wives!' and he flew away and travelled in a circle, coming back to where they were, thinking that he would find out their secret fire. But they were too cunning. They saw by his action that he began to be suspicious.

'Eat my wives, you are both looking hungry. Eat and be strong.'

'Not until you bring us some fish,' answered the wives.

So the Eagle Hawk flew away across the mountain until he came to a billabong. And he sat upon a limb of a large gum tree, with his keen eyes fixed upon the surface of the water. A perch feeding among the [reeds] rose a little, a whirr, the Eagle shot like an arrow straight upon its prey and struck its talon deep into the flesh of the fish, then rose and hastened back to his wives, who were sitting down sunning themselves.

When they heard the flap of the wings of their Lord and Chief they rose hurriedly to greet him, and he gave them the much sought-for food and asked them to have their meal.

'But,' said his wives, 'we have just finished our meal and are feeling satisfied. We go to rest with your kind permission.'

The Eagle began to become uneasy about their conduct, since he smelt cooked food. So he went away and met the Magpie and told him about the suspicion he had about his wives.

'Now what shall we do to find out whether they really have the lost secret of fire? Would you mind going among the tribes and asking for volunteers?'

So the Magpie went and asked the Cockatoo. 'Oh yes, I shall endeavour to find out where they hide the fire.'

So he set off and spent days and days waiting round watching for signs of smoke. He said to himself: 'Well, if they should make a fire I shall notice smoke rising.'

So he waited and waited and began to get uneasy. So he thought he would try another plan, and would follow after them when they received the allowance of food from their husband.

When the Eagle returned with the spoils, he gave them their portion and when the Eagle went to have his afternoon rest, the wives sneaked away to cook their food and the Cockatoo followed. And his clumsy feet became entangled in the boughs of the shrubs and he stooped and used his beak as a snip to cut his way through and they would click, a noise which would give a warning to the Kryang yartooka, who snuck away from their fireside and lay quietly among the bushes. Cocky would sit still, and after thinking that he had waited long enough, would begin to go forward. Again his feet became entangled in a creeper and he fell down scared, thinking someone had tripped him, so he screeched and, of course, the Snakes would just simply leave the place.

The Cockatoo returned to the Magpie and told him of his failure. Then the Magpie asked the Emu, thinking that he would, by having a long neck, see farther. He tried but failed.

'Now,' said the Magpie, 'this will never do. The King of Birds, the Eagle Hawk, will make a proclamation that should any fail in future, they shall be slain or put in prison. Now we must make a mighty effort. Let us form a circle round about them and draw closer and closer until we shall come upon them. Then someone must see them, surely.'

So they all agreed and set off on their mission. There were the Magpies, Cockatoos, Butcher-birds, Kookaburras, Emus, Wrens, Little Wrens, and Willy Wagtails, and a great many other members of the Bird tribe, forming a large circle, coming nearer and nearer. And the Cockatoo, with his clumsy feet gripping and falling, caused the Koo ka kee a great deal of amusement, and just as they got very near to the Kryang yartooka they could scent the smell of flesh cooking. All eyes were strained before them, stretching their necks and tip-toeing, when the Cockatoo slipped and fell. The Kookaburras could not resist it any longer and burst into laughter and spoilt the show. They sneaked off, feeling ashamed of themselves.

Then they called for the assistance of the Animal tribe but they were a greater failure than the Birds, because when they came within a certain distance their mouths would water when they smelt the appetising food that was roasting and they would hurry forward and come tumbling over twigs and sticks, and the Kryang yartooka would hear them coming and would disappear into the grass and bushes.

They began to become very desperate and threatened the Kryang yartooka that they must reveal the fire; if not, they would be killed.

The Magpie said: 'Why should you keep from all the tribes a much needed want?'

But the Kryang yartooka said to them: 'You forget we are wives of the great Bird Chief, and you cannot force us to tell.'

And they were all astounded at this reply, which they all recognised. And in shame of defeat, with heads bowed, they all disappeared to their own mia mia. As the Kookaburras were walking homeward enjoying jokes of their defeat, they came across a Lizard tribe, who had just returned from a hunting expedition with their great spoil of game and were making their mia mia to camp for the night. They asked the Kookaburras to spend the night with them, to which they willingly gave their consent. And as they were sitting down enjoying as best as possible their evening meal, one of the Bun bar rang—for that was the name of this little family of Lizards—said: 'Oh, if we could only have the long-lost fire, what a happy evening we should be spending—cooked food and light and warmth.'

'Well,' said a Koo ka ka, 'there is fire and we must make an effort to take it from the Kryang Marrallang, the Snake sisters, wives of the Eagle Hawk; they have the secret. We have tried all the smart hunters to wrest the secret but they all failed. We tried all in a body, formed a large circle around them but the Cockatoo at the last moment got his clumsy foot into something and fell. This happened to him and you know how excitable he is; he screeched and howled, and we thought that Muldarpie had him. Of course the noise warned the Kryang of our approach; and now perhaps you may be able to suggest means by which we shall procure the secret from them.'

The little Bun bar rang thought and thought all through the long hours of the night, and then he quietly went to bed and slept soundly. And in the morning some of the Bun bar rang began their journey homeward. But this one particular little Lizard expressed a desire to stay with the other tribe to try and help to procure the light. So he went out to the place where the two Kryang usually spent their time in the absence of their husband.

Now the little Bun bar rang came back to the camp and told the Cockatoo, Magpie, and others of that tribe, as well as the Animal and Lizard tribe, and asked that some of the picked men of each tribe, recognised hunters, should accompany him. He asked them to follow in his trail at a distance. So they all set off, the Bun bar rang leading about a hundred yards or more, winding his way in and out of the bushes and shrubs until they came to the spot that made every one excitable, because they could smell something like food cooking.

So the little Bun bar rang suggested that he should go by himself until he reached a certain spot where he thought it likely the Kryang would lie; on his way he would crawl flat upon his belly for a few yards, then stand upon his three legs and hold up the fourth one to beckon the others to follow or stop, just as the case may be. Then he would go forward through bush and grass, then take another glimpse to see how far away the Kryang were; in this he would hold up one of his front hands and beckon them to keep perfectly quiet, then he would put the hand down and raise the other—perhaps the right hand. He saw the Kryang busy cooking their food with fire that was cunningly hidden in the disused Ant-bed and the Kryang sitting behind the Ant-bed enjoying their meal.

The Bun bar rang crept up cautiously, stopping now and again, beckoning first with the right and then with the left hand. All this while he carried a grass-tree stick and when he came near enough he poked the grass-tree stick into the Ant-bed and allowed it to remain a few moments, then withdrew it, and it was alight. When he saw that the grass-tree stick blazed he ran away towards where the others were waiting, and on his way he set fire to grass and bushes and the country was all ablaze.

The Kryang became very angry indeed when they saw that their secret was discovered; they swore vengeance upon all life that came within striking distance—they would inflict a wound that would cause death. They also became the most dreaded enemy of the Animal, Bird, and Lizard tribes since that day when the little Bun bar rang stole their secret and spread the fire all over the country, and they themselves were deprived. The Kryang were able to use fire only when it was embedded within the Ant-bed, and now since it was taken from the ant-bed the Kryang are unable to restore or use it.

Now the action the little Bun bar rang adopted on that day was so trying that, although many and many years have passed, you will see him anywhere among the bushes or rocky country crawling and stopping, and raising first one front leg and then the other, as if in the act of giving a sign to stop, or beckoning to come on. This is one of the peculiar habits of the little Bun bar rang that he still retains in memory of that far-gone day when his ancestor gave the then world or restored the gift of fire to become the property of all.

Yara Ma Tha Who

There were many strange beings who lived a long while ago, many, many years, before Captain Cook found a landing at Kurnell. Some took the form of the mythological Bunyip, the Tuckoonie, and the Thuyoaniperrie (a queer little red man). Now, this little man of ours was an exceptionally funny fellow. He stood about four feet and he had such a big head for such a small body; in fact, the biggest parts of this little man were his mouth, throat, and belly, with no teeth in his jaw, and he would just simply swallow his food. And the strangest part of all was that this little fellow would swallow an ordinary man you see in the streets of our towns or cities. His head and mouth was something like a snake's head and he would open his mouth just as you see the snake do.

These little people or beings did not hunt their food or make spears, Nulla nulla, or boomerangs like their bigger brother Man. But they were in possession of a queer hand; at the points of their fingers were cup-shapes, like the suckers of the octopus, and so were the tips of their toes. And they lived mostly in thick bough trees and preferred the Wild Fig-tree. Now, during the summer months, men, women, and children often would come and seek shelter from the burning rays of the sun, or in winter they would be protected by the thick boughs from rain and hail. So that is where these little men (Yara ma tha who) chose to live, because it would save them the trouble of going about hunting for food.

Now, when a little boy would be by himself, he fell an easy prey to the Yara ma tha who and everybody dreaded this queer chap and would often go and seek shelter in caves or under ledges of rock on the mountain-side. Now, this Yara ma tha who had a strange way after he captured a person. He would pounce upon him like a cat does upon a mouse; only in this case, the Yara ma tha who is smaller than his prey, but when he springs and captures his victim he places his hands and feet upon the body, which sucks the blood from the victim and leaves him helpless upon the ground.

I may say that he does not try to suck all the blood from the body but leaves sufficient to keep him alive while he walks round to raise an appetite, which causes him to return, and he will first lie upon the ground facing the victim and crawl like a goanna and open his mouth wide and suck the food down head-first, then he will rise and stand on his little leg and dance and dance around until the person is well inside his belly. Then he goes away to a river or pool of water and drinks and drinks, and then goes to some valley near by and lies down to sleep. And when he wakes he will do just what the whale did to Jonah—spew him out.

The person would still be alive, lying upon the ground, quietly feigning death. The Yara ma stands beside him, and then walks away a few yards (say, about five paces) and suddenly turns round, walks back and probes the victim in the side with a stick to see whether he is alive. If the person shows no sign of life the Yara ma walks about ten paces, turns suddenly, and goes to the side of the victim and this time tickles him under the neck or arm. If the person again shows no sign of life, he repeats this but goes further (say about fifty yards) and comes back and tickles the person; and then lastly he goes away and sits behind a bush, watching the victim.

Now, every child is taught that should they be captured, to offer no resistance, because they have a better chance of escape to allow themselves to be swallowed and the Yara ma to spew them out, as it was the custom of all Yara ma to do from time immemorial. Should the Yara ma fail to do this, then the Spirit of the Wild Fig-tree would slay him by entering into his head through the ear and cause such mumbling noise ending with intense silence, and the Yara ma spirit would leave the rude body and become cold fungus that grows upon the trees which shed a dull glow at night.

The Yara ma, after spewing the person out and going through his performance, seeks a bush and lies down to rest, sleeping soundly. And the victim seeks his opportunity and runs away. And should the Yara ma hear the sound of running feet, he would rise very suddenly and give chase, shouting all the while: 'Yara ma, Yara ma, which way hast thou gone, which way hast thou gone, my victim, my victim?'

One advantage that the victim has is that the Yara ma is not able to run very fast; he has the gait or wobbling style in walking like the Cockatoo.

Failing to again capture his prey he would go away where there were rock-holes or waterholes and drink up all the water there. This he would do to deprive the people of their water supply. Then they would go in search of the wild apple-tree and strip the bark, and sometimes the water would come forth from a cavity between the bark and trunk of the tree. Now this would give the Yara ma another opportunity to capture a person because he was more able to attack his prey from a tree thick in boughs than attempting to do so upon the ground.

Supposing the same person was caught and swallowed again, or should it happen three times, the first time he was swallowed he would become shorter in stature, the second time shorter still, until the last time he would become and resemble the Yara ma, only in this first stage of transformation the victim's skin would become very smooth, with visible signs of hair on the body and head. They would remain thus for a short time and then long hair would begin to cover the body very thickly indeed. And in this way the people were gradually changing from ordinary human beings into the little mythical beings that roam about among the dense forest along the coast of the Pacific Ocean.

This is one of the stories told to bad children: that if they do not behave themselves the Yara ma tha who will come and take them and make them to become one of their own.

How Teddy Lost His Tail

Once upon a time, long, long ago, before the Animal, Bird, Reptile, and Insect life came to Australia, they occupied the many islands that existed in the ocean Karramia, a place of the beginning of day, where all is peace and rest. The Kangaroo tribe lived upon one island, the Eagle Hawk tribe upon another, the Iguana tribe upon another.

Now, upon one beautiful island, with high and lofty mountain peaks reaching into the sky, and with deep valleys clothed with great giant gum trees, there lived the Teddy Bear with his tribe. The Teddy Bears were a wise and intelligent tribe. The elders would take the young Teddy Bears up into the mountains and instruct them in the knowledge of astronomy. One night as they were gazing into the sky their attention was drawn to a streak of light away in the south.

'That is strange,' said the elder of the tribe, staring at the light in the south.

Then he looked to the north and saw another light shining against the northern sky.

Night after night the elders of the Bear tribe would climb to the mountain top to hold a consultation as to this mysterious light that appeared at intervals during the night. The elder of the tribe, a venerable old Bear, eventually felt convinced that he had arrived at a solution to the mystery, and he said: 'Children, tomorrow, just as day breaks, let every man Bear, woman Bear, and child Bear gather and carry to yonder mountain a bundle of sticks. This must be done for seven sun risings.'

So every Bear able to work began the tedious labour of carrying sticks to the mountain top. On the evening of the seventh rising sun, everything was in readiness. The great Philosopher Bear gave instructions that all the Bears should attend and watch, and they all congregated on the mountain where the sticks were stacked. Then the Philosopher with another elder of the tribe sat upon the mountain to watch the result.

At sunset everyone was awaiting instructions. Presently the small voice pierced the air: 'Fire the wood-heap.'

They began rubbing the sticks together until they kindled a spark and the wood-heap was set ablaze. It made a huge bonfire, and the flames leapt up lighting the darkness for miles around and across the sea. The Elder Bear, who was sitting gazing intently through the darkness, saw answering flashes around the horizon: north, south, east, and west.

'The problem is solved,' said the Philosopher Bear. 'We shall discuss it further tomorrow.'

Next morning all the Bears rose early and sat around in orderly groups on ledges of rocks, on boughs of trees, and in every available place, awaiting the arrival of the Philosopher Bear. Then they started to chatter among themselves, and their voices gradually grew louder. One of their number, seeing the Philosopher approaching, shouted: 'Order!' The Elder took his place among them and commenced to address them. There was an instant silence, as they strained their ears to hear what he was about to say.

'Children,' he said, 'there are other lands like ours all around us, which are occupied by strange and queer people I am not able to describe, as I have never seen them; but I do say that there are other forms of life. Prepare your canoes, north, south, east and west, and scour the oceans and bring me information.'

The male Bears dragged their canoes into the water and set out on their voyage of discovery. They paddled for a long time until they eventually landed in beautiful new countries and they went about among the new tribes, noticing their customs and the kind of people they were, and when they had learned all they could of them they returned to the Elder. Each explorer told his story, one describing the Kangaroo, one the Emu, and another the Iguana, the Platypus, the Eagle Hawk, the Lyre Bird and so forth. And very wonderful the descriptions sounded to the people who had never seen any land but their own.

After a week the Elder gave instructions to build many, many canoes, saying: 'We will paddle our way to the great new country.'

All the male Bears set to work making canoes, some making as many as a dozen. At last they were completed and they paddled across the sea till they reached Australia. The landing-place was at Shoalhaven. After they had lived in Australia for some time, wandering away into the Blue Mountains and up and down the Parramatta, Hawkesbury, Hunter, and the great Murray rivers, they thought it would be nice to ask the Kangaroos, the Emus, the Eagle Hawks, the Iguanas, and all the Animal, Bird, Reptile, and Insect tribes to come down and share this wonderful country. So once more they set out in their canoes and brought them back with them, distributing to them various parts of Australia.

When they returned to their home at Shoalhaven, they met with stormy weather and paddled through the angry surf, their canoes being so tossed about that every Bear fell out of the canoes and had to swim ashore. The hungry sharks followed them and bit their tails off, and that accident completely subdued the adventurous spirit of the Teddy Bears.

GLOSSARY

This glossary is not intended to reproduce contemporary linguistic orthography; it is rather intended as a simple guide for the readers of this book. Not all spelling variations found in the text are included. These variations, where they occur, should be clearly seen as the same word or words. There are a few phrases appearing in the text which we have been unable to gloss.

Unaipon used an anglicised spelling system, and chose to spell each word syllable by syllable (with a gap between each syllable), supposedly to aid pronunciation. Often the word breaks do not correspond to contemporary practice. For instance, his *Rich er rook itty* (Willy wagtail) would now be rendered *ritjaruki*.

Most of the words are taken from Unaipon's own language, Ngarrindjeri. But there is no comprehensive contemporary dictionary of the Ngarrindjeri language one can consult for comparative purposes. Interested readers can cross-check Unaipon's words with the old written sources of Ngarrindjeri words, such as those prepared by missionaries H. A. E. Meyer (1843) and G. Taplin (1879), or examine the original texts with interlinear translations produced in Berndt (1993).

BANN KA GEE (RANKAGEE)	Boomerang
BARRAAL	Wallaby
BOONAH	Earlier name for Narroondarie
BROO PAR	Platypus
BUN BOON	Sacred meeting ground
BUNYIP	Monster

BYAMEE	Father of all
CHILLI	Gnats
COOLAMON (KOOLUMOON)	Long wooden dish
COONGNURRIE	Swan or tribal name
CORROBOREE	Ceremony with dance and song
CUL PAR RIE	Widgeon duck
GHERAWHAR	Goanna
GO ROOL	Bandicoot
GOOL LUN NAGA	Green Frog
GOON NA GHUN	Starfish
HICK KA	Is that so? (also 'Be it as you wish')
HYARRINUMB	Great Spirit; Whole Spirit
ITTY ITTA	Kangaroo rat
JEIR ELL ANG	Star
KALLITTHIE	Hail spirit
KAMILAROI	Language group, northern NSW
KARLDOOKIE	Flower tops of reeds
KARNARK, KANNARK	Weapon or Nulla nulla
KARRAMI	East
KARRAMIA	The eastern sea
KARROONNOO	Sister
KAY HEY	Hurrah
KAY KAY	Well done
KELI	Dog
KEY KEY (KYKIE)	Reed spear
KINDIE	Raft
KOL KA NIA	South Sea
KOLKAMI	South
KOO KA KA (BURRA)	Kookaburra
KOONE	Game
KORN MAR CULDAR (KOMNUKALDA)	Mankind
KORNMUND	Full manhood
KORRAWALDI (KOWRAWALDI)	Tribal name
KREEL THOOL LIN	Fish spearing
KREEL THOOL LIN YERI	Fish-spearing expert
KRINGAL	Grow
KROO WULTHIE	Fire-flies

KROOLTHUMIE	Owl
KROWALLIE	Blue crane
KRY YIE	Tiger snake
KRYANG YARTOOKA	Maiden snakes
KRYUNDA	Snake
KUK KOO LOON	Calling out, making a noise
KULE THOU OO	In the long ago
KULLEE EM BEEN	Platypus
KUTCHLE KUTCHLE	True, let it be as you say
KUTHUWARR	Cockatoo
LAWARRIE	Cape Barren Goose
LAWRAWAL	Upwards
LOO LOO POON COLD	Northwest
MANPARRIE	Frogs
MAR KAR REE	Moon
MAR RALLANG	Pages Island
MARDPUNG	Stone axe
MARPUNGIE	Weapon
MARRI	Hairy; fur
MARRUNGARIE (THARRANGIE)	Crow
MARRUNHONIYIE	Tribal name
MEE WEE	Powerful (spiritual) feelings, usually located in the stomach
MEE WELL LUM	Mind of my tribe
MEEMUND	Full womanhood
MEMINAN	Young women
MEMINIE	Woman
MIA MIA	Shelter
MIN KERRIE	Flirt
MIYUNDI	Wind
MONARRIE	Blue-tongue Lizard
MOOKPOOL THOU WONG	Place name
MOONCUMBULLI	Wise old man
MOOR ANG ENG	Place name
MOOR RUCK ALL	Take the weapon
MOURN BOUNE	'Fur tribes'
MULDARIE	Magpie
MULDARPI	Evil spirit; devil-devil

MULLOWIE	Variety of fish
MUMGUNG	Encore
MUNDI	Home
MUNGUNGEE	Star
MUNMUNDI (MOON MUN DIE)	Festival
MY A MIN	Swan in distress
MYEYEA	Wind spirit
NABOOLEA (NEBULLE; NEBULEE)	Great man of the stars, Ruler of the heavens
NARPANGE KRYE	Carpet snake
NARPINUNDA	Husband of mine
NARPUND	Wife
NARROONDARIE	Sacred man
NEIL YERI	Pointing bone
NHAR ULL LIN	Flight
NHUNG E UMPIE	Navel cord relationship
NHYANHUND	Father of All
NOL KAL UNDUTCH	Control of appetites and desires
NOO PAA	Tribal name
NOUTHONGIE (NOUGHOUNGIE)	Instrument of witchcraft
NOW WARRIE	Star
NOW WONDIE	Camp, belongings, etc.
NUGOONGIE	Human hair
NUKONE ILLAWIN	Children
NUL THEE	Flesh or muscle
NULLA NULLA	a weapon, a club.
NUP ILL GHEE IN ILL	Now I leave you
PA NEE	Rain spirit
PAK IRRIE	Song
PALLETIS	Grub
PAM ERIE	Shadow
PAMP PARL LOWA	Do unto others as they would do to you
PANKUGGEE (PAA KUGEE)	Weapon
PA NOONDI	Hail
PAR BAR RARRIE	Springtime
PAR OUNG DE KULD	Leaders

PAR RUCH EL HOW	Rise and follow me
PARRAM PAIRRIE (PARRIMPARRIE)	Place name
PARRIMPARRIE	Good or evil spirit
PEANG EE	Fish
PONDI	Murray cod
PEEL LANGGA	Eyes
PEENJULLIE	Emu
PEEWINGIE	Eagle hawk
PHULL LIE	In the by and by; until we meet again
PIL LUL KIE	Perch
PINT	Fishing spear
PLONGEE	Weapon, a club
PLOONGIE	Fish
PON EL ITCH	Dead
POOL JARRA WALLUL	Curse
POOL LOO WE WULD	Place name
POOP PILL LA	Water rat
PORUN	Remember
PREE GHEE	Messenger
PRILL THUN YERI	Tribal name
PRONHOOKIE	Water
PROOLGIE	Spirit, Native Companion bird
PRUCKOOL LOW	Rise at once!
PUCK NOWIE	Grandmother Spirit
PUL JUNG KGEE	Ball
PUMBALA	Place name
PUMMAR	Girls aged eight to fourteen [pl]
PUMMERIE	Catfish
PUMMI	Girl aged eight to fourteen
PUNBARLIE	Tribe of the Coorong
PUNERRIE	Picture
PURSECHOUL	Call of daylight
RANIJERI	Tribal name
RARRABARR	Small throwing waddy
RETCULDIE	Water rat
RHINGARRIPARRIE	Tribal name
RHONGHUND UN	Brother-in-law

Rich er rook itty	Willy Wagtail
Rowhokkun	Place name (Raukkan; also known as Point McLeay)
Rroararund	Thunder
Tarrarrie	Lump of fat
Tatearra	Place name
Tcherie	Freshwater bream
Thalung	Tongue
Thar na wun	Snake and lizard tribes
Theen who ween	Emu (ancient name)
Thildarrin	Lightning
Thoo ee	Charmed human hair rope
Thooree	Tribal name
Thoo roo	Snake
Thookerri	Bony bream
Thooyoungie	Goanna
Thow Pulthook	Don't be afraid
Thul lang	A language
Thun tul how	Sleep thou must
Thunk cum bulli	Lizard
Thuyoaniperrie	Impish red man, mythical
Thymie	Instrument of witchcraft
Thyrallgie	Throwing stick
Tintinarra	Place name
Tolkami	West
Tontick nubbie (Thookabbie)	Tortoise
Tuckoonie	Mythical little man
Uoo goo nook	When
Wachan	Stabbed
Wail lar roo mundi	Large camping-ground
Wak kuldi	Small shield
Walkund	North
Wandhillie	Porcupine
Waradjuri	Language group, Riverina, NSW
Warrawaldie	Tribal name of Unaipon's group
Whalie	Camp made of boughs and rushes or reeds

WHANGUNHUND	Kangaroo (formal address)
WHINGAMMIE	Kangaroo
WHIT WHIT	Small egg-shaped hunting weapon
WHY YEE	Brown snake
WING GARRAWARN	Place name
WIRRI	Gum tree
WIRRIE	Pointing bone
WOLKUND	North
WON OO WEE	Uncle
WONDANGAR	Whale
WY YOUNG GURRIE	Sacred man (meaning he who returns to the stars)
WYERRIEWARR	Heavens
YAKA YAKATUMBURRA	Oh, I pity
YAR NA BARRIE	Waddy
YAR RALD DE KULD	Language of the Yaraldi group
YARNABARR	Weapon
YARTOOKA	Adolescent girls
YARTOOKIE	Girl
YING GAWATCHERIE	Tribal name
YOLDIE	Cormorant
YONGULJEE	Flint knife
YUN MUNDI	Conference
YUN NA MIN DIN	Speak as if addressing a human being
YUN WHO NOOM ME	Court
YUNDI	Spear

Bibliography

Alexander, J. 1997, 'Following David Unaipon's Footsteps,' *Journal of Australian Studies*, no. 55, pp. 22–9.

Bell, D. 1998, *Ngarrindjeri Wurruwarrin, A World that Is, Was and Will Be*, North Melbourne: Spinifex Press.

Berndt, R. M. 1993, *A World that Was: The Yaraldi of the Murray River and the Lakes, South Australia*, Carlton: Melbourne University Press.

Beston, J. 1979, 'David Unaipon: The First Aboriginal Writer', *Southerly*, no. 3, pp. 334–50.

Carey, H. M. 1998, '"The Land of Byamee": K. Langloh Parker, David Unaipon, and Popular Aboriginality in the Assimilation Era', *The Journal of Religious History*, vol. 22, no. 2, June, pp. 200–18.

Davis, J., Muecke, S., Narogin, M., Shoemaker, A. (eds), 1990. *Paperbark: A Collection of Black Australian Writings*, St Lucia: University of Queensland Press.

Frow, J. 1998, 'Public domain and collective rights in culture', *Intellectual Property Journal*, vol. 13, no. 1, pp. 39–52.

Gale, M.-A. 2000, *Poor Bugger Whitefella Got No Dreaming: The Representation and Appropriation of Published Dreaming Narratives with Special Reference to David Unaipon's Writings*, PhD thesis, University of Adelaide.

Hosking, S. 1995, 'David Unaipon—His Story', *Southwords: Essays on South Australian Writing*, ed. Philip Butterss, Kent Town: Wakefield Press, pp. 85–101.

Jenkin, G. 1979, *The Conquest of the Narrindjeri*, Adelaide: Rigby.

Johnson, C. [Mudrooroo], 1965, *Wild Cat Falling*, Sydney: Angus & Robertson.

Jones, P. 1996, 'David Unaipon', *Australian Dictionary Of Biography*, ed. J. Ritchie, vol. 12, Melbourne: Melbourne University Press, p. 304.

Mathew, J. 1899, *Eaglehawk and Crow: A Study of the Australian Aborigines including an inquiry into their origin and a survey of Australian languages*, London: David Nutt; Melbourne: Melville, Mullen and Slade.

Meyer, H. A. E. 1843, *Vocabulary of the language spoken by the Aborigines of the southern and eastern portions of the settled districts of South Australia, preceded by a grammar*, Adelaide: James Allen.

Muecke, S. 2000, '"Between the church and the stage": David Unaipon at the Hobart Carnival, 1910,' *UTS Review*, 6:1, 2000, pp. 11–19.

—— 1992, *Textual Spaces: Aboriginality and Cultural Studies*, Sydney: University of NSW Press.

—— 2000, and Adam Shoemaker, 'David Unaipon,' *Oxford Companion to Aboriginal Art and Culture*, ed. S. Kleinert and M. Neale, Melbourne: Oxford University Press, p. 724.

Shoemaker. A, 1989, *Black Words White Page: Aboriginal Literature 1929–1988*, St Lucia: University of Queensland Press.

Slattery, L. 1998, 'How our hero was robbed of his mythical tales for £150', *The Australian*, 22 October, p. 1.

—— 1998, 'The $50 tragedy', *The Weekend Australian*, 24–5 October, p. 32.

Smith, W. Ramsay. 1930, *Myths & Legends of the Australian Aboriginals*, London: George G. Harrap.

—— 1998, *Myths & Legends of the Aborigine*, Middlesex: Tiger Books International.

Sorensen, R. 1998, 'Read between the lines on literary theft, expert urges', *The Courier Mail*, 23 October, p. 5.

Taplin, G. 1878, *Grammar of the Narrinyeri Tribe*, Adelaide: Government Printer. (Also in Taplin 1879.)

—— (ed.) 1879, *The Folklore, Manners, Customs, and Languages of the South Australian Aborigines*, Government Printer, Adelaide. (Johnson Reprint 1967.)

—— 1873, *The Narrinyeri: An Account of the Tribes of South Australia Inhabiting the Country Around the Lakes Alexandrina, Albert, and Coorong, and the Lower Part of River Murray: Their Manners and Customs.* Also, *an Account of the Mission at Point Macleay*, in Woods (ed.), 1879.

Unaipon, D. 1924–1925 *Legendary Tales of the Australian Aborigines* (manuscript and typescript), Mitchell Library, ms. nos A1929–A1930.

Unaipon, D. 1925, 'The Story of the Mungingee', *The Home*, pp. 42–3.
—— n.d. (1929?), *Native Legends*, Adelaide: Hunkin Ellis and King.
—— n.d. (1927?), *Aboriginal Legends*, no. 1, Adelaide: Hunkin, Ellis and King.
—— n.d. (1951?), *My Life Story*, Adelaide: Aborigines' Friends' Association.
—— 1954, 'How the Tortoise Got His Shell', *Dawn*, vol. 3, no. 11, 1954, p. 9.
—— 1955, 'Why all the Animals Peck at the Selfish Owl', *Dawn*, vol. 4, no. 4, pp. 16–17.
—— 1959, 'Love Story of the Two Sisters', *Dawn*, vol. 8, no. 9, p. 9.
—— 1959, 'The Voice of the Great Spirit', *Dawn*, vol. 8, no. 8, p. 19.
—— 1959, 'Why Frogs Jump in the Water', *Dawn*, vol. 8, no. 7, p. 19.
Walker, K. [Oodgeroo Noonuccal] 1964, *We are Going*, Brisbane: Jacaranda Press.
Watson, B. 1998, 'Justice at last for a brilliant Aussie', *Aussie Post*, 21 November, p. 14.
Wilmott, E. 1989, *Inaugural David Unaipon Lecture*, Adelaide: South Australian Institute of Technology.
Woods, J. D. 1879, (ed.), *The Native Tribes of South Australia*, Adelaide: E. S. Wigg and Son. (Also, Australiana Facsimile Edition no. 215, Adelaide; Friends of the State Library of South Australia, 1997.)